PC Hardware Configuration Guide
for DOS and Solaris™

Ron Ledesma

SunSoft Press
A Prentice Hall Title

Editorial/production supervision: *Ann Sullivan*
Manufacturing manager: *Alexus R. Heydt*
Cover designer: *Wanda España*
Acquisitions editor: *Phyllis Eve Bregman*

The publisher offers discounts on this book when ordered in bulk quantities. For more information, contact: Corporate Sales Department, PTR Prentice Hall, 113 Sylvan Avenue, Englewood Cliffs, NJ 07632. Tel.: (201) 592-2863; Fax: (201) 592-2249

10 9 8 7 6 5 4 3 2 1

ISBN 0-13-124678-X

SunSoft Press
A Prentice Hall Title

This book is dedicated to the memory of Domenic Ledesma and LeGrande Coates. They touched our hearts for such a short time but left such a great impression.

Contents

Preface

This book takes direct aim at the underlying cause of x86 hardware installation and configuration problems — no enforceable configuration standards. Every system configuration can literally be unique!

Anyone who has ever configured a personal computer or added an option card to one can tell you horror stories about configuration conflicts with interrupts, memory addressing, I/O port addressing, or BIOS memory location. You may have been able to get by with a trial-and-error approach in the past, but installing the Solaris operating system demands compatible x86 hardware and precise configuration of each system component.

After building and configuring untold numbers of x86 systems; after dealing with constant frustration; and, after listening to so many others with the same experiences, I found myself saying, "Enough Is Enough! There has to be a better way to configure a personal computer." The good news is — there is a better way; but the bad news is — there is usually no one available who can tell you what it is!

This book provides you with a simple structured approach to hardware configuration that enables you to avoid the pitfalls associated with configuring hardware for demanding operating systems such as Solaris® x86. You not only discover how to take the mystery out of technical configuration details, but you are guided through step-by-step procedures for building x86 hardware systems and networks.

CHAPTER 1

What is Solaris x86?

The first chapter provides an overview of the Solaris operating environment and the many features associated with it. The MS-DOS® and MS-Windows® environments are also discussed, and comparisons are made with the Solaris environment to help you understand the similarities and differences between them.

Concepts such as multiuser, multitasking, distributed processing, networking, and enterprise management are discussed and explained in easy-to-understand terms.

CHAPTER 2

What is x86 Hardware?

Personal computer hardware comes in an infinite variety of sizes, shapes, performance levels, prices, and you name it! This chapter focuses on those aspects of x86 hardware that are most likely to affect your ability to properly configure a system for the Solaris environment. Chapter 2 contains a summary of the most important facts about the x86 system configuration such as:

- Minimum x86 component requirements
- Definition of compatible x86 components
- Explanation of x86 bus architectures
- Explanation of memory configuration requirements
- Explanation of I/O port address assignments
- Explanation of BIOS memory address assignments
- Explanation of RAM memory address assignments
- Explanation of DMA level assignments
- Explanation of IRQ level assignments
- Overview of recommended configuration methodology

CHAPTER 3

Network Hardware

One of the least understood areas of computing is network hardware. Chapter 3 provides simple descriptions and examples of the most basic and essential network components and how they connect systems together, taking most of the mystery out of networking. You will need to read this chapter if you plan to build a network of any size. If you already know how to build a network, you will probably be familiar with much of this material.

CHAPTER 4

Planning Your Installation

Once you read the first three chapters you should have enough information to begin the planning process. The discussion in Chapter 4 addresses planning for such needs as:

- Upgrades to existing systems
- Stand-alone configuration installations
- Small work-group network installations
- Large-scale enterprise network installations

Planning includes needs assessment, hardware selection, and scheduling.

CHAPTER 5

Designing Your Network

Before you run out to buy network hardware, you will need to design your network. Chapter 5 will provide you with a basic approach to network design. Some of the issues you will have to consider are:

- Choosing media
- Choosing topology
- Drawing a logical network
- Drawing a physical layout
- Creating a bill of materials

CHAPTER 6

Partitioning Your Hard Disk

This topic is important enough to rate a chapter of its own. Disk partitioning is one of the first and most critical tasks in preparing x86 hardware to receive the operating system software. Partitioning requires planning and an understanding of your long-term needs. Chapter 6 will help you through the partitioning process and will also provide simple recommendations for building multiple partitions on multiple disks for multiple operating systems.

CHAPTER 7

MCA Installation

Once the planning process is completed and you have all your required x86 MCA bus hardware components, you will be ready to assemble and configure your system. This chapter is a step-by-step description of the installation, verification, and testing sequence you will use to prepare your MCA hardware to receive the operating system.

A checklist and configuration worksheet are provided to give you a quick look at the process and a place to record your final configuration details.

CHAPTER 8

ISA Installation

Once you are done with your planning and you have all your required x86 ISA bus hardware components, you are ready to assemble and configure your system. This chapter is a step-by-step description of the installation, verification, and testing sequence you will use to prepare your hardware to receive the operating system.

A checklist and configuration worksheet are provided to give you a quick look at the process and a place to record your final configuration details.

CHAPTER 9

EISA Installation

Once you are done with your planning and you have all your required x86 EISA bus hardware components, you are ready to assemble and configure your system. This chapter is a step-by-step description of the installation, verification, and testing sequence you will use to prepare your hardware to receive the operating system.

A checklist and configuration worksheet are provided to give you a quick look at the process and a place to record your final configuration details.

CHAPTER 10

Installing Solaris x86

If you did your homework and configured your hardware as recommended, loading the operating system is trivial. The information in Chapter 10 gives an overview of the steps required to install the operating system from both a local CD–ROM and from a network install server.

Additional information is provided to explain the process for setting up network boot servers and diskless (no local hard disk) workstation clients.

CHAPTER 11

Troubleshooting

If you are a person who likes to put everything together, button down the covers, connect all the cables, say a prayer, and then flip on the power, you may be in for a terrible shock. That method will usually not work with sophisticated systems. If the system does not work as expected when you apply power, numerous things could be wrong, and it may take you hours to to find the problem — if you can!

It is easier to configure and install your system in stages and work out the bugs as you go. The troubleshooting approach for x86 hardware is simple:

- Configure your system in stages
- Verify and test at the end of each stage
- Troubleshoot and fix any problems before going to the next stage

The installation sequences recommended in Chapters 7 through 9 will guide you through stages of installation that can be easily verified and tested. The troubleshooting information in Chapter 11 will help you make it through each stage of the installation with a minimum of frustration and loss of time.

APPENDIX

References and Details

The appendix contains specific configuration information for the most common compatible x86 components, a list of known compatible systems and components, and a list of vendors and suppliers of compatible systems and components.

Such a great deal of information exists that is specific to individual hardware components that it was necessary to add an appendix for each component listed below:

- Motherboards
- Disk controllers
- Video display cards
- Audio cards
- Network cards
- CD–ROM drives
- I/O cards
- Modem and FAX cards
- Magnetic tape units
- Mice and keyboards
- Monitors
- Disk drives
- Printers

Acknowledgments

NCA COMPUTER PRODUCTS

My sincerest thanks to Tony Ghanma, president of NCA Computer Products, for providing me with the lab space, systems, and technical support to configure and test the examples provided in this book. I am grateful for his unconditional support.

To all the crew behind the scenes at NCA, I want to say thanks for accepting me as one of your own. I could not have written this book without your help.

Larry Adler	Darrell L. Burrell	Frank Camodeca
Malo Collins	David Dear–Johnson	David DeHaven
Dave Gorman	Ricardo Hernandez	David Jarvis
Keith Kurup	Daryl Lang	Luluina Lepue
Travis Moretti	Mike Nealon	Douglas Paiso
Siralotonga Paletaoga	Anthony Rosado	Michael Scuderi
Chris Shaheen	Sami Shahin	Nicolas Silvam
David M Soden		

The equipment used for writing this book was provided courtesy of NCA Peripherals of Sunnyvale, California.

The cover photo was taken by photographer Bob Cronin and provided courtesy of NCA Computer Products.

SUN MICROSYSTEMS

SunSoft

Thanks to the many people at SunSoft who shared their offices, equipment, and experience with me. A special thanks to Karin Ellison, my friend and editor.

Vicki L. Abe	Armand Aghabegian	Juzer Bannister
Monica Bouweraerts	Lynette Case	Patrick Curran
Chris Dotson	Lorna Dreisbach	Cindy Ellenberg
Paul Fronberg	Kira Hartz	Hae Hirdler
Robert Hosale	Connie Jong	Gerard Kam
Judy Little	Mark Logan	Mike Lovas
Dennis Mangrobang	Patrick Moffitt	Cathleen Reiher
Alan Yoshida		

SunService

Thanks to my workmates at SunService who supported me during this project.

Davinder Atwal	Terry Bond	Russell Chang
Ginny Charles	Gary Croak	Ken Jones
Ken Marks	Bill Norton	Mike Persichetty
Don Roach	Steve Rogers	Warren Rogers
Jim Smith		

Last but not least—

I owe my greatest thanks to my family, who have always been an inspiration to me. I love you all, but especially you know who.

Donna Anderson	Desiree Burns	Ronnette Coates
Darlene Kennedy	Albert Ledesma	Eric Ledesma
Mike Ledesma Jr.	Brad Rothrock	Adeline Teague
Arlene Valdez	Tom Wiant	Terry Yednock

A special thanks to my favorite son-in-law Michael Coates for his enthusiastic and "liberal" use of red ink on my first-draft manuscript.

Thanks to my Mom, Elynor Gutierrez Perea, for her love and caring. I love you Mom.

And last, thanks to my wife and best friend, Gail Benson Ledesma, who encouraged me to write this book. She told me I could do it and, of course, I had to prove her right. I love you Gail.

What Is Solaris x86? 1

What is Solaris x86? To the average person, this seems like a simple question. The answer, however, is the stuff books are made of. In simple terms, Solaris x86 is the SunSoft™ PC version of UNIX® SVR4 with some desktop tools and a windowing interface thrown in for good measure.

If you are already a UNIX user, you probably know that the simple answer just given does not begin to do justice to Solaris x86. You would probably relate better to a definition that declares Solaris x86 to be nothing less than a world-class, multiuser, and multitasking operating system with incomparable networking and windowing capabilities.

For the rest of us (needing to know more about Solaris x86), a more complete and objective definition is required before we can appreciate this truly amazing operating system (OS).

Solaris x86 is:

- A computer operating system (based on SunOS™ 5.x)
- UNIX SVR4 (a worldwide standard for compatibility)
- A file system (everything has its place)
- Networking (teamwork between computers)
- OpenWindows™ (a better view of your work)
- Utility programs (controls to tune your engine)
- A shell (to translate your wishes to computer commands)
- An AnswerBook™ (30 lb of technical literature on 2 oz of CD)

SOLARIS IS SUNOS 5.X

Solaris x86 is based on the Sun Microsystems Inc. (SMI) operating system known as SunOS 5.x. Sun Microsystems has been instrumental in the development and promotion of UNIX as the operating system of choice in the high-end engineering, education, and commercial computer markets.

Solaris x86 was born with a heritage of excellence that spans two decades and is recognized all over the world. It is not a "new" operating system. It is actually the same SunOS source code used on Sun™ SPARC® computers. The Solaris x86 code was ported (adapted) for use on x86 hardware. It is very likely that parts of the Solaris x86 source code were already 20 years old before it was released.

SunOS 5.x means very little unless you already know what an operating system is. Let's take a look at the more generic definition of an operating system before we discuss other aspects of Solaris x86. Most computer systems require three primary components to be of any use to humans. They must have (1) the hardware to run on, (2) the operating system to control the hardware, and (3) the software applications that are used to get work done.

Three Basic Components for Useful Computer Systems:

- Hardware to run on
- An operating system to control the system resources
- Applications that do your work

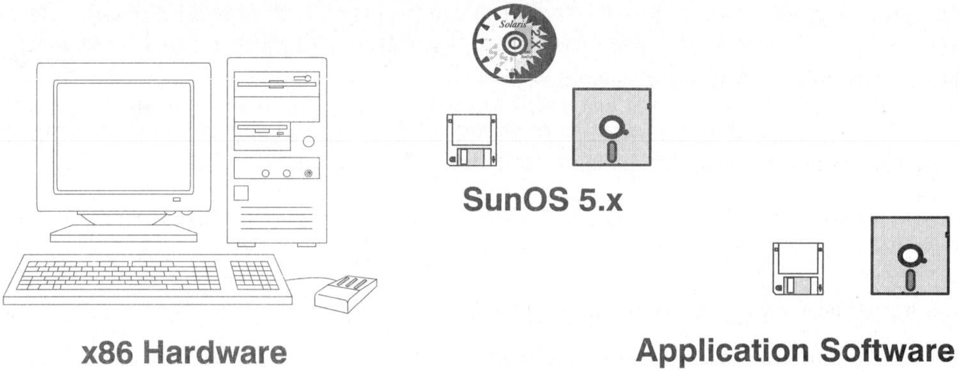

Hardware can be described as a set or configuration of interconnected system components such as a keyboard, a mouse, a printer, a monitor, and a central processor unit. The hardware components chosen to be joined together with the operating system must be perfectly matched and compatible if the marriage is to work.

Note: *Compatibility is the key to a successful and happy marriage between hardware and software. If anyone tries to tell you otherwise, they may be trying to wreck the marriage. If you do not have hardware and OS compatibility, adding application software will be like adding fuel to a fire. Above all else, do your best to ensure that the system components you assemble are compatible.*

You could say that the operating system is the executive in control of all resources. As executives go, SunOS 5.x is one of the finest made. It is capable of controlling the action on a single home computer and equally as capable of controlling the action on a worldwide enterprise of computers. It can allow multiple users to access its resources simultaneously, and it can allow each user to execute multiple simultaneous tasks. You could literally be performing thousands of tasks for countless users at one time on one computer.

The hardware components under control of the OS are diverse, and each component speaks a different control language. The printer, the display, the keyboard, the modem, and the disk drives all speak unique languages and respond to commands only in their own native language. The application software also speaks a unique language. This would be confusing except that the OS speaks all languages, and when the OS speaks everyone listens! The OS also understands commands from humans (you are the board of directors). You are actually in charge and the OS works for you to keep things running smoothly on your computer. The operating system is your best friend!

The OS is usually the first software loaded onto your new hardware. The typical installation procedure is:

- Configure the compatible x86 hardware (the focus of this book).
- Install the operating system from distribution media onto x86 hardware.
- Use OS control to install application software from distribution media.

A few years ago you needed to own a bank or run the local university to be able to afford or obtain an operating system as sophisticated as Solaris x86. Today, because of cost reductions and advances in desktop computer technology, anyone can install and use an OS that was in the past reserved for the most elite of techno-wizards (highly respected gurus in the computing world).

SOLARIS IS UNIX SVR4

Solaris is not just any operating system. It is a UNIX operating system. Just as it is important to have hardware compatibility, it is also important to have software compatibility. The OS and the application software must be compatible. UNIX SVR4 forms the basis for insuring that Solaris x86 is compatible with UNIX software applications.

Solaris is based on the UNIX System V Release 4 standard (commonly known as SVR4). This is very important to you as a user wanting to purchase compatible software. Independent software vendors (ISVs) develop software to meet the most popular standards. This enables developers to reach the largest possible market for their software with the least effort. It is by no coincidence that UNIX SVR4 is such a popular OS for ISVs. Over the years it has established a huge installed user base. In fact, there are proportionately more ISVs developing products for UNIX SVR4 than for other OS types in the same class.

Just as it is easy to find a wide variety of useful accessories for popular automobiles, it is also easy to find useful application software for popular operating systems. SVR4 is extremely popular; therefore, you are extremely lucky if your OS is SVR4 compatible.

SOLARIS X86 OPERATING ENVIRONMENT FEATURES

It takes a combination of things to create an environment. The key features of Solaris x86 environment are:

- SunOS 5.x, a 32-bit UNIX operating system based on SVR4
- ONC+, the standard for heterogeneous networking technology
- OpenWindows Version 3.x, SunSoft's network-based windowing system
- WABI, SunSoft's windows application binary interface
- DeskSet Version 3.x, an integrated desktop including 16 productivity tools

MINIMUM HARDWARE REQUIREMENTS

Standalone System Hardware

The following minimum requirements are for a standalone system configuration. Some networked configurations require less hardware because of dependence upon a network server for disk and CD–ROM access. Your first system must at the very least have the CD–ROM and disk space required to load and boot Solaris x86. The minimum standalone system requirements are:

- 386 with 387DX coprocessor (33MHz minimum speed), or
- 486SX with 486SX coprocessor (25MHz minimum speed), or
- 486DX (25MHz minimum speed), or
- 486DX2, or
- Pentium, and
- 16MB memory
- ISA, EISA, or MCA motherboard bus
- SCSI or IDE hard disk controller
- 200MB hard-disk space
- SCSI CD–ROM

The enormous variety of PC hardware available today can make hardware selection extremely confusing. Chapter 2 will provide you with a more detailed explanation of minimum requirements and key factors in choosing the products that will work best for your desired system. Compatibility and performance are the two critical issues to consider when hardware is selected. If you have severe budget constraints, you will also find some guidance on cutting costs (usually at the expense of performance).

Network Connection Hardware

The basic thin Ethernet network configuration is simple enough for just about anyone to build. The cable and connectors are prefabricated and can easily be plugged into one another to form a network of computers. The minimum thin Ethernet hardware requirements are:

- Network card (thin net Ethernet)
- Cables (thin Ethernet)
- Two terminators (one at each end of the networked string of computers)
- T connectors (one for each computer)

The building (premises) environment, the number of computers, the distance between furthest nodes (computers), and the type of media (cable) all have a bearing on the hardware requirements. You will find more information on these items in Chapter 5.

SOLARIS X86 VS. MS–DOS™ WITH MS–WINDOWS™

The Friendly Argument

As a regular user of DOS with Microsoft Windows and Solaris, I find myself discussing the relative attributes of each with anyone who seems even remotely interested. More often than not, there is a coffee room discussion (argument is perhaps too strong a word among friends) about which is better; and then we all choose sides, proclaim our respective brand loyalties, and return to our desks just as set in our ways as when the discussion first started. You may have had similar experiences.

If you are a DOS user thinking of switching to Solaris x86, or if you are a new user deciding which operating system is best for you, the following comparisons should prove helpful.

Ubiquitous DOS

If you know anything at all about personal computers, you probably know that MS–DOS and MS–Windows are the operating system and window interface of choice for the majority of PC users. It is hard to imagine a PC without DOS. That is like trying to imagine a dog without fleas, nachos without cheese, or chips without dip.

DOS is everywhere! Even people who use alternatives to DOS keep a copy of DOS someplace on their PC. It seems obvious that if there were a contest for the most popular operating system, DOS would win. Just ask the billionaire who runs the company that makes it. DOS is even more popular than UNIX.

Yes, DOS with Windows is truly remarkable and you won't catch me trying to tell you otherwise. However, there is a life after DOS, and for many of us, Solaris is the light that leads to a new and exciting world of UNIX. Don't run out and delete all your copies of DOS just yet. But let's take a closer look at what could motivate you to leave a trusted friend like DOS and to pick Solaris x86 as your primary operating system. You may even decide to choose both, since they can coexist on the same hard disk.

Would Someone Please Hand me a Screwdriver?

The best way to describe the two operating systems is to say that if DOS was a screwdriver, then Solaris would be a hardware store! Well, maybe I am a bit more enthusiastic than I should be. Just for the sake of modesty, let's say that Solaris would be a box full of tools.

I see DOS as a very fine screwdriver. It is handy, fits in small places, and performs its intended function better than anything else. Over the years my DOS screwdriver has grown with snap-on bits and attachments. It even has added cordless power to make my life easier. I love my favorite screwdriver.

Note: *Techno-wizards have tool boxes that are full of tools specialized for working on computers. I always refer to my computer tools as a tool kit — not a tool box.*

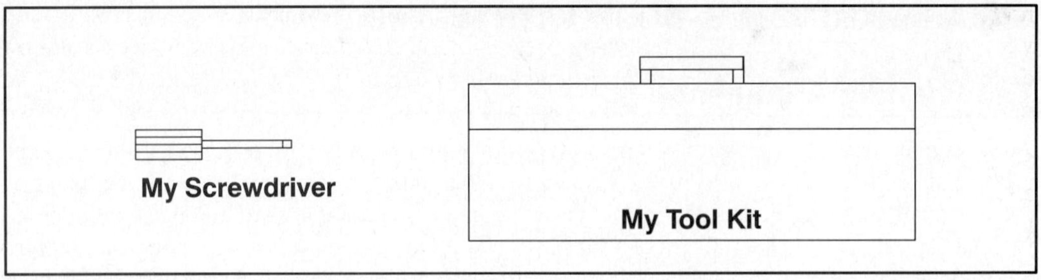

I have tried to do everything with my screwdriver that you could imagine. I have used it to stir paint, poke holes in walls, pry open crates, chisel wood, and a host of other things that are too numerous to mention. I have found my screwdriver to be indispensable. Together with a few other well-chosen tools I went along happily for years. After I became an expert with the screwdriver, I discovered that I could do more if I had more tools. Eventually I talked my wife into buying me lots of tools for Christmas because I found it difficult to spend so much money on myself. Of course, now I am happily obligated to build nice things for my loving wife with my new tools.

The point of this story is that I still use my screwdrivers, but my collection of tools has grown to fill my garage and the things I build reflect the craftsmanship that I have acquired through the use of many tools.

Big vs. Small — Just Look at the Size of It!

Based on the minimum space requirements for a standalone installation, Solaris requires at least 200 megabytes of hard-disk storage space. This is roughly ten times more than DOS and Windows require. Just as a tool kit is larger than a screwdriver, Solaris is larger than DOS. This creates some unique differences.

The most obvious difference is in the distribution media. Solaris x86 is distributed on CD–ROM and floppy disk, while DOS is distributed on floppy disks. This of course means that a CD–ROM player becomes a necessity for standalone configurations. The larger Solaris x86 operating system promises greater performance and flexibility, but in return demands a great deal of space! If you are serious about using UNIX, then get used to the idea of big disks, tape backup, and CD–ROM. You won't get much use out of your floppy drives once you load Solaris x86.

In another comparison of big and small, Solaris processes data in big 4-byte (32-bit) chunks. DOS still uses smaller data chunks and cannot use the full processing potential of the computer hardware. In this case DOS is smaller and slower than the chunkier but speedier Solaris.

Single-tasking vs. Multitasking — One Thing at a Time Please

DOS does not know how to execute more than one task (application program) at a time. The concept behind DOS is that when you issue a command to begin a program task, DOS loads the program and services it until the program reaches completion. Once the task is completed, DOS reasserts control of the computer hardware and waits for your next command. There are some variations on this theme where several programs are linked together sequentially or loaded directly from memory (quick access), but only one task at a time is in control of the system resources.

Solaris x86 is a multitasking operating system. You can command Solaris x86 to execute additional tasks until you reach a practical limit, at which point your computer hardware no longer has the ability to perform the tasks fast enough to be useful. It is difficult to choke a Solaris system, but if you try hard enough it may cough at you.

Single-user vs. Multiuser — One Person at a Time Please

DOS is a single-user operating system. As far as DOS can tell, there is only one person at the controls at a time. You have no identity under DOS. The assumption is that you are authorized to use the computer by virtue of the fact that you are using it. It is very easy to access data on a DOS system, and there is little you can do to keep unwanted eyes from viewing your files.

In contrast to DOS, Solaris x86 can support many users simultaneously. Solaris provides for user login identification and password access. You cannot access any file on Solaris x86 without the permission of the file owner. The first thing you will notice on a Solaris x86 system is the ever present "login" message prompting you to type your login name.

Security — Is There a Lock on This Door?

Security is paramount on networks where data is shared by many users, and the information put into the system is confidential or proprietary. Solaris abounds with security features to keep all unwanted persons from breaking into your computer. The tough security that you find in operating systems like Solaris is demanded by sensitive users such as government agencies, banks, and just about any business that has trade secrets to protect.

DOS has no security features built into it. As indicated above, there is less of a need for security on single-user systems. Most standalone DOS system users do not perceive security to be a top priority. Nonetheless, there are some products available for DOS and Windows that provide some modest levels of security that would keep the average person locked out of your system.

Home Alone — Just Me and My DOS

DOS works great with Windows on a standalone PC in your living room. If your PC is at home, and you are not a bona fide techno-wizard, you will probably want to curl up with your DOS system and run your favorite Windows program while lounging in your slippers and bathrobe. DOS fits right into the suburban lifestyle.

If you are a techno-wizard, you probably already decided that DOS isn't enough to keep you happy at home or at the office. You will want to install Solaris on your standalone machine just because you can. You do not need to own a race track to want a red sports car with wire spoke wheels, so you do not need to own a network to want Solaris. I do not own a sports car, but I do have Solaris in my living room. In fact, I am typing this sentence on a standalone Solaris system. I probably do not need it, but I am unwilling to part with it either.

My wife is using the DOS PC across the room at the moment. I just looked over my shoulder to check on her. We are both dressed for work, but there have been days when we work for hours at the computer before looking up and realizing that we are still in our robes. If you use computers as much as we do, I would not rule out any operating system, but if you are a casual standalone system user at home, stick with DOS until you need a challenge.

Networking — Just Me and My Enterprise

Solaris has outstanding networking capabilities. You won't find a better equipped operating system to run on a heterogeneous (multivendor hardware and software) network. The bigger the network, the more you will appreciate the features that sets Solaris aside from all others. When your network grows to enterprise (really big) proportions, Solaris becomes a must and you will be forced to forsake your old friend DOS.

Multitasking is the single most valuable feature that Solaris employs in network management and communication. Solaris can simultaneously communicate with other computers and operating systems, share files, and share tasks. While you are working with a spreadsheet displayed on your monitor, Solaris can be transferring mail to your associate in Toledo, receiving a letter from a friend in Germany, sharing a database file with another system in your office, or providing directory assistance for a user on the network trying to locate your E-mail address. All of this, of course, is totally transparent to you.

There is a saying at Sun, "The network is the computer." DOS cannot compete with Solaris in a networked environment.

Applications — So What's a WABI?

Eventually you will reach a point where you will actually be accomplishing something productive on your computer. You will be running a software application program that you purchased to perform a specific task. Two of the things you must consider are protection for your existing software investment and flexibility for your future software investments.

DOS and Windows have plenty of software available for home and business use. You may find it a bit difficult to find home applications for Solaris, since the majority of UNIX applications cater to the networked commercial computing environment. If you have a networked commercial computing environment, you will find thousands of applications available for UNIX SVR4 operating systems.

If you are a Windows user, you may have a large investment in Windows software to protect. With that thought in mind, SunSoft created WABI (Windows application binary interface). WABI is the name of the software that was bundled with some early promotional versions of Solaris x86. If you do not get WABI with your version of Solaris x86, it is available as a product from SunSoft. WABI software allows Solaris OpenWindows to execute your Windows programs without Windows. WABI is wonderful! Of course, Windows is wonderful, too, if all you have to work with is DOS.

There is a liberal supply of software that will run on both DOS and Solaris. Since Solaris can run Windows applications, your Windows software investments are not lost when converting to Solaris.

Ease Of Use — Installation From Hell

I decided to write this book to help you get through the arduous task of configuring a PC to run Solaris x86. Needless to say, if you are reading these words, you probably figured out that installing a sophisticated configuration of PC hardware and setting up a network of PCs is not something to take lightly. With good documentation (this book of course) and simple procedures, you should be able to make it through this process with a smile on your face and the feeling of accomplishment that can only come from success.

DOS and Windows hardware requirements are much looser than those for a high-performance operating system like Solaris x86. Your hardware must be configured absolutely correctly, or the stress of performance will result in some type of unforeseen failure. One of the most often heard laments of a user with installation trouble is: "It worked on DOS."

DOS and Windows installation is no picnic, but Solaris x86 demands a confident and patient installer with good preparation. This book addresses the preparation required, but you will have to supply the patience, read the appropriate chapters in this book, and forget about short cuts. If you are skilled enough to install your own disk drive and controller, you are skilled enough to configure a high-performance UNIX PC.

Which Is Better — DOS or Solaris?

You're right. "Which is better?" is a trick question. The real question is "What do you need?" Both operating systems provide excellent value and do exactly what they advertise. The bottom line is that you should make sure your needs are met first, and then if you have some flexibility, make sure you get what you want!

I'll take the red convertible with the wire spoke wheels!

What Is x86 Hardware? 2

READ ME FIRST — OR ELSE

"Read me first" is a term you often find within technical documentation. It usually is intended to catch your attention in the hope you will not proceed until you have first read that documentation. In this case, I am giving you notice that the information contained in this chapter must be read before attempting to configure your hardware. This is the chapter that will save you hours of frustration and grief.

HARDWARE OVERVIEW

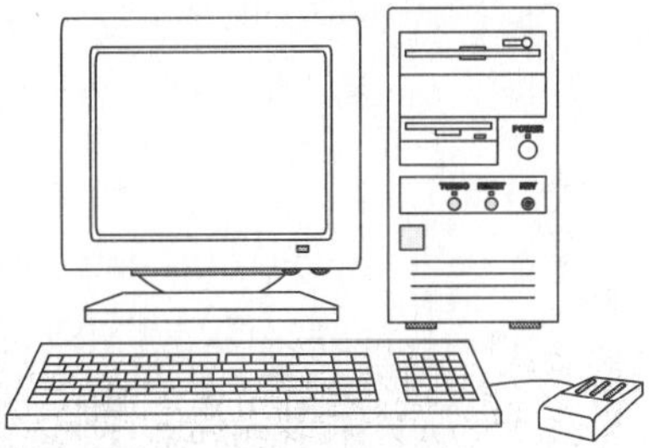

The PC architectures and component descriptions in this chapter will give you a perspective in understanding the scope of available hardware options. More details on hardware components are provided in the Appendices.

Motherboard

The heart of any system is the motherboard, which has the CPU, memory, and Input/Output (I/O) bus slots. The type of I/O bus supported on a motherboard varies from board to board.

CPU (Central Processing Unit)

- Solaris 2.1 minimum requirement is 33MHz 386DX with a math coprocessor.
- Solaris 2.4 minimum requirement is 33MHz 386DX.
- Minimum recommended is 33MHz 486DX.
- Multiple processors are supported in releases after Solaris 2.1.

For best performance, a 486DX, a 486DX2, or a Pentium CPU is recommended. I would not recommend anything less than a 33MHz 486DX CPU. After visiting my local computer retailer, I was surprised to discover that most 386DX systems are no longer being sold, and that the 40MHz 386DX was the slowest CPU available. The cost of a 486DX is so close to that of a 386DX that it makes no sense to buy a 386DX or 486SX and then have the added expense of a math coprocessor (Solaris 2.1 only). Just buy the best CPU available in your price range, provided a math coprocessor is included. Solaris 2.4 does not require a math coprocessor but performance is disappointing without it. If you already have a motherboard with a 386DX CPU, upgrade it to a 486DX CPU motherboard!

COMPONENT	MINIMUM REQUIREMENTS
Motherboard Several x86 bus architectures are supported. • Industry Standard Architecture (ISA) • Extended Industry Standard Architecture (EISA) • Micro Channel Architecture (MCA) • VESA Local Bus • PCI bus *Compatible Products* Most recently manufactured clone motherboards are compatible. Incompatible boards can be easily upgraded at very low cost. Existing CPUs and memory can be reused in new boards. • AMI Enterprise and Voyager • Micronics EISA and ISA	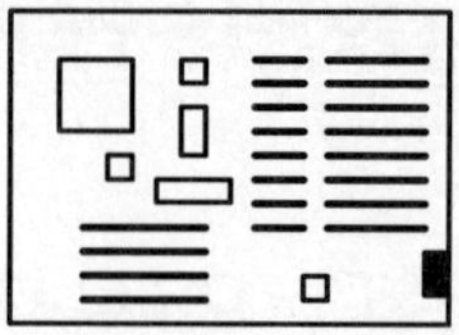 □ 12MB Memory (16MB recommended) □ 386DX 33MHz with Math Coprocessor 386, 486, and Pentium processors can be used provided they have either internal or add-on coprocessor units.

Any of the following CPU combinations will work:

- Intel 386DX/33 Mhz with 387 coprocessor
- Intel 486DX or 486DX2
- 486SX w/ 487SX coprocessor
- Intel Pentium

Performance on a network file server can be greatly improved through the use of multiple processors. Multiple processors are controlled by the Solaris x86 operating system. Tasks are balanced between processors, and overall system performance is enhanced.

A Bus For All Occasions

There are five common I/O bus architectures supported:

- Industry Standard Architecture (ISA)
- MicroChannel Architecture (MCA)
- Extended Industry Standard Architecture (EISA)
- Video Electronic Standards Association (VESA) local bus
- Peripheral Component Interconnect (PCI)

Each of the bus architectures have both good and bad points. The type of bus you choose depends on your application and resources. Any one of the five architectures can serve you well, provided you understand its value with respect to your unique application. Chapter 4 provides information to help you choose the bus architecture best suited for your needs.

ISA Bus

The 16-bit ISA I/O bus is the most common of the bus architectures. It is the original AT bus that has served for years with distinction on millions of personal computers. It isn't the fastest or most sophisticated bus, but it is the most popular and most cost effective of the three. Optional ISA adapter boards are reasonably priced, readily available, and made to meet your every need.

- Original 16-bit AT bus design
- Older technology with limited I/O bus speed
- Lowest cost
- Manual configuration
- Excellent support and availability
- VESA local bus adds significant performance boost

Configuration of optional adapters on ISA bus systems is almost always done by manipulating jumpers or switches. The configuration process on ISA bus systems requires an informed approach and should not be attempted without careful planning.

The ISA bus connector illustrated below has two edge connectors with one row of connections on each edge. When fully inserted, the edge connectors make contact with the female motherboard bus slot.

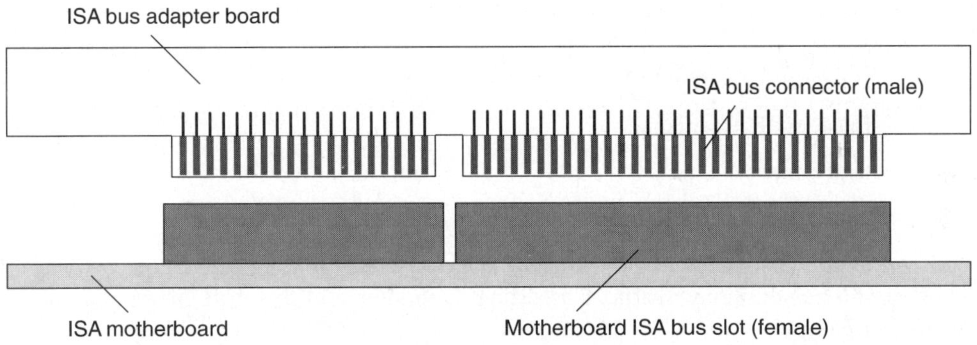

If you don't mind the bit of extra effort required to configure the ISA bus system, it is an excellent choice for everyday use as a workstation. You won't be disappointed with the flexibility and cost savings associated with the ISA bus. Furthermore, you will have no trouble finding ISA bus products at your local retail computer store.

VESA Local Bus

Recent implementation of VESA local bus (VL) standards have extended the useful life of the ISA bus by providing high-speed 32-bit CPU bus access for local bus adapters such as IDE disk interface adapters, video display adapters, and SCSI (Small Computer System Interface) bus adapters. By allowing data transfer between the CPU and adapter boards on the CPU bus, the older and slower ISA I/O bus can be completely bypassed. A properly configured ISA bus system with local bus capability can achieve respectable performance when compared to more powerful EISA and MCA bus architectures.

More recently, VL bus Version 2.0 was introduced to improve the performance of the original design. Version 2.0 supports 50MHz CPU clock rate, and is expanded to a 64-bit data path. The performance improvement keeps the VL bus competitive with the PCI bus.

Note: *Motherboards can only have a maximum of three VESA local bus slots due to limitations in the CPU bus driver circuitry. Each VESA local bus device places an additional load on the CPU bus. Three devices on the local bus will push the CPU to its limits. It is always a good idea to use a CPU cooling fan or CPU heat sink on VESA local bus systems.*

VESA local bus adapters are similar in appearance to ISA boards. The obvious difference is the third paddle connector that connects to the VESA local bus. Local bus adapter boards require more insertion force than ISA boards because of the additional connector. The local bus adapter must be inserted carefully and with a firm rocking motion.

If you choose the ISA bus for your system, make sure to get one with the VESA local bus. The premium you pay for the VESA local bus is almost nothing — get it, or you will regret it!

MCA Bus

The MicroChannel bus was designed by IBM. Commonly referred to as the MCA bus, it has the following features:

- Designed to be the 32-bit bus of the future
- Excellent Performance
- Higher cost
- Automated configuration

The MCA bus was designed with performance and ease-of-use in mind and could easily be rated as the best x86 bus design available. The design is unique, and therefore not compatible with previous bus designs.

The MCA bus design uses more than one edge connector size to accommodate 16- and 32-bit bus data widths. The example illustrated below has one edge connector. It is important to note the types of available slots on a system before shopping for adapter boards.

The intent was to design the bus from scratch without the limitations that can result from compatibility requirements. The designers met their performance goals at the expense of vendors and users who had made huge investments in ISA bus technology. Incompatibility is the only wall standing between the MCA bus and success.

This bus is not nearly as common as the other two; costs can be higher for options, and availability is limited. You won't find many MCA bus systems to choose from at the local computer store, and

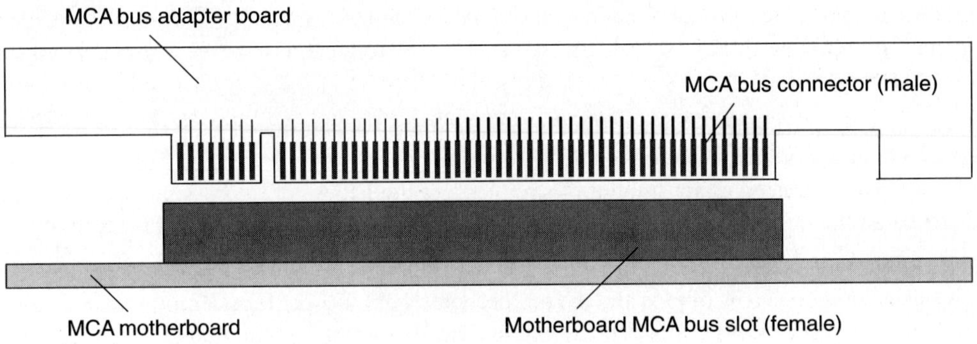

replacement parts and upgrades can be quite expensive. MCA bus designs are more likely to be proprietary and less likely to enjoy the lower costs of the more common ISA and EISA bus motherboards.

If you need performance, have a reliable supplier, can negotiate reasonable prices, and are planning to install and configure a large number of systems, you should consider this bus as a good option. This is a good bus that just hasn't caught on yet. If you feel lucky, don't hesitate to invest in a good MCA bus product. It stands uncontested as the overall performance leader.

EISA Bus

- Extension of original ISA bus design
- Performance close to MCA bus
- Compatibility with ISA boards
- 32-bit high-speed I/O bus
- Partially automated configuration
- Good availability

The introduction of the incompatible MCA bus caused such a stir in the ISA bus vendor and user communities that many of the vendors gathered to design their own bus. They wanted a bus that would provide the performance improvements associated with the MCA bus and yet maintain compatibility with existing ISA bus products. The result of their effort is the 32-bit EISA bus.

You usually get what you pay for. In the case of the EISA bus, you will have to pay more to get more. EISA products generally cost more than similar ISA products, but performance and ease-of-use are usually much better.

Backward compatibility with ISA bus adapters is an important design feature of the EISA bus. Ideally, you should avoid the use of ISA boards on the EISA bus because of the resulting performance and configuration penalties. If you plan to use the EISA bus, you should also plan to use available EISA bus adapters wherever possible. This is not as easy as it sounds. It is difficult to find video, audio, and I/O port EISA option boards. On the bright side, ISA option boards for modems, I/O ports, and audio boards can be used effectively because they are not performance bottlenecks on the bus.

Another benefit of using EISA boards is that configuration is automated. You should not have to fiddle with jumpers and switches on EISA option boards. This is not to say it is easier to configure. You still need a fair amount of savvy to get the EISA configuration correctly entered and stored on the motherboard CMOS or NVRAM (nonvolatile random access memory).

The EISA bus edge connector illustrated below is similar to the ISA bus edge connector, but the EISA bus has a second row of pins and the motherboard has a deeper female slot with two rows of corresponding connections. This design enables the EISA bus to maintain ISA bus connector compatibility (first row of connections) while providing additional bus lines (second row of connections. When ISA adapter cards are inserted into an EISA motherboard slot, only the first row of ISA adapter connections can make contact with the EISA bus.

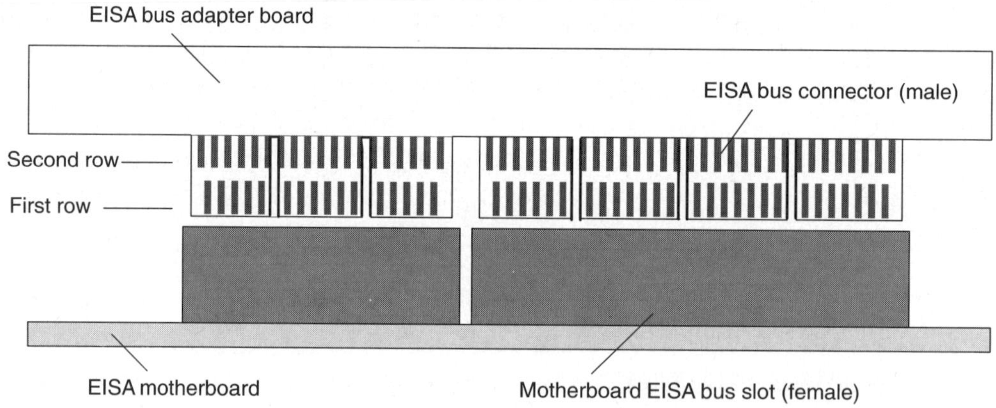

There are also hybrid motherboards available that provide EISA and ISA bus slots with the VESA local bus to give you a wide range of performance options. These hybrid motherboards usually have two VESA local bus ISA slots, three EISA slots, and three standard ISA slots. My experience with hybrid boards has been negative thus far. I tried configuring two separate motherboards (both used the HINT chip set), but was not able to get them to run reliably. Avoid any hybrid board that is not on the hardware compatibility list (see Appendix A).

The 32-bit EISA bus system is ideal for the performance demands of servers and engineering workstations. A server usually requires more bus slots, more power, fast I/O bus transfer, multiple disk controllers, multiple network adapters, specialized terminal controllers, and huge chunks of memory.

Most computer retail outlets carry a line of EISA products. If you need power and you can afford the modest cost premium, go for the EISA bus system.

PCI Bus

Gaining in popularity, the Peripheral Component Interconnect (PCI) bus was developed by Intel to provide a fast 32-bit or 64-bit interconnection between the CPU, peripheral chips, and optional adapter boards. As with the VESA local bus, the PCI bus should be compatible with DOS and Solaris.

The PCI bus could very well be the standard bus architecture of most future motherboard designs. It is receiving wide acceptance with motherboard manufacturers because it offers excellent performance and the promise of true plug-and-play simplicity.

As with the VESA local bus motherboards, PCI designs are generally available with a combination of ISA and PCI slots on the same motherboard. The only drawback to the PCI bus is that optional adapters are sometimes difficult to find. I expect this problem to be short-lived.

The most significant feature of the PCI bus is that it is not directly connected to the CPU bus, as is the VL bus. Because of this feature the PCI bus is generally referred to as a mezzanine bus. The PCI bus takes its timing from the CPU but is buffered from it. The result is that the PCI bus supports five adapters versus a maximum of three on the VL bus. What I find even more interesting, is that this feature enables the PCI bus architecture to work with CPUs other than the i486. Within a year or so we will probably see the PCI bus on PowerPC CPUs, on SPARC CPUs, and on Pentium CPUs.

It will take some time before plug-and-play BIOS support and plug-and-play hardware support are available to fulfill the promise of hassle-free installation. Once the industry can agree on a plug-and-play standard, look for the PCI bus to dominate the market.

PCMCIA

The Personal Computer Memory Card (PCMCIA) interface is available on many laptop computers today. This interface enables small credit-card-size adapters to plug into external system slots. This interface is not currently supported by Solaris. This could change. Check Appendix A for current compatibility information.

Proprietary Motherboards

You have probably seen countless magazine ads for closed architecture computer systems that include I/O ports, SVGA graphics, floppy disk controller, mouse port, and hard disk controller on the "motherboard" — all standard! These valid offers are usually made through large mail-order firms or factory-direct channels. This is usually good news for the consumer looking for low prices and lots of features. PC manufacturers can lower costs by adding functionality to the motherboard and reducing the number of components required to build a system. The result is a proprietary board that is low in cost and unique in the PC industry.

Proprietary motherboards are not good news for power users looking for standard products with open architecture and easy upgrade paths. Your only path for proprietary upgrades is through the original manufacturer. This can be very costly as new technologies emerge. Be cautious when investing in proprietary motherboard designs. You must verify compatibility with the operating system before you purchase proprietary hardware.

Minimum Memory Requirements

- 12MB of motherboard memory is required.
- 16MB of motherboard memory is recommended.
- All the memory you can afford to buy is recommended.

16MB is the minimum amount of motherboard memory that I would recommend. You can get the operating system to work with 12MB, but performance will be degraded, and you may have some problems getting the operating system installed. This is not an area where you should try to save money by just meeting the minimum requirement. If you are a power user, you should plan on at least 24MB or more.

Some 386 designs will not support more than 16MB of memory. It is always a good idea to verify memory capacity before buying a motherboard or system.

Note: *You can improve system performance substantially by adding to your memory. Buy as much memory as you can afford, and check your motherboard memory requirements to ensure that the memory is fast enough to support your processor speed (70 nanosecond memory is usually fast enough).*

Disk Subsystem

Both IDE and SCSI hard disks can be used but there are major differences in functionality. IDE does not provide a CD–ROM or magnetic tape interface.

Hard-Disk Interface

- Both IDE and SCSI hard disks are supported.
- SCSI HBA is recommended.

Hard-Disk Capacity

- Requirements vary according to system use.
- 350MB hard-disk drive is "recommended" (200MB minimum).
- Networked systems can boot without hard disks.

The SCSI host bus adapter (HBA) is the recommended disk controller because of its flexibility and high performance on network file servers. It can simultaneously control seven separate SCSI device targets such as disk drives, CD–ROM drives, magnetic tape units, printers, and scanners. Each of the seven devices is assigned a unique target address between 0 and 6.

If you plan to have a standalone system or a network file server, you will need the SCSI HBA for your CD–ROM and magnetic tape unit. Note that application software distribution is usually via CD–ROM, floppy disk, or magnetic tape cartridge.

COMPONENT	MINIMUM REQUIREMENTS

SCSI Subsystem

Standalone configurations work best with SCSI controllers and devices. The most common SCSI devices are:

- Hard disk drive for file systems
- CD–ROM for data/program input
- Magnetic tape for file system backup

Compatible Products (See Appendix C for complete list)

- Adaptec – 1540/1542B, 1540/1542C
- Adaptec – 1640/1642
- Adaptec – 1740/1742A, 2740/2742
- BusLogic – BT542B, BT545S, BT742A, BT747S
- DPT – 2011, 2012, 2021, 2022
- IBM – PS/2 SCSI

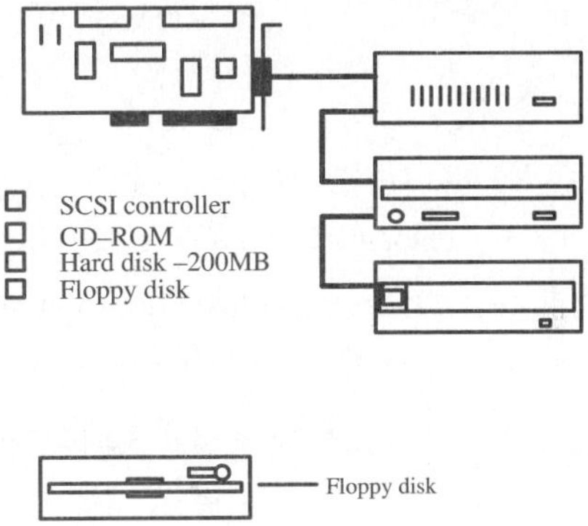

You will not need a hard disk if you only intend to boot off a network server, but in all other cases the hard disk is required. Even on systems that boot off the network, a hard disk is useful and should be included in the configuration.

The recommended disk capacity is 350 megabytes if you are configuring your hardware for a full operating system installation. You could get by with less local disk capacity if a network server is providing added disk space, or if you are only running a few applications that require little or no disk space. A minimum Solaris installation requires 200MB (not including the DOS partition) of disk space, but this is insufficient for most purposes.

Note: *The term SCSI host bus adapter (HBA) is the formal description of the SCSI adapter boards that are connected to a PC bus. The SCSI HBA is also commonly called the SCSI adapter, the SCSI controller, the SCSI interface, or the SCSI host adapter. SCSI controller is the general term used throughout this book to describe the SCSI HBA (adapter board) or the embedded SCSI chip found on some proprietary motherboard designs.*

CD–ROM Drive

- ***Operating system distributed on CD–ROM***
- ***CD–ROM must be a SCSI device***

The operating system software is distributed on CD–ROM. The distribution package also includes two diskettes (one in each format). The diskette is used as the initial boot media, and contains the software drivers required to install the operating system from CD–ROM, hard disk, or network install server.

If you are not installing from a network install server, you will require a CD–ROM device. The operating system only supports SCSI CD–ROM.

Floppy-Disk Drive

- This drive is required for installation of operating system software.
- 3.5-inch 1.44MB floppy drive is recommended.
- 5.25-inch 1.2MB floppy drive is handy to have.
- Floppy and hard disk controllers are packaged together.

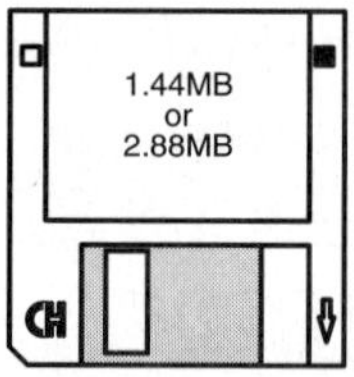

The floppy disk drive is invaluable and is a requirement for loading the operating system boot disk. You can get by with one floppy disk drive in either the 3.5-inch 1.44/2.88 MB format or the 5.25-inch 1.2MB format. If you are limited to one choice, pick the 3.5-inch 1.44MB drive. The 5.25-inch format is older technology and will be used less as time passes.

Having both formats can prove to be a lifesaver because you cannot predict which disk format vendors will supply with their products. If space in your computer case is at a premium, I recommend installing a combination floppy disk that fits in one 5.25-inch slot, but supports both 5.25- and 3.5-inch formats.

The floppy disk controller is usually a part of the hard-disk controller option board or included on the motherboard. Both IDE and SCSI disk controller boards have models that include or exclude the floppy-disk drive controller. Appendix C contains more details on disk controllers.

Deciding on the right capacity disk or disks for your configuration is a topic described further in Chapter 4.

IDE Disk Drives

COMPONENT	MINIMUM REQUIREMENTS
IDE Disk Drive IDE disk drives are compatible with Solaris x86, but they are more difficult to configure with SCSI controllers in the same system. Motherboards with onboard IDE and floppy interfaces are most difficult.	☐ Hard disk – 200MB 

The IDE disk drive and interface performs well and is a low-cost alternative to SCSI disk drives. It is the interface of choice on most PCs sold today. It is inexpensive and relatively fast. You will likely see this interface on proprietary motherboards that have on-board video, floppy, serial port, parallel port, and hard disk support.

Following are some important issues to address when IDE drives are used:

- AT/IDE is not suitable for high performance servers.
- AT/IDE is limited to two disk drives.
- IDE and SCSI may conflict.

The IDE interface will only support two IDE disk drives (designated master and slave). This leaves little room for expansion, which is critically important if you plan to use IDE drives on a server. The performance and expansion issue is one that you will need to address when you plan your configuration.

When I refer to a server, I picture a system sitting in a computer room cranking out transactions for 20–100 users at a time. This type of server needs top-of-the-line performance. If your definition of a server is a system supporting a few people in a small company, please adjust your thinking to compensate for the difference. A small business server may perform its task perfectly well with IDE drives.

IDE and SCSI can peacefully coexist on a system, provided the right conditions are met. The biggest obstacle to overcome is proprietary motherboard compatibility. Standard ISA and EISA motherboards do not have onboard IDE interfaces. Proprietary designs such as Dell motherboards may have onboard controllers and I/O ports. If the floppy and IDE drive controllers can be disabled or can function without conflicting with the SCSI controller, you will have no problem. If you are not sure about IDE compatibility, stick with standard motherboard designs.

Video Chip or Adapter

Standard ISA or EISA motherboards do not have onboard video capability. Video adapters are attached via the motherboard bus. This open architecture is easy to configure. All you have to do

COMPONENT	MINIMUM REQUIREMENTS
Video Chips and Adapters Most standard motherboards use video adapters connected via the I/O bus. Some proprietary boards use onboard video chips. The onboard chips should be checked to verify compatibility. *Compatible Products* • ATI Mach 32 and Mach 8 (ATI mouse OK) • Chips – S386C805, S386C911, ET–4000, S3 • Orchid Fahrenheit 1280, VA, and Pro Designer II • STB PowerGraph Ergo • Paradise Accelerator (WD90C31) • IBM XGA • Compaq QVision 1024	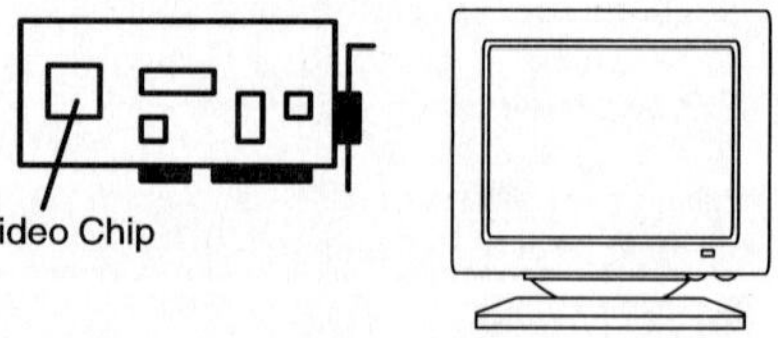 Video Chip □ 1024x 768 SVGA

is choose the compatible video adapter you need and plug it into the bus. Upgrading the video capabilities on open-architecture systems is simply a matter of removing the current video adapter and replacing it with a new one.

Proprietary motherboard designs may include onboard video capability. This presents a unique problem. The video capability is provided by a chip on the motherboard. You must know the type of chip on the motherboard to determine if it is compatible with the Solaris operating system.

Video chips and video adapters usually have one thing in common — software setup. Graphic accelerator chips may be customized under DOS to operate in different display modes. Software utilities are provided for this purpose and also for testing all of the available display modes. The video software utilities are copied to the DOS partition during DOS installation.

Monitor

The monitor must match the video adapter resolution and scan rates. Before choosing a monitor:

- Review the specifications of your video adapter.
- Determine the maximum resolution and scan rate required (i.e., 1280×1024).
- Determine the frontal screen performance required for your applications.

A good quality high-resolution monitor is the single most expensive component of most computer systems. Take the time to view as many monitors as possible before deciding on a purchase. See Appendix L for more details on monitor features.

Network Adapter

A network adapter is required if you intend to use the system in a network. Ethernet and token ring are both supported by the Solaris operating system. The hardware compatibility list (see Appendix A) contains a complete list of compatible adapters.

COMPONENT	MINIMUM REQUIREMENTS
Network Adapter Token Ring and Ethernet are supported. • Industry Standard Architecture (ISA) • Extended Industry Standard Architecture (EISA) • Micro Channel Architecture (MCA) • VESA Local Bus *Compatible Products* • SMC – WD8003, WD8013 • 3Com – 3C503, 3C509, 3C529, 3C579, 3C507 • 3Com – TokenLink III 16/4 • IBM – Token Ring 4/16 • See Appendix F	 ☐ Any compatible network adapter Avoid using older 8-bit cards such as the 3C503. Throughput will be severely limited. The 3C503/16 is okay.

The network adapter board, more than any other, is the cause of configuration conflicts on the system. The network adapter factory default settings are usually the source of the problem. In almost all cases you will have to manually set ISA network adapters to new settings before you can use them. Plan on it!

Software is usually included with network adapters. The software is used to test and configure the adapter. Like most other PC adapter utilities, the network adapter software is DOS based. You will need to run your diagnostic and setup programs from the DOS partition.

Mouse and Keyboard

Many of the pointing devices available are compatible with the Microsoft bus mouse and Microsoft serial mouse specifications, thus assuring a wide variety of choices.

Solaris x86 supports a variety of languages and thus a variety of keyboards. You can use keyboard layouts in:

- U.S. English
- U.K. English
- French
- Canadian
- German
- Italian
- Dutch
- Portuguese
- Spanish

COMPONENT	MINIMUM REQUIREMENTS
Mouse *Compatible Products* • Appoint – Thumbelina • Dyna Point – Dyna Track • Interlink – PortaPoint • Kraft Systems – Micro Track • Logitech – MouseMan, C7, C9, Trackman • Microsoft – Serial Mouse, Bus Mouse, PS/2 Mouse • Mouse Systems – New Point • MicroSpeed – Microtrac	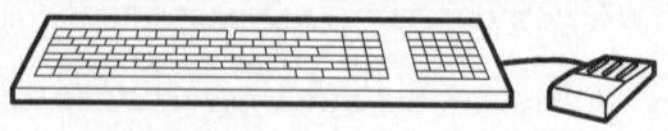 ☐ Any AT keyboard ☐ Any compatible mouse

Printers

PostScript printers are common and readily available. The average cost of a PostScript printer is a bit higher than most other types because of the built-in PostScript processor. PCL format is also supported.

Printer technology continues to improve at an amazing pace. When shopping for a printer, get the highest resolution you can afford. I personally wouldn't settle for anything less than 600×600 dpi. A 300-dpi printer is fine for almost all routine printing jobs.

COMPONENT	MINIMUM REQUIREMENTS
Printer • PostScript compatible printers are supported • Parallel interface recommended • Buy the highest resolution you can afford *Compatible Products* • Any serial or parallel Postscript printer	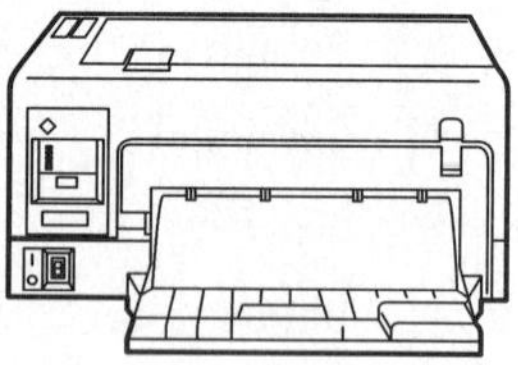 ☐ PostScript ☐ PCL

Audio Board

COMPONENT	MINIMUM REQUIREMENTS
Audio Board Sound is fully integrated in the Solaris operating system. Sound is extensively used to enhance the functionality of desktop tools. Servers make little use of sound. *Compatible Products* • Sound Blaster Pro	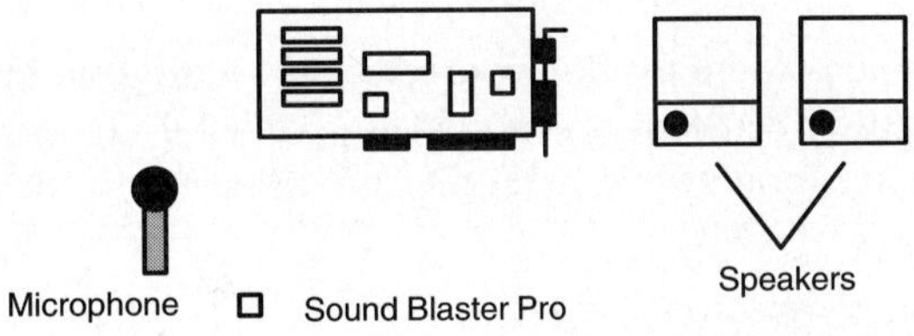

The audio adapter will enable you to use the full range of sound input, editing, and output capabilities provided with the Solaris desktop tools. This feature is optional.

CASES

- Slim-line desktop
- Full-size desktop
- Mini tower
- Medium tower
- Large tower

There are many types of PC cases to choose from. The size and type of case you choose should reflect the type of use you expect for your system. Since the power supply is usually included with the case, it is important to choose a case with adequate power.

Slim-Line Desktop

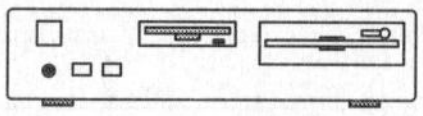

The slim-line desktop case is a compact design for desktop use. The monitor can be placed on top of the case to save desktop space. There is little room for expansion of boards or peripheral devices, so the small power supply is adequate for this case.

There is room for floppy drives and a hard disk, but not much else. This case can be effectively used on desktops where added peripheral devices are not required. This would make a good choice for network nodes that are diskless or limited to small disks.

Standard Desktop

The full-sized standard desktop is probably the most common of the cases available today. There is adequate room and power for most needs, and it is widely available at a reasonable street price. The main drawback in this design is the large desktop footprint.

This is a good general purpose design that has been around for a long time. Since the design is old, the case does not work well with smaller 3.5-inch peripherals. The case was originally designed for 5.25-inch peripherals and is not organized to take advantage of smaller peripheral devices. If you want to use this case, give some thought about the placement of your peripherals.

This design does not provide external 3.5-inch bays to install a 1.44-MB floppy disk drive. If you use this type of case, buy a 5.25-inch half height bay mounting kit for your 1.44-MB floppy disk.

Mini Tower

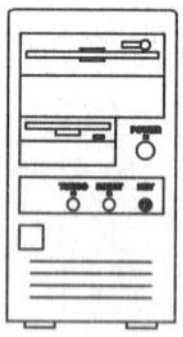

The mini tower is very popular for low-end systems that do not require large power supplies or room for major expansion. These cases are made to accommodate the 3.5-inch devices and provide efficient use of internal space.

This is a desktop case with a small footprint. It is usually placed beside the monitor on the desktop and has the convenience of a front-mounted power switch that is characteristic of the tower design. Peripherals such as floppy disk and CD–ROM are also easy to access.

The major drawback is the lack of internal space for setting up the system. This type of case can be tough for a technician to work on.

The internal bays on this case sit above the motherboard and will inhibit the use of full-sized cards in the first few bus slots. This may be a serious problem on motherboards with local bus slots in the first two positions. If you cannot insert your adapter board, you will have either to change the motherboard or use a medium-tower case.

Medium Tower

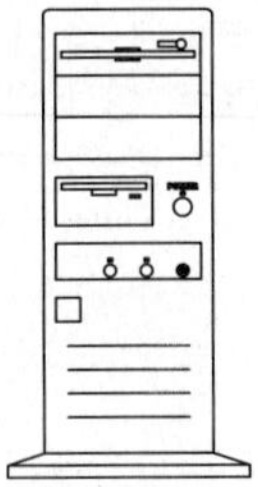

The medium tower case is just about the right size for a power user or standalone system. It has just enough room and power to expand gracefully. It will easily support a CD–ROM, magnetic tape unit, and floppy drives in the available external bays, and still have room for at least two 3.5-inch disk drives in the internal bays. Check your cable lengths on this tower. You may find yourself with cables that don't reach your topmost drive.

This case is barely small enough to fit on the desktop but can be safely placed on the floor. It is the most practical system case for power users and can be configured as a low-end server.

As with the mini tower case, the internal bays on this case sit above the motherboard and can interfere with the placement of full-size adapter boards in the first two slots.

I strongly recommend this size tower as the minimum requirement for a standalone single user configuration. Anything smaller might not adequately serve your expansion needs.

Large Tower

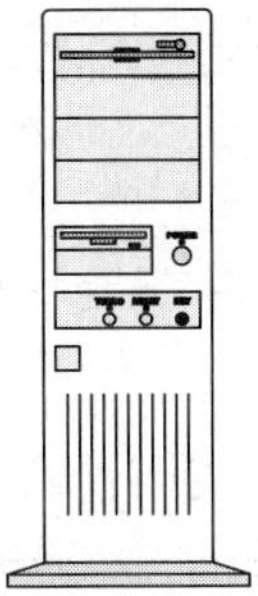

The large tower is made to be freestanding on the floor. It is just right for server applications. This type of case usually has a high-capacity power supply and enough room inside for a full complement of SCSI peripherals.

There is plenty of space inside for the technician to work, but sometimes all that room can be a problem. The distance between the topmost peripheral bay and the motherboard is typically much further on this case than on the others. Many disk controllers and floppy controllers come with short cables that do not reach far enough to connect the components. There is also the possibility, if you use the space to load your system with peripherals, that the cables provided with your adapters may not have enough connectors! Tower configurations can present you with some difficult installation problems.

Some full tower designs do not provide external 3.5-inch bays to install a 1.44-MB floppy disk drive. If you use this type of tower, buy a 5.25-inch half-height bay mounting kit for your 1.44-MB floppy disk.

THE TECHNICAL FACTS ABOUT x86 HARDWARE

There are more things to know about x86 hardware than you or I could write about for the rest of our lives. Fortunately, we don't need to know everything ever written about PCs to configure the hardware correctly. The topics discussed here are the ones most likely to help you in your quest for the perfectly executed configuration:

- BIOS (Basic Input Output System) memory address allocation
- RAM (Random Access Memory) address allocation
- I/O port address allocation
- Interrupt request (IRQ) level allocation
- DMA channel allocation

Before we can get into specifics about hardware configuration, we need to review main memory and how hardware configuration fits within the structure of the x86 memory map. Main x86 memory has some well–defined boundaries, and some not-so-well-defined boundaries. Hardware configuration problems usually surface in areas where the memory boundaries are not clear, or where the boundaries are intentionally left open to interpretation.

Memory Map

Many of the difficult decisions made during system configuration are related to the mapping of memory space occupied by host bus adapter boards. The task is made difficult by the absence of standards governing memory space usage within the range of C8000 to F0000 hex.

To get around this ambiguity, most hardware manufacturers have designed their adapter boards with some degree of flexibility. This is good news because you can have several optional adapter boards from different vendors use the free memory space without conflict. This is also bad news because there is no easy way to configure all the variables on the optional adapter boards. Conflicts between boards are responsible for the majority of problems during installation.

BIOS Memory Address Allocation

When you apply power to your system, it springs to life with a series of ticks, beeps, messages, and assorted lights and sounds that combine to tell you the system BIOS has taken control of the hardware.

The acronym "BIOS" refers to the *basic input output system* that is included on the motherboard. The BIOS program is stored on a motherboard chip and starts when you first turn on the computer. The BIOS provides the first level of intelligent program code on the computer. The BIOS will always run at startup, provided your motherboard is not damaged or defective.

- BIOS is a program stored on a computer chip.
- Motherboard BIOS executes when power is applied.
- Motherboard BIOS runs power on self test (POST).
- Motherboard BIOS program finds adapter board BIOS chips.
- BIOS programs display information during initial system boot.

Memory Map

Memory addresses are represented in several ways. The three most commonly seen in x86 specifications are decimal digits (dec), hexadecimal (h or hex) digits, and kilobytes (K or Kbytes). The translation table below demonstrates the relationship between the three types of numbers

Decimal numbers are cumbersome and most references to memory are in Kbytes or hex. The map on the right is broken into 16K blocks with marks at 4K intervals.

Decimal	Hex	Kbytes
1,032,192	FC000	1,008K
1,015,808	F8000	992K
999,424	F4000	976K
983,040	F0000	960K
966,656	EC000	944K
950,272	E8000	928K
933,888	E4000	912K
917,504	E0000	896K
901,120	DC000	880K
884,736	D8000	864K
868,352	D4000	848K
851,968	D0000	832K
835,584	CC000	816K
819,200	C8000	800K
802,816	C4000	784K
786,432	C0000	768K
770,048	BC000	752K
753,664	B8000	736K
737,280	B4000	720K
720,896	B0000	704K
704,512	AC000	688K
688,128	A8000	672K
671,744	A4000	656K
655,360	A0000	640K

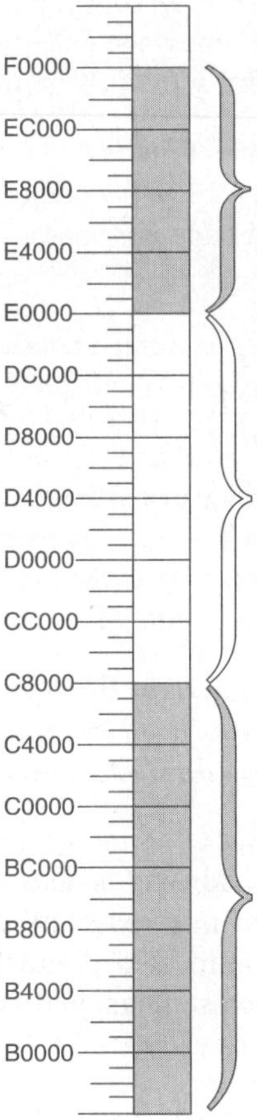

DOS Expanded Memory Page

This area of memory should not be assigned to any option board if you plan to use a DOS partition that requires expanded memory.

You may use this space without reservation if you plan to run the Solaris operating system exclusively or if you have only a token DOS partition that is only used for system configuration.

Available Memory Space (Yours!)

This area of memory is available for your use in configuring your option boards.

The boards that will contend for this space are usually limited to SCSI controllers and Network interface boards. There is sufficient space for two or three boards to share, but larger configurations require careful planning to avoid memory conflicts.

Video Memory Space (Not Available)

The area of memory between A0000 and C8000 hex is not available for optional adapter board use. It is always reserved for your video display adapter. The usable address space starts at about C8000.

For all practical purposes, you can forget that it exists. It takes care of itself!

Note: *The area of memory between 00000 and A0000 hex is not shown as a matter of convenience. The range of addresses shown is the range of available memory that is directly affected by hardware configuration.*

Scanning for BIOS

One of the first things your BIOS will do is scan memory for other valid BIOS programs, and then attach and execute them. Motherboard BIOS begins to scan for other BIOS chips within the first megabyte of memory. Some of the chips it is likely to find are:

- Video adapter BIOS
- SCSI controller BIOS
- Network adapter BIOS

The memory space is scanned sequentially. The first BIOS found is usually the video adapter which is within the A0000–C7FFF hex memory space. When the video BIOS is found, a message is displayed on the screen. This "banner" message usually states the name and revision level of the BIOS. The video BIOS banner is usually the first item displayed during the boot process.

The scan continues until each BIOS chip is found. As each chip is found, a banner (message) is displayed. The SCSI controller is usually found second at address C8000 hex. The address may vary depending on the setting on the SCSI adapter board. The scan will find the SCSI BIOS chip at the address set on the SCSI controller.

Adapter BIOS addresses must be unique. You must configure each adapter with a unique BIOS address before you attach them to the bus. Not all adapters have or need a BIOS program. Check your adapter documentation for more details.

BIOS programs such as the SCSI controller usually do more than just display a banner. In most cases the adapter BIOS will attach itself to the motherboard BIOS program and become a permanent part of the system BIOS. In this way the system motherboard BIOS program dynamically configures itself to accept the newly found BIOS as its own.

Note: *The important thing to remember is that the BIOS program on the adapter board must have a unique address in memory to avoid loading itself into memory space already occupied by another program. You are responsible for setting the BIOS address on some option boards, so be sure to plan ahead.*

As a rule, the area of memory available for any adapter BIOS address is the 96K block from C8000 to E0000. You can use the memory map (page 29) as a visual guide to help you determine where your selected BIOS addresses are located. To make it even easier, I have suggested a standard for adapter board BIOS address settings, and for your convenience, I have included those addresses in the configuration worksheet (page 55).

There are usually only one or two boards on a system that require a BIOS address setting. With the aids provided in Chapter 4, you should have no trouble determining your BIOS address configuration requirements.

RAM Address Allocation

RAM address space is similar to BIOS address space in that it must occupy unique space. The RAM space is memory space that the adapter board must reserve for its unique purpose. The memory is usually set aside as a buffer space for temporary storage of data. Some network cards require a RAM page of 16K for data. Check for RAM requirements when you configure your network board.

RAM space is not detected by the motherboard BIOS scan. RAM space is an area of blank memory space that is reserved for use only when the adapter is in operation. The rule for RAM space is much the same as for BIOS space: Avoid using space that will overlap memory already assigned to another function.

I/O Port Address Allocation

I/O ports are the pigeonhole-type memory locations a bus adapter uses to pass information to and from the operating system. Unlike 4- to 16-Kbyte BIOS or RAM requirements, the I/O ports are usually only 10 or 20 memory locations.

You will most often see I/O port addresses stated in the form "1F0-1FF Hex" or just "1F0h." In the first form you are given the range of first and last port addresses. In the second form you are only given the starting address of the port range.

Even when only one port address is shown, it is safe to assume it is only the starting port address and there is more than one port address used. The number of port locations used is rarely more than 16 memory locations for a single board such as a SCSI, async adapter, parallel adapter, or network card.

I/O Port Address Table

I/O Port Address Table		
Common Port Addresses	**Function**	**Comments**
000–01F	DMA Controller 1	
020–03F	Interrupt Controller 1	
040–057	Timer	
060–06F	Keyboard	
070–07F	Non Maskable Interrupt	
080–09F	DMA Page Register	
0A0–0BF	Interrupt Controller 2	
0C0–0DF	DMA Controller 2	
0F0–0FF	Math Coprocessor	
1F0–1F8	AT Hard Disk	
200–20F	Joystick	Sound Board
220–233	Sound	Sound Board
278–27F	Parallel Port 2	
2E8–2EF	Serial Port Com4	
2F8–2FF	Serial Port Com2	FAX/Modem
330–333	Hard Disk Controller	Primary Disk Controller
338–389	FM Synthesizer	Sound Board
378–37F	Parallel Port 1	Postscript Printer
3B0–3BF	Mono Display Adapter (MDA)	
3BC–3BE	MDA Parallel Port	
3C0–3CF	EGA	
3D0–3D7	CGA	

Common Port Addresses	Function	Comments
3E8–3EF	Serial Port Com3	
3F0–3F7	Floppy Disk Controller	Primary Disk Controller
3F8–3FF	Serial Port Com1	Serial Mouse

Interrupt Request (IRQ) Allocation

IRQ conflicts are like mosquitoes at sunset. They fly right to you if you are crazy enough to stand still for the attack. I have been bitten countless times by both beasts. The easiest way to avoid IRQ conflicts is to plan your installation as described in Chapter 4.

IRQ Table

Interrupt Request Table			
IRQ	**System IRQ's**	**Standards to follow:**	**Recommended:**
0	Timer Output		
1	Keyboard		
2			
3		Standard for Com2 (tty1)	FAX/Modem or Network Adapter
4		Standard for Com1 (tty0)	Serial Mouse
5		Standard for Parallel Port 2	Sound Board
6	Floppy Disk		
7		Standard for Parallel Port 1	System Printer
8	Real Time Clock		
9			Available
10			Network Adapter
11			Available
12			Available
13	Math Coprocessor		
14	Primary Hard Disk		Primary SCSI or IDE
15			Secondary SCSI

Use the interrupt request table to familiarize yourself with the System IRQ assignments (preassigned), the standard IRQ assignments used by most adapters (preassigned), and the IRQ settings recommended for your additional adapter boards.

As you can see in the IRQ table above, there are enough IRQ levels available to install a hard disk controller, network card, printer, mouse, and FAX/modem card, with a few left to spare. This is usually good news, but unfortunately the reason IRQ assignments are so difficult is that most older adapter boards only allow two or three IRQ choices. Avoid using them. Most of the main offenders are network adapters.

The interrupt controller assigns priority from 0 to 7, with 0 assigned the highest priority. Because the interrupt controllers are cascaded using IRQ 2, the resulting priority sequence is not obvious. The second interrupt controller assignments IRQ 8 to 15 are assigned to fit between IRQ 1 and 3. The resulting interrupt priority sequence thus becomes:

IRQ 0, 1, 8, 9, 10, 11, 12, 13, 14, 15, 3, 4, 5, 6, 7

IRQ 2 is linked or cascaded to IRQ 9, and, therefore, does not appear in the priority list. Once linked, IRQ 2 and 9 are actually the same IRQ. The IRQ priority sequence is for the most part "techno-trivia." The most important IRQ configuration information to remember is to assign a unique IRQ setting to each adapter.

See Appendix F for information on which network adapters can cause IRQ problems. The best way to avoid network board problems is to choose the right board. There are excellent boards available that are virtually trouble free.

DMA Channel Allocation

Direct memory access (DMA) is a technique used by some adapter boards to read and write directly to memory without the aid of the central processor unit (CPU). DMA transfer of data is commonly used on network adapters, sound cards, and disk-controller adapters.

DMA Table

DMA Table			
DMA Level	**Reserved**	**Recommendations**	**Transfer Size**
0	Memory Refresh		8 bits
1		Sound Board	8 bits
2	Floppy Disk		8 bits
3		Available	8 bits
4	Cascade		
5		SCSI Adapter	16 bits
6		Available	16 bits
7		Available	16 bits

Network Hardware 3

This chapter provides a brief overview of the basic components required to build a network. Solaris x86 supports both ethernet and token ring, but since ethernet is more commonly used in the Solaris environment, ethernet was used in the examples and illustrations. The principles explained here for the most part apply to both ethernet and token ring. A complete list of supported ethernet and token-ring network adapters is contained in Appendix A.

If you are not attaching your system to a network, you can skip this chapter and move on to Chapter 4.

NETWORK ADAPTER BOARD

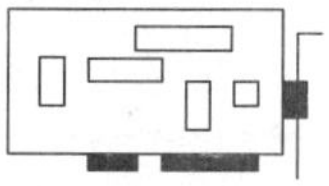

Most x86 computers are configured for standalone use and are not usually connected to a network; therefore, it will be necessary to add a network adapter board to provide the necessary network interface circuitry. In contrast to x86 systems, most engineering workstations are designed with integrated network interface circuitry.

Some server configurations may contain multiple network adapters. The ability to connect a server to more than one network allows the server to act as a network bridge and router.

PHYSICAL MEDIA

Physical media refers to the wires or cables that are used to carry data on the network. Ethernet networks can transfer data through many types of physical media. The most common types of physical media are:

- Coaxial cable
- Unshielded twisted-pair cable (telephone cable)
- Fiberoptic cable

Some specialized applications may require a wireless network solution. Wireless networks are not widely used and are not discussed in this chapter.

The most popular media today is unshielded twisted-pair telephone cable. The low cost, ease of use, and flexibility of twisted-pair (10BASE-T) cabling is the main reason for its popularity. The example network I used for this book is based on a coaxial cable (10BASE-2) segment connected to an unshielded twisted-pair (UTP/10BASE-T) hub.

Coaxial Cable

Coaxial cable comes in two popular types:

- 10BASE-5 thick-net
- 10BASE-2 thin-net

Thick-net

Many early network backbones were based on thick-net, also known as 10BASE-5. This type of coaxial cable can span 500 meters per segment, as compared to only 185 meters per segment on thin-net 10BASE-2 coaxial cable. Buildings wired with thick-net typically have one or more long segments of coaxial cable snaking throughout the ceiling to provide taps for individual drops and drops to concentrators or hubs.

Up to 100 transceivers can be connected to a cable segment. Transceivers are spaced on the cable 2.5 meters apart. Proper spacing will avoid the possibility of interference from standing waves on the cable.

Thick-net Segment Example

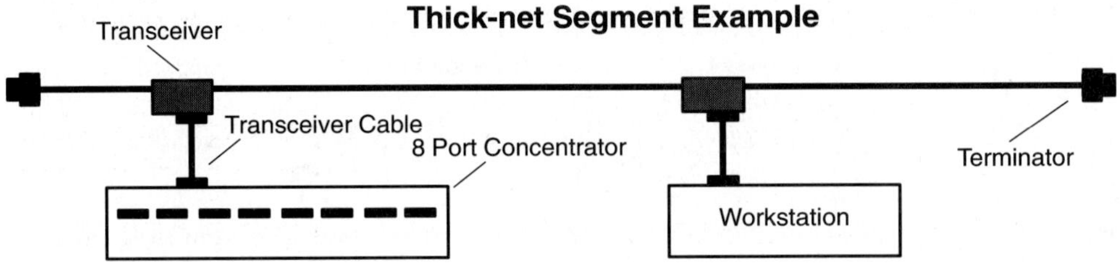

Transceiver AUI Cable Connector Pin Assignments

1	Shield to connector shell		
2	Collision +	9	Collision –
3	Transmit +	10	Transmit –
4	Reserved	11	Reserved
5	Receive +	12	Receive –
6	Power Return	13	+ Power
7	Reserved	14	Reserved
8	Reserved	15	Reserved

The transceiver drop cable can extend up to 15 meters from the backbone and has a 15-pin D-series connector at each end. Thick-net transceiver AUI (Access Unit Interface) cables are bulky and hard to handle when they are routed through walls.

This type of network cabling was effective for many years, but as technology improved, better and cheaper methods were developed. Fiberoptic cable has replaced coaxial cable for most high-speed long-haul applications.

Thin-net

Thin-net 10BASE-2 coaxial cable is a less expensive alternative to thick-net cabling schemes but does not work well in large building implementations. Thin-net is most often found on small local area networks that do not span great distances. A small office network of 5–30 nodes can be easily constructed simply by connecting a thin-net cable between each node and terminating both ends.

Each thin-net coaxial cable segment is typically routed in series to a BNC type T connector at each node on the network and terminated at each end with a 50-ohm terminator. There is no drop cable between the coaxial cable and the network node. The T connector is always attached directly to the BNC connector on the network node.

I do not see much use for thin-net cabling to network nodes in new network construction. Twisted-pair is much more flexible for workstation connections. Thin-net is, however, handy for backbone use to connect wiring closets and active hubs together. In the thin-net example diagram, a server is connected via thin-net coaxial cable to UTP concentrator hubs. The hubs can be located in wiring closets throughout a building, and nodes can be connected to the hubs using UTP telephone grade wiring.

Thin-net Backbone Example

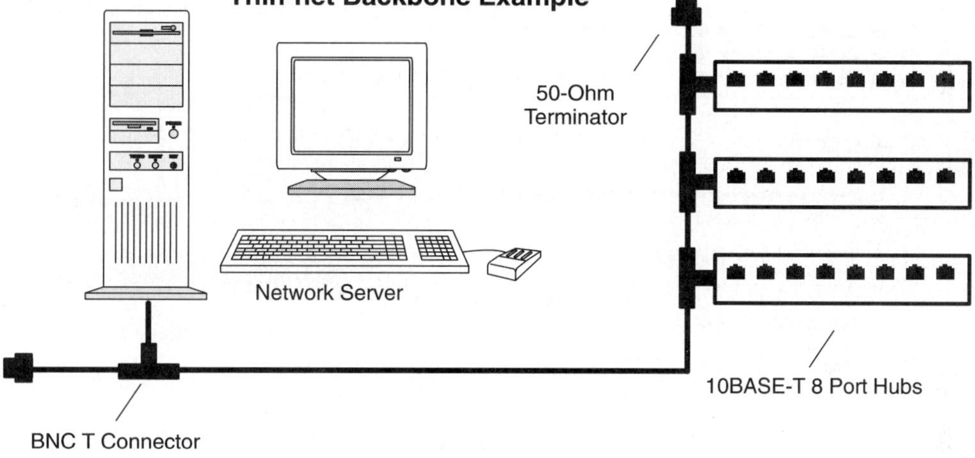

Thin-net uses coaxial cable type RG58 A/U or C/U, 50 ohm, with a single shield and BNC connectors. This type of cabling is limited to 185-meter segment lengths, 30 nodes per segment, 1024 nodes per network, and total network span of 925 meters. Minimum space between nodes is 0.5 meter.

Unshielded Twisted-pair (UTP) Cable

Unshielded twisted-pair cabling is 24-gauge solid conductor copper telephone wire with each pair tightly twisted together to provide noise cancellation. It is inexpensive, easy to install, and many buildings are already wired with UTP for network use. UTP is the cabling system of choice for most large building or premises wiring schemes. Most new building construction can easily incorporate data network requirements using existing telephone wiring techniques. The 10BASE-T network example illustrated below shows how a typical building would be wired to accommodate networked office computers.

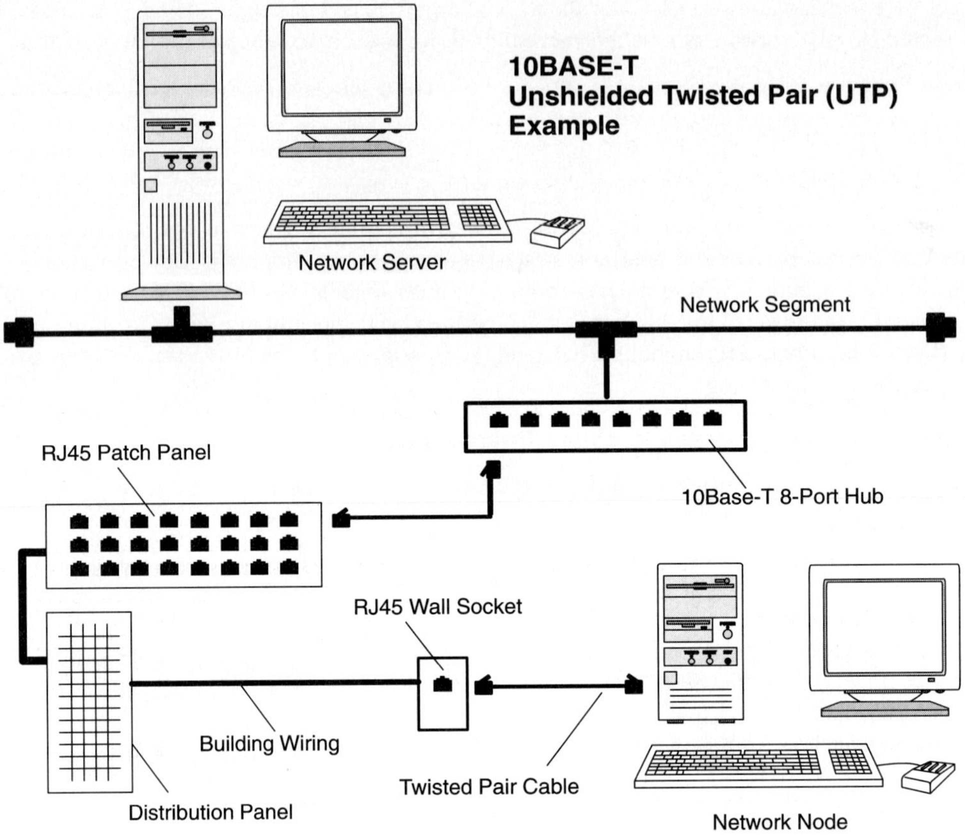

UTP wiring is especially valuable for connecting computer systems in offices to a network backbone. Many networks are setup to connect servers together on very high-speed backbones to increase performance, while at the same time using less expensive UTP technology to connect individual network nodes to the backbone through a concentrator or hub. The office computer node can be connected to the network by using a simple RJ45 telephone cable between the node and the RJ45 modular 8-pin wall plug. It is not uncommon to see both data and telephone on the same wall plug. These dual-function wall plates usually have two clearly marked jacks (phone and data).

RJ45 wall outlets are connected via UTP cabling to wiring closet distribution panels within the building. The distribution panels are in turn wired to patch panels that provide a simple and versatile way to connect a network hub port to any office data outlet via a patch cable. This ability to easily connect and disconnect office data outlets is extremely valuable.

UTP connections are limited to a maximum of 100 meters between the network node and the hub. Plenum grade wiring may be required in some buildings, but standard telephone cable is most often used.

RJ45 Modular 8-Pin Connectors

When RJ45 jacks (ISO 8877 8-pin modular) are used, the wiring of the plugs should conform to ANSI/EIA/TIA 568-1991 standards.

- ANSI - American National Standards Institute
- EIA - Electronic Industries Association
- TIA - Telecommunications Industry Association

Two pairs of wire are required to connect each node to the network. The two pairs are wired to RJ45 plugs using the pins indicated in the following example.

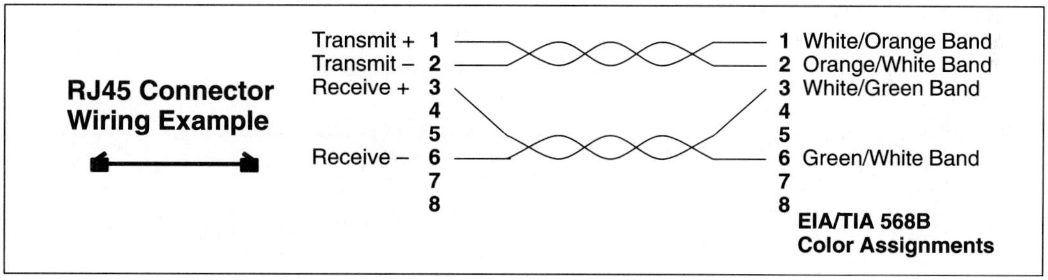

Fiberoptic Cable

Fiberoptic cable is most often used to interconnect buildings, floors, computer rooms, and wiring closets within a building. Fiberoptic cable is not affected by electromagnetic fields and can be used in environments that are hostile to coaxial cable.

Fiberoptic cables are more difficult to work with and require experienced installers. This medium is much too expensive for use at the network node level. Using fiberoptic connections to each node on the network is only done in cases where there is a special need, such as security (cannot be tapped), hostile environment, or speed.

TRANSCEIVER

A transceiver is a simple device that connects dissimilar media by providing two different types of connectors. You may have a network node with a UTP RJ45 connection that you want to connect to thick-net 15-pin AUI drop cable. A simple transceiver can be used to connect to the

AUI cable on one side and to the UTP connection on the other side. The transceiver handles any signal conversion required. All you have to do is plug it in.

BRIDGE

Repeaters can be used to add segments or to expand a local network until it reaches the design limits imposed by the network topology, such as furthest distance (time delay) between two nodes, total number of nodes on the network, and performance.

A bridge is similar to a repeater in that it connects two network segments. The difference is that a bridge joins two separate and different networks, while a repeater only joins two segments of the same network. The bridge can be used to expand a local area network by transparently linking additional local area networks.

The bridge connects the two networks in such a way that communication across the bridge is transparent to the communicating nodes. Nodes on both sides of a bridge appear to be on the same network.

2 Networks Joined by a Bridge

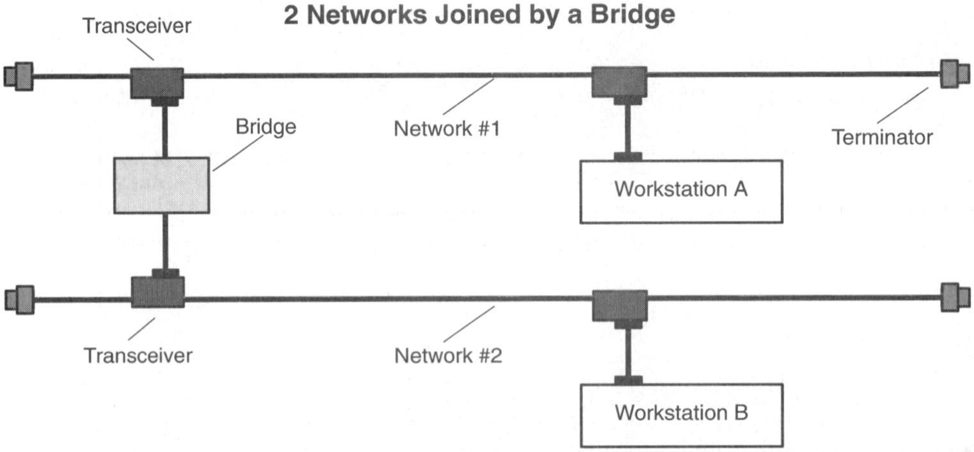

The bridge can provide performance gains by filtering the traffic that flows across both sides of the bridge, allowing only traffic across the bridge when the destination is on the other side. This one simple characteristic of the bridge has a profound influence on network performance. Separating workstations into balanced workgroups is a basic technique used by network administrators to tune a network for maximum performance. The bridge is the primary tool that allows this kind of tuning.

One slight drawback of the bridge is that it is a store-and-forward device. It saves packets in a temporary storage until the first available opportunity to forward the packets through the bridge to their destination. This delay is a small price to pay, considering the enormous benefit derived.

REPEATER

A network can be constructed from several segments that are joined by a repeater that passes the network data between segments. At the same time, the repeater cleanses the signal and restores signal timings to their optimum levels.

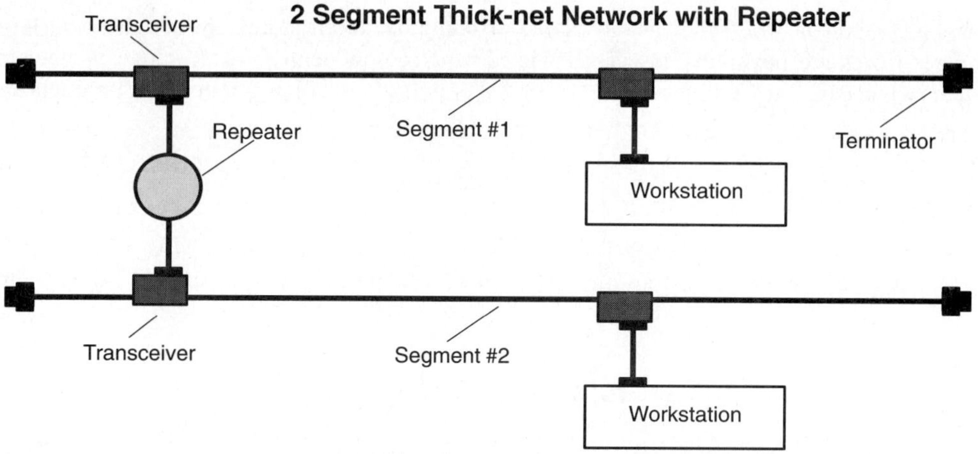

Repeaters can also be used to connect segments of dissimilar media. You could, for instance, have two segments of coaxial cable in two buildings with a fiberoptic segment running between buildings to join the two coaxial cable segments. All you need is a repeater that supports input from both types of media. This is actually very common, and repeaters are available in all types of configurations to accommodate this type of need.

HUB

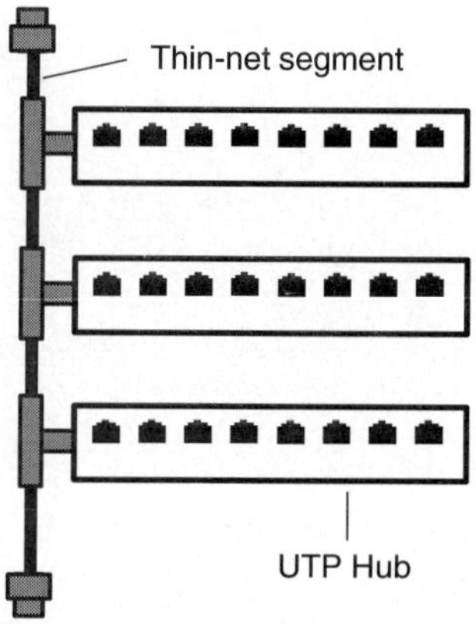

The hub or concentrator is a convenient and efficient way of providing multiple connections to the same network segment. The hub has the added benefit of functioning as a transceiver, thereby connecting many nodes of one medium type to a network segment of another medium type.

You will most often see hubs in wiring closets or in computer room groupings. The hub will support multiple ports of one medium type, and also will provide for a single connection to another media such as coax or fiberoptic cable.

Hubs come in a variety of shapes and sizes, but they all perform the same basic functions. Some more sophisticated hubs can report status of the ports and gather valuable performance data that can be sent to a network manager. Large networks need hubs capable of supporting up to 1,024 nodes on a single network. Larger hubs are mounted in racks and can be expanded to meet the changing requirements of large network configurations.

HARD TO FIND COMPONENTS

Network components are often not available at computer retail stores. Although some large computer stores are beginning to carry basic network components, a wide range of network products wll necessitate finding a dealer or service provider specializing in network products and services.

Planning Your Installation 4

THINKING AHEAD

Computer installations always require some level of planning. Whether you plan to upgrade your desktop system, install a network of system nodes, or build a standalone system for your personal use, you will always need to consider the consequences of your decisions before acting on them.

Consider the problem of installing untested upgrades to a manufacturing network server at the month's end. Think about how you would explain your timing to the president of the company if the end-of-month revenue shipments out of manufacturing were delayed. You would get little sympathy from anyone if you kept the network off line for an extra day because you did not have the right connectors or cables.

In my case, I usually have to explain to my ever–enduring wife why I picked the day before her "big" presentation to upgrade the motherboard in her computer. I can tell you with certainty that I will not make that mistake again. Scheduling well in advance is on my planning checklist!

Planning is not difficult. The process is outlined below:

- Analyze your needs
- Write down your configuration details
- Procure the proper hardware and software
- Schedule the installation time
- Gather everything you need in a clean work space
- Go for it — install!

ANALYZE YOUR NEEDS

The amount of analysis required will vary depending on the size and complexity of the installation. You may have to do some extensive research if you are planning a network installation with many systems and many software applications. Research can help you determine the unique requirements of each system, such as performance, size, connectivity, and flexibility.

The analysis process includes a variety of variables such as:

- Applications
- Application growth

- Performance
- Size of installation
- Network servers
- Engineering workstations
- Network nodes
- Workplace environment
- Upgrades
- Printing

Applications

What business are you in? The best way to analyze your application needs is to review the way you do your business and then determine which computer applications can contribute to improving your productivity. Common types of applications include computer-aided design and engineering, software development, desktop publishing, database management, and graphics.

Determine which applications will be supported on each system you install and match the system functionality to meet your application. Several configuration choices can be directly linked to the application requirements. Applications generally require sufficient memory and disk swap space to function properly, or may require a sharply focused display with accelerated graphics.

If you are not sure about your application requirements, you will have to do some research. Do not proceed with hardware choices until you are confident that your applications will work well in the hardware environment you wish to create.

Growth

Growth is difficult to deal with in a networked multiuser environment. It seems that the more you have, the more you need. Take a long and thoughtful look into the future and plan for inevitable expansion. Memory and hard-disk space are two components that will certainly require expansion as your applications grow.

Always configure systems with excess capacity to absorb at least the first year of expansion. Plan an easy upgrade path by anticipating the additional space requirements for new peripherals.

Performance

Take a global approach when considering performance. View the network or system as a whole. Make sure the operating system, the network, and the hardware are sharing the performance load. A performance bottleneck anywhere within the network could potentially bring the entire system to its knees.

When evaluating performance, consider:

- CPU speed for compute-intensive applications
- SCSI data throughput for database applications
- Network data throughput for optimum number of network nodes
- Display speed for graphics applications

Computer applications seem to consume gains in technological performance as fast as they are realized. Based on the past, it seems applications will always grow to fill the performance surplus left in the wake of advancing hardware technology. You could be led to conclude there is never enough performance, and you would not be far from the truth.

There is no end in sight for the technology and performance explosion, and there is no accurate equation to determine the correct performance level for any specific system configuration. This may seem like bad news, but it is actually quite good. The benefit to you from investing in industry standard technology is the upgrade path to ever-increasing performance.

The best way to maintain a performance edge is to use the best and most stable hardware available today, and to plan a hardware migration path that maintains a parallel course with industry standards. Avoid investment in a proprietary product unless it is an enabling technology that is critical to your business. Configuring a computer system that follows industry standards is your best assurance that performance will always be there when needed.

Size of Installation (Number of Systems)

As with most system projects, there is some economy of scale to be gained when many systems with similar configurations are built on an assembly line. After the first of a group of systems has been built and tested, the remaining systems will require less of your effort to achieve the same result.

Single-system installations require a greater effort per system, much like building prototype airplanes or cars. If each system is unique, special care and effort must go into its creation and maintenance.

The Single-System Strategy

Get it right the first time! Do not experiment with untested hardware or cutting-edge technology (you might get cut). Most hardware vendors will be of little help if you have incompatibilities or unexplained failures. Stick with proven, reliable, and compatible components.

Treat a single system as you would your primary mode of transportation. You must depend on your car, bike, or motorcycle to get you to places on time. You want your vehicle to be reliable, easy to use, and easy to maintain.

The Multiple-System Strategy

Experiment with hardware components to get the best performance and lowest cost! Find a vendor willing to work with you to configure, test, and maintain evaluation systems. If you plan to buy a large quantity of hardware, you should have little problem finding a helpful vendor.

Once you are satisfied with the components you test or evaluate, you can easily order systems from your vendor that are preconfigured and ready to install. If your vendor will not agree to build systems to your specifications, the answer is simple — find another vendor!

The network is a major consideration when installing multiple systems. The network hardware must be designed, configured, and installed before systems can be connected. On new networks, servers should be installed and operational before adding network nodes and workstations.

The Solaris operating system network installation process relies heavily on network resources. One of the first things you will need on a new network is an installation server that enables network clients to install the operating system without the need for local CD-ROM or hard disk.

It is extremely helpful to build and test a prototype network when evaluating components. You can use a test network setup similar to the basic network example used in Chapter 3.

Network Server Configurations

Do you need a network server? The network server is on the high end of the performance and feature scale. When you think server, think big!

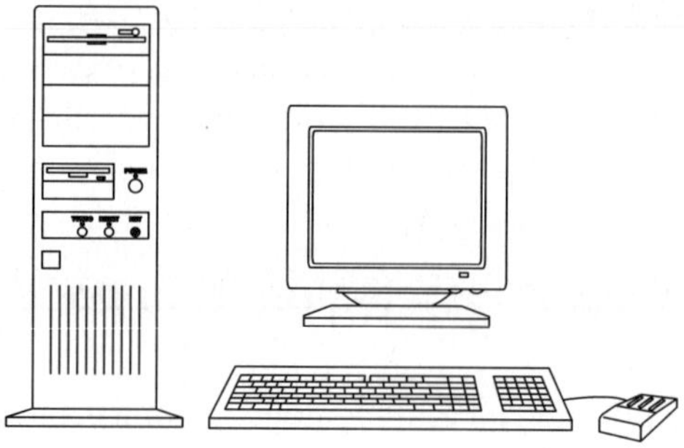

The main visual characteristic of a server is large physical size and shape, usually a freestanding full tower case. The large physical size and big power supply are required to accommodate the server's large complement of peripheral devices and option boards. A typical server may include:

- Full tower case with 300-350 watt power supply
- 486DX CPU on EISA or MCA motherboard
- 32MB or more of main memory
- Fast SCSI II hard-disk subsystem
- Fast SCSI CD–ROM
- Fast SCSI magnetic tape unit
- 3.5- and 5.25-inch floppy drives
- Fast network adapter
- Postscript laser printer
- High-speed FAX/Modem

A network server should be used exclusively for providing network resources. It should not be additionally used as a personal workstation. The only exception to this is on a small office network of less than 12 systems. The network overhead would be light enough to make a dedicated server impractical. In cases such as this, the system administrator would most likely use the server as a personal workstation.

Motherboard

The typical server is configured with either an EISA or MCA motherboard. Avoid using ISA motherboards on servers, as they are limited in performance and expandability. Only EISA and MCA motherboards can provide the bus width and DMA transfer speeds required to support multiple fast SCSI controllers.

Multiple Processors

Multiple processor configurations are becoming commonplace on network servers. When computing power is critical to the applications, look for EISA or MCA systems equipped to support multiple processors. Check Appendix A for a list of compatible multiple processor systems.

ISA Boards in EISA Motherboards

When using the EISA motherboard, it is critical to match the network adapter and SCSI controller to the bus. Do not use ISA adapters such as network and SCSI boards in EISA motherboard slots unless you have determined that ISA performance is adequate for your applications.

System performance will be somewhat limited by ISA boards on the EISA bus, but the added expense of EISA components may not be justified for some applications.

Memory

Memory can dramatically affect server performance. A server may need more than 32MB of main memory to perform even routine tasks. The application demands placed on the server usually determine the correct amount of memory to install. The important thing to remember is to choose a motherboard equipped to handle main memory requirements of 128MB or greater.

SCSI II Subsystem

SCSI II is the current widely available SCSI standard. SCSI I is out of date and not a viable option. SCSI III is in the future, but it will not be the focus of this book. SCSI II is available and it is dependable. Check the documentation supplied with your SCSI HBA and SCSI devices to determine if you have SCSI I or SCSI II. See Appendix C for more details on SCSI.

The SCSI controller is a general purpose interface. It can support a variety of devices such as hard disks, CD-ROM drives, printers, scanners, and tape drives. The SCSI controller and SCSI devices combine to form a subsystem that can be tested and configured to meet changing requirements. The components of the SCSI subsystem are:

- SCSI host bus adapter
- SCSI bus internal and external cables
- SCSI devices
- SCSI terminators

In most cases the hard-disk drives are the most used and most important devices on the SCSI bus. Performance varies from controller to controller. The current performance standard is 10 megabytes per second (10MB/s) SCSI bus transfer rate in synchronous mode. This is generally referred to as fast SCSI. A fast SCSI II subsystem is the only viable server option. Anything less would limit performance.

Additional SCSI controller features you may need to consider are caching and redundancy. Servers providing database access could benefit greatly from the enhanced performance of a fully cached SCSI controller. In addition, many applications require the security of fully mirrored or redundant disk subsystems. If you are planning to configure a large-capacity high-performance disk subsystem, spend extra time researching these optional SCSI controller features.

SCSI CD-ROM drive technology continues to improve. Review the drives available and compare access speed and data transfer rates. Choose a compatible drive with the best performance characteristics. Avoid using drives with access times greater than 265ms or with transfer rates slower than 300kb/sec.

The magnetic tape unit (MTU) is available in a variety of shapes and sizes. Servers require high-capacity tape units with fast transfer rates. Older SCSI I MTU devices may limit the overall throughput of the SCSI controller. Some SCSI II controllers cannot negotiate fast 10MB/s synchronous transfer rates if a slow SCSI I device is on the SCSI bus.

The server MTU should have a capacity of at least 2GB per cartridge. File system backup is critical on a server, and the MTU is the primary backup device. Consider the size of the server file systems when selecting your MTU.

Floppy Disk

Floppy disk drives are inexpensive commodities. Configure your server with both 3.5-inch 1.44MB and 5.25-inch 1.2MB drives. You will need both formats. Other formats are available but unnecessary. All the software distributed on a disk is on one of the two recommended formats.

Network Adapter

The network adapter can be a performance bottleneck. The server must have a high performance network adapter matched to the EISA or MCA bus. Do not use an ISA network adapter on a server. It may work, but it also may choke the network!

Printer

After the water cooler, the printer is the next most popular place for people to congregate. Everyone appreciates a good, fast laser printer. Think of your printer as a workhorse. It must be reliable, able to handle the heavy loads, and friendly to users. A server should have a durable 300-dpi (dots per inch) PostScript printer with at least 4MB of memory and a speed of eight pages per minute.

For best performance, avoid using printers with a serial interface; the parallel interface is much faster. A serial interface has the benefit of being able to span greater distances than the parallel interface, but it should only be used when the printer must be located apart from the server and out of range of the parallel interface. The parallel printer interface should not be used to span distances greater than 5 to 7 meters.

Printer furniture is often overlooked. The printer will need a table to sit on as well as space to store supplies and a place to sort and store printer output.

Monitor, Sound Board, Keyboard, and Mouse

The audio board, mouse, keyboard, video display adapter, and monitor are not very important on a dedicated server unless it is used by a system administrator for network management. If the server is not used regularly, you can save money by using a less expensive keyboard, mouse, and monitor.

Floor Space

Server configurations can grow quickly (much like bamboo), so make sure you have plenty of room to expand. It is very likely you will need room for additional equipment, such as peripheral expansion boxes, printers, and modems.

External cables can be tough to manage on a server. Think about the number of telephone lines, terminal lines, printer lines, power lines, and other network lines that can spill over into adjacent areas.

Technical Skill Level

Server configuration will challenge your technical skills. Complex configuration conflicts are more likely to occur on servers because of multiple SCSI controllers, multiple processors, multiple network cards, and multiple terminal controllers.

If you consider yourself a novice, make sure you have a skilled technical person available to help out when things get tough. Setting up a server on a network requires experience and a lot of patience.

Engineering Workstation Configurations

Do you need an engineering workstation? The engineering workstation is in the middle of the performance and feature scale. This type of system is usually personalized to meet the specific needs of a power user. The main characteristic of the engineering workstation is a subset of local resources that are usually found only on the server. Engineering workstations are often standalone configurations.

The engineering workstation can depend on a network server for most resources, but duplication of network resources often occurs for the sake of convenience and productivity. The resources on the engineering workstation should be configured to match the needs of the power user. Engineering workstations are quite often standalone (not dependent on a server) systems that are installed, configured, and maintained by a power user.

Most engineering workstations contain:

- Medium or mini tower case with 200-300 watt power supply
- 486DX 33MHz CPU on ISA, EISA, or MCA motherboard
- 24MB or more of main memory
- Fast SCSI II hard-disk subsystem
- Fast SCSI CD–ROM
- Fast SCSI magnetic tape unit
- 3.5- and 5.25-inch floppy drives
- Fast network adapter
- High-performance display adapter with 17-inch monitor
- Sound board
- Quality keyboard and mouse

The Power User

A power user can be a programmer, a technical writer, a draftsman, an engineer, or anyone else who regularly places a heavy load on the workstation or the network. A programmer may require greater computing power to execute lengthy compiler tasks, while a technical writer would benefit more from a personal printer to handle large print jobs. Adding a printer to a technical writer's system can also provide a productivity boost for network printer users who otherwise would have long delays because of large jobs in the print queue.

Motherboard

The engineering workstation can be designed using any of the motherboard bus types. The ISA motherboard with a VESA local bus is ideal for the entry-level workstation. The VESA local bus slots provide good performance at a reasonable cost. The EISA bus and the MCA bus motherboards are better choices for the high-performance workstation.

At a minimum the motherboard should have a 486DX 33MHz processor. Most motherboards provide for upgrades to faster CPU speeds. Confirm the upgrade path on the motherboard. Replacing the CPU with a faster version is relatively painless.

EISA

Whenever using an EISA motherboard, it is important to ensure that the network adapter, the video display adapter, and the SCSI controller adapter are true EISA bus adapter boards. These three types of boards require high-speed bus data transfer to and from memory, and have a significant effect on overall system performance. Using ISA versions of these boards will severely limit performance.

Some ISA boards such as multi-I/O boards, modem boards, and audio boards can be used on EISA bus slots without a performance penalty. These boards have a very low throughput rate and will not adversely affect overall system performance. In fact, you may have a difficult time finding anything but ISA boards of this type. I do not remember ever seeing an EISA bus modem, I/O board, or audio board.

Memory

The engineering workstation may need more than 16MB of main memory to meet the performance expectations of the power user. The application demands placed on the workstation should be evaluated to determine the correct amount of memory to install. Choose a motherboard flexible enough to handle main memory requirements of 64MB or greater.

SCSI or IDE Disk Subsystem

Disk drives and floppy drives are critical components for any engineering workstation configuration. Both IDE and SCSI disk drives can be used. IDE is a good choice on systems not requiring SCSI peripherals such as CD–ROM or magnetic tape.

If you need SCSI peripherals, you will need a SCSI controller. Once you install a SCSI controller, it is best to avoid using IDE on the same system. Use only SCSI peripherals if possible.

The CD–ROM, MTU, hard disk-drive, and floppy-disk drive are necessities on a standalone workstation.

Monitor and Video Adapter

Engineering workstations usually require superior quality and performance from the display. Look for a monitor that will support 1280×1024 non-interlaced resolution at 70Hz refresh rate. The minimum monitor size should be 17-inch. Many applications require 19-inch or 21-inch monitors. It is very important to see a monitor model before buying one. Be prepared to spend as much for a quality 21-inch color monitor and adapter as you do for the rest of the system.

The video adapter will directly affect overall system performance. Avoid using average performing video adapters.

Audio Board

An audio board and speakers are optional, but the multimedia capabilities included with the Solaris operating system take advantage of these built-in features.

Keyboard and Mouse

This is an area of great concern because of repetitive stress syndrome. The mouse and keyboard should be ergonomically designed to protect the user from undue stress. Track balls are good alternatives to the mouse.

Printer

Printers are optional personal productivity tools. Adding a printer to a workstation can provide network benefits as well as quick access for the workstation owner. All printers can be shared on the network, so any workstation printer could serve several people in a small work group.

Workstations with printers will require some additional disk space for spool files (10MB or more) depending on the type and volume of printing done. The root partition of the operating system is where the extra space is required.

Client Configurations

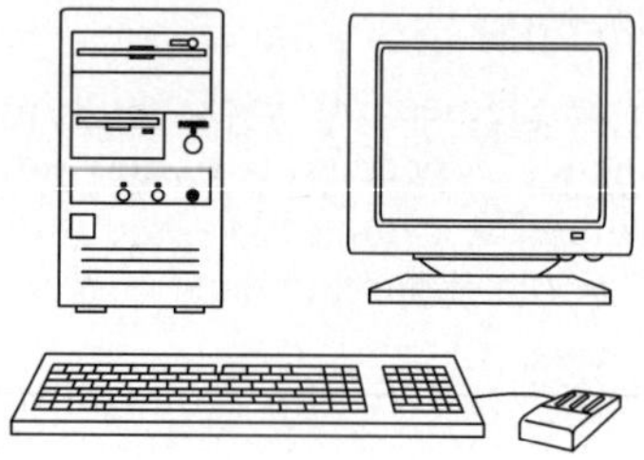

Do you need a client system? The network client is at the bottom of the performance and feature scale. This type of system is usually widely distributed on the network and dedicated to basic business applications such as word processing, electronic mail, inventory management, order entry, and information services.

The main characteristics of a client system are:

1. Used mostly by nontechnical personnel
2. Installed, configured, and maintained by a dedicated system administrator
3. Dependent on the network server for access to printers and file systems

The network client in the client-server model is usually referred to as a diskless client or diskfull client.

A typical entry-level network client system configuration includes:

- Mini tower or desktop slim-line case with 200-watt power supply
- 386DX 40MHz CPU (with math coprocessor) on ISA motherboard
- 16MB of main memory
- 40MB IDE disk (diskfull)
- 3.5-inch floppy disk
- Fast network adapter
- 1024×768 display adapter with 15-inch monitor
- Sound board (optional)
- Quality keyboard and mouse

The network clients depend on a network server for most resources. This is the most common network configuration because sharing server resources is cost effective.

Network Performance

Without local resources to draw from, the client places heavy loads on the network. The network must be designed to accommodate the peak traffic demands of clients. This is one of the main reasons why networks are broken into local areas. The number of nodes in a local area network is balanced to match the load capacity of the physical network medium. Network client performance is sensitive to improperly balanced or poorly designed networks.

Motherboard

ISA motherboards can work well for network client use. Motherboards with 486DX processors and VESA local bus slots can provide excellent performance for the majority of applications.

One possible drawback of ISA motherboards is the poor availability of network cards for VESA local bus. If network throughput is critical, MCA bus or EISA bus motherboards may be the better choice.

Memory

16MB is the recommended minimum memory. This is adequate for most applications on a network client.

IDE Disk Subsystem

I would not build a system without at least a small IDE hard disk for the DOS partition. Instead, I recommend that each network client have at least enough disk space for root and swap partitions. This will enhance performance on both the network and the client. A 200MB IDE drive would provide plenty of space for two primary partitions, and would minimize network loads.

Color Monitor and Video Adapter

A good quality 15-inch monitor with 0.28mm dot pitch and 1024×768 noninterlaced resolution will work fine for most network clients. You can find very inexpensive monitors in the 15-inch range, but I would avoid low-quality monitors that flicker or have large dot size and poor focus. The monitor is arguably the single most important component on the system.

Audio Board

The audio board and speakers are purely optional system components. They enable the use of some multimedia services available within the Solaris desktop tools.

Network Requirements

The network client depends on the network. Install the fastest network card you can afford. Network throughput is important. Do not use older technology 8-bit network cards. Older cards will work, but they are slow enough to make an insomniac yawn.

Physical Environment

The working environment is becoming a critical issue. Check the lighting, keyboard height, monitor height, and chairs for good ergonomic design. Proper placement of monitors and keyboards can help workers avoid undue glare on the monitor (to avoid eye strain) and undue stress on the wrists.

Some monitors may be sensitive to electromagnetic interference. Check building plans to avoid placing systems close to major power conduits or next to main power transformer facilities.

Upgrades

If you are upgrading a system, review the existing system components and documentation. Plan to rebuild your system from scratch, keeping only those components you can use. Do not try to make your new system fit within the limits of your existing hardware, but try instead to fit salvageable hardware into your new configuration.

When you decide to keep an existing component, verify that it is compatible with the operating system and make sure you have all the original documentation and software. If you do not have the documentation or software you need, get replacement copies from the manufacturer or local computer dealer.

You may have to upgrade your case, your cables, your motherboard, and your peripherals. Upgrade everything at one time. You will not want to add more upgrades and in a month have to repeat the installation process.

If you are upgrading, there is a reasonable chance you have existing data on the target system. Backup your data and think about how you will restore your files on the upgraded system. You may have a problem restoring the old files in the new environment if you do not give it some thought now!

Inherited Hardware

It is always possible you inherited system hardware that was passed from one corporate owner to another. If this happens to you, take inventory of the system components and locate any and all original documentation, drivers, or utility software. As with all upgrade projects, you should contact the original component manufacturer for documentation and lost or misplaced software.

CONFIGURATION WORKSHEET

Once you have completed your analysis, begin developing a system requirement specification or worksheet. This is nothing more than writing down a list of the components you need for each system, and determining the correct configuration choices. By resolving configuration conflicts on paper, you will avoid the misery of endless hours of troubleshooting.

You can design your own worksheet or use the one provided on page 55. If you are configuring several systems, copy the worksheet and use one for each unique system. The worksheet will prove extremely valuable when you are ready to negotiate the purchase of your components or systems.

Note: *Appendix A contains a list of Solaris x86 compatible hardware.*

Configuration Worksheet

Host Name: ______________________ **Date:** ______________________

IP Address: ______________________ **BIOS:** ______________________

Domain Name: ______________________ **Description:** ______________________

1. Motherboard

Type
- ☐ ISA
- ☐ EISA
- ☐ MCA
- ☐ VESA Local Bus
- ☐ PCI
- ☐ Proprietary
- ☐ PCMCIA

CPU
- ☐ 386DX
- ☐ 486SX
- ☐ 486DX
- ☐ 486DX2
- ☐ 486SLC
- ☐ Pentium
- ☐ Other ______

Speed
- ☐ 25MHz
- ☐ 33MHz
- ☐ 40MHz
- ☐ 50MHz
- ☐ 66MHz
- ☐ Other ______

Memory
- ☐ 12MB
- ☐ 16MB
- ☐ 24MB
- ☐ 28MB
- ☐ 32MB
- ☐ Other ______

Case
- ☐ Slim Line Desktop
- ☐ Full Size Desktop
- ☐ Small (Mini) Tower
- ☐ Medium Tower
- ☐ Full Height Tower
- ☐ Other ______

2. Video Adapter

Manufacturer: ______________________

Model or Chip Type: ______________________

Refresh Rate: ______________________

Does your video display adapter support optional features such as mouse or sound? If yes, record the IRQ, I/O port, DMA, or other required settings.

- ☐ IRQ# ______
- ☐ I/O Port ______ ☐ Other ______

Features
- ☐ VESA Local Bus
- ☐ Mouse Port
- ☐ Sound Support
- ☐ 24bit Color
- ☐ PCI Bus

3. Monitor

Model: ______________ *Resolution:* ______________

VRAM Size: ______________ *Refresh Rate:* ______________

Size
- ☐ 15"
- ☐ 17"
- ☐ 20"
- ☐ Other______

4. Mouse

- ☐ Serial
- ☐ Bus

______

Keyboard
- ☐ English
- ☐ Other

______

5. Primary Disk Controller

Floppy Controller

Port 3F0–3F7

- ☐ Enabled
- ☐ Disabled

IRQ 6 *DMA* 2

Recommended Configuration

	IRQ#	*DMA*	*BIOS*	*I/O Port*
SCSI Setting	11	5	C8000	330
IDE Setting	14	None	None	1F0–1F7
Record your board setting here				

6. Floppy & Hard Disks

Complete this section for your primary disk controller, either SCSI or IDE — not both.

- ☐ IDE
- ☐ SCSI

Floppy Drive
- ☐ 1.2MB Floppy
- ☐ 1.44MB Floppy
- ☐ 2.88MB Floppy

IDE Disk Drive Assignments

		Make	*Size*
1	Master		
2	Slave		

ID	*Suggested*
0	Hard Disk
1	Hard Disk
2	Open
3	Open
4	Mag Tape
5	Open
6	CD–ROM

Termination
- ☐ Internal Only
- ☐ External Only
- ☐ Internal & External

SCSI Target ID Assignments

ID	*Device Type*	*Size*
0		
1		
2		
3		
4		
5		
6		

Configuration Worksheet — continued

7. Second SCSI Controller

Floppy Controller
☐ Enabled
☐ Disabled

Recommended Configuration

	IRQ#	*DMA*	*BIOS*	*I/O Port*
For SCSI #2	15	2	D8000	230
Record your settings				

If you only have one controller in your system, this section does not apply to you.

IDE is not recommended for your second disk controller. There are some intelligent IDE adapter boards that will allow two IDE boards to co-exist on the same bus, but most IDE boards do not properly disable the floppy controller and therefore, will not work.

The second SCSI adapter does not require floppy disk capability. It is assumed that you configured the first disk controller with a floppy controller enabled.

You cannot boot from the second SCSI controller. The system will always try to boot from the boot disk on the primary (first) disk controller.

ID	*Suggested*
0	Open
1	Open
2	Open
3	Open
4	Open
5	Open
6	Open

Termination
☐ Internal Only
☐ External Only
☐ Internal & External

SCSI Target ID Assignments

ID	*Device Type*	*Size*
0		
1		
2		
3		
4		
5		
6		

8. Network Adapters

Not all network boards use IRQ, BIOS, or DMA settings.
Cross out the settings that do not apply to your board.

Model: ______

Eternet Address ______

☐ UTP ☐ Token Ring ☐ Other
☐ Thin Net ☐ Ethernet ______

Recommended Configuration

	IRQ#	*DMA*	*BIOS*	*I/O Port*
First Board	10		CC000	300
Record your settings				

Model: ______

Ethernet Address: ______

☐ UTP ☐ Token Ring ☐ Other
☐ Thin Net ☐ Ethernet ______

	IRQ#	*DMA*	*BIOS*	*I/O Port*
Second Board	12		DC000	
Record your settings				

9. Audio Card

Model: ______

FM Synth Port
338–339

Game Port
200–207
☐ Enabled
☐ Disabled

	IRQ#	*DMA*	*BIOS*	*I/O Port*
Recommended	5	1	None	220–233
Record your settings				

10. I/O Board

Game Port
200–207
☐ Not Present
☐ Enabled
☐ Disabled

COM1 ☐ Yes ☐ No
Port 3F8–3FF
IRQ ☐ IRQ 4 ☐ Other ____

COM2 ☐ Yes ☐ No
Port 2F8–2FF
IRQ ☐ IRQ 3 ☐ Other ____

LPT1 ☐ Yes ☐ No
Port 378–37F
IRQ ☐ IRQ 7 ☐ Other ____

LPT2 ☐ Yes ☐ No
Port 278–27F
IRQ ☐ IRQ 5 ☐ Other ____

COMPONENT PROCUREMENT

After completing your needs assessment and configuration worksheet, you are ready to spend some money. All you need is a place to spend it! You have several options:

- Mail order
- Direct from manufacturer
- Local retailer

For single-system installations and upgrades you can use any convenient product source. If you are installing multiple systems, you might consider the benefits of dealing with a reputable manufacturer or local dealer that will build to your specifications and provide technical support.

Preconfigured Systems

Most systems can be correctly preconfigured for you by a computer manufacturer or computer dealer, provided you can define the configuration requirements.

It might seem reasonable to assume that any system you purchase will be delivered with all the parts properly configured and ready to use. However, the reality of the situation is that you cannot assume the dealer understands your requirements. You must be very specific when ordering your hardware and you must be very specific about your setup requirements. You cannot state your requirements in general terms such as:

- CD-ROM
- SCSI controller
- 500MB hard disk
- Mouse

You must state your requirements clearly, for example:

- Brand Name Model 3401XT CD-ROM
- Brand Name Model 1744D SCSI Controller with 2MB Cache
- Brand Name Model CP02540 SCSI II Hard Disk
- Brand Name Serial Mouse

Specify the brand and model you want. Do not leave it up to the dealer to decide which components to use on your system. Make sure your dealer knows how you intend to use your system. Discuss your expectations before finalizing your order.

Verify that each component on your system configuration is a known brand name and compatible with the operating system. If you are well prepared, you can instruct the dealer, in writing, to configure your components preset to the IRQ, DMA, BIOS, RAM, and I/O Port settings on your configuration worksheet. This will save you time and work.

SCHEDULE THE INSTALLATION

Make sure you have considered the timing of your installation. Pick a day and time when technical support is available, and give yourself plenty of time to complete your work without interfering with others.

ASSEMBLE YOUR COMPONENTS IN A CLEAN WORK SPACE

This is only important if you want to stay healthy. You will be working with electricity, and you do not want to work in a hazardous environment. Make sure that you have adequate space and safe power connections.

Lay out your tools, components, software, and documentation so that you have everything you need before you begin the installation. Give yourself at least three hours of free time to focus on the installation without interruption.

INSTALLATION DAY PLANNING

A last caution — you should not begin the installation procedure until you have completed the planning process. At this point you should already have planned all of your system settings such as BIOS memory addresses, I/O port addresses, IRQ settings, and SCSI device addresses. Without planning you may find yourself stuck in the middle of your installation with a short cable, a disk drive you cannot address correctly for lack of a jumper block, or with the wrong type of SIMM (single in-line memory module).

You can cut your installation time down significantly by reviewing your installation worksheet and setting all of your hardware jumpers and switches before you begin to assemble and test your system. The most time-consuming aspect of installation is setting the jumpers and switches on each component.

Installation Procedures

The installation procedures in Chapters 7 to 9 are written as a guide for power users or experienced technical staff. If you are a novice, you can use the Appendices to help you with aspects of installation not familiar to you.

If you are a techno-wizard, you probably will jump right to the checklist and bypass the procedure altogether.

The keys to success are to plan the installation ahead, follow a predetermined sequence (the installation procedures in Chapters 7 to 9), verify each stage of the installation before going to the next, avoid short cuts, and give yourself plenty of time. The best attitude to maintain in this situation is patience and a willingness to go with the flow.

YOU ARE READY TO INSTALL!

After reviewing the planning checklist on page 59, you will be ready to begin the installation procedure.

PLANNING CHECKLIST

This checklist is a quick guide through the planning process. Review this list to see if you have considered the major planning details.

Needs Analysis

Go through this checklist early in the planning phase of your installation. This is a minor planning activity if you are installing a standalone system, but could require weeks of research for a large network project.

- ❑ *Applications*
- ❑ *Environment (Physical Space)*
- ❑ *Growth*
- ❑ *Network Tuning*
- ❑ *Hard Disk Subsystem*
- ❑ *CPU Performance*
- ❑ *Network Server Systems*
- ❑ *Engineering Workstation Systems*
- ❑ *Network Node Systems*
- ❑ *Disk Partitioning*

Network Readiness

The network should be up and running normally before you attempt to add new systems. Network Information Services (NIS or NIS+) should be setup and updated to include new systems.

- ❑ *Install Server Operational*
- ❑ *Network Information Services Available*
- ❑ *Backup File Systems*
- ❑ *Network Connections Available*
- ❑ *Network Printer Available*

System Components

Gather everything you need at the installation site. Use a dealer or supplier willing to configure systems and provide support.

- ❑ *Operating System Software*
- ❑ *Hardware Drivers and Utility Software*
- ❑ *Case and Power Supply*
- ❑ *Magnetic Tape Unit*
- ❑ *CD-ROM*
- ❑ *Sound Board and Speakers*
- ❑ *Keyboard and Mouse*
- ❑ *I/O Ports*
- ❑ *Internal Cables (Power and Signal)*
- ❑ *Motherboard*
- ❑ *Memory*
- ❑ *SCSI II Controller*
- ❑ *Hard Disk*
- ❑ *Floppy Disk*
- ❑ *Network Adapter Card*
- ❑ *Video Adapter and Color Monitor*
- ❑ *FAX/Modem*
- ❑ *IDE Controller (Optional in Place of SCSI))*

Installation Day

Check scheduling to avoid conflicts with other events.

- ❑ *Power Strips Available*
- ❑ *Installation Work Space Available*
- ❑ *Tools and Misc. Hardware Screws, Jumpers, Etc.*
- ❑ *Plenty of Time!*
- ❑ *Hardware and Software Components*
- ❑ *Component Documentation*
- ❑ *Technical Support Backup*

Designing Your Network 5

Network design and installation are not trivial. Designing and installing a small network of ten systems in a small office environment could be done by an experienced system administrator, but large buildings have specialized requirements that are usually beyond the capabilities of untrained installers.

Building codes, fire codes, performance tuning, and complex network hardware interconnections are just a few of the issues that will confront the network designer. If you want to design and install a small network, this chapter will help you.

If you need a large network installed in a commercial building, you should call in a network design consultant. The information in this chapter will help you to understand the process a network design consultant must go through during the course of the design. The design process is the same for any size network; the only difference is in the level of complexity.

ASSESSING NEEDS

- Nodes on the network
- Room to grow
- Distance spanned by network cabling
- Media/cable type

Nodes on the Network

You should know the approximate number of nodes that will be installed and the general design of the office or building. This information will help you to decide whether the complexity of the project requires the aid of a network design consultant. You will also need this information to formulate a budget. Don't forget to include printer nodes or other workstations that are used for specialized purposes.

Room to Grow

Consider your future growth before deciding on a network design. Examine the building or premises to determine how expansion of the network could be done. Also consider your long-term business needs.

Distance Spanned by Network Cabling

The distances spanned by network cabling are important for two reasons. You will need to estimate the amount of material required to cable the network, and you will also be required to stay within the distance limits imposed by the type of cable used. If you are cabling a small office this is not an issue, but large buildings or several interconnected network segments could exceed the maximum distance allowed for the type of cable.

If the installation is big enough to require a consultant, then let the consultant worry about maintaining legal cable lengths.

If you are installing your own small network in one physical location, don't worry about exceeding maximum distances. The chances of that happening are extremely remote. If any of your cables exceed 100 meters, you should take a closer look at your maximum distance limits.

Medium/Cable Type

- Fiberoptic cable
- Unshielded twisted pair (UTP)
- Thin coaxial cable
- Thick coaxial cable

You will more than likely need twisted pair or thin coaxial cable for a small installation. Twisted pair is the easiest to work with, and in many buildings the existing phone wires can be used as network data cables. Thin coax can be best used to interconnect hubs or distribution closets within a building. Twisted pair is ideal for cabling between the workstation and the hub or distribution closet.

SITE SURVEY

One of the most valuable documents you will need is the building plan or blueprints. If you can't get a copy of the building plans, you will have to draw your own. The plan should be drawn to scale in order to accurately measure distances.

Walk through the installation site. Follow the proposed cable plant path through the building to ensure there are no obstacles that could affect the installation.

A walk-through survey should take no more than one hour on a small installation. In large installations, you would probably perform the survey with the aid of a network design consultant and a facilities representative (building manager).

During your site survey:

- Review building floor plans for component placement
- Decide on cable scheme (UTP, thin coax, fiberoptic, etc.)
- Decide on method of termination for network drops (wall plates, etc.)
- Identify component placement throughout the building
- Specify printers, modems, etc.

Example Site Survey Building Plan

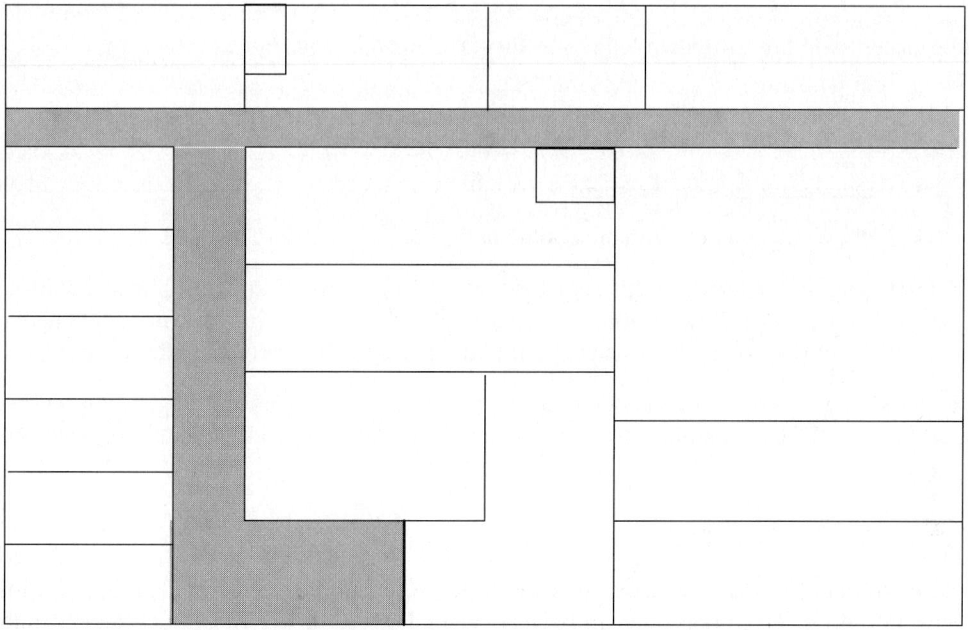

Component Placement

The site survey gives you an opportunity to check each room on the building plan and determine where network components would be located. This is especially important for location of hubs, distribution panels, wall plates, and cables.

Don't forget to check for power outlets where you plan to install components. You could have a serious problem installing a hub in a wiring closet that is without power.

Cable Scheme

As you survey the site, keep in mind the kind of cable you will be routing through walls and offices. You may find a need to use more than one type of media to complete your project. You may need to use fiberoptic cable to route near an area of intense electromagnetic interference, such as close to a power conduit.

Some cables may need to meet fire-code ratings when routed through plenums or vertical risers. Once again, it is wise to use a qualified network consultant to avoid violating local fire codes.

DESIGNING THE NETWORK

The network design should be put on paper as soon as possible after the site survey is complete. It will be easier to do the design while the site survey is fresh in your mind.

- Add drop and component locations to the building floor plan
- Draw and label the logical topology of the network
- Draw each network segment
- Draw each unique drop or set of drops

Do not get hung up on details at this stage of the design process. Take your time and start with simple drawings. If you follow this process, you should be able to design your own small network without much help. You can always have your plan reviewed by a specialist after it's completed.

If you are buying network components from a local vendor, you may be able to get some technical support for free. Let your component vendor review your plan as you will probably get some good feedback.

Revise the Floor Plan

The first step in designing the network is to mark the location of network components on the building floor plan. The floor plan can be used as a guide for you or for professional installers during installation. Show where the cables are routed, where wall plates are to be installed, where distribution panels are to be located, and where other network components will be installed.

It would also be helpful to show the location of workstations and show the cable lengths required to connect each workstation to the wall plate.

The cable and floor plan example on page 65 shows the relationship between a cable drawing and a floor plan. The cable drawing can help you to visualize the cables and components required for the network. A cable drawing can be comprehensive enough to include all components on the network. This can be helpful when you are making a bill of materials.

Draw Logical Topology

Use a blank piece of paper to sketch a drawing showing just the network components. Include all of the network components on the drawing.

The network topology drawing is a useful tool for showing the logical network components. On large networks it is important to have a topology drawing. Managing a large network would be impossible without a complete and detailed topology drawing.

Example of UTP Cabling Plan

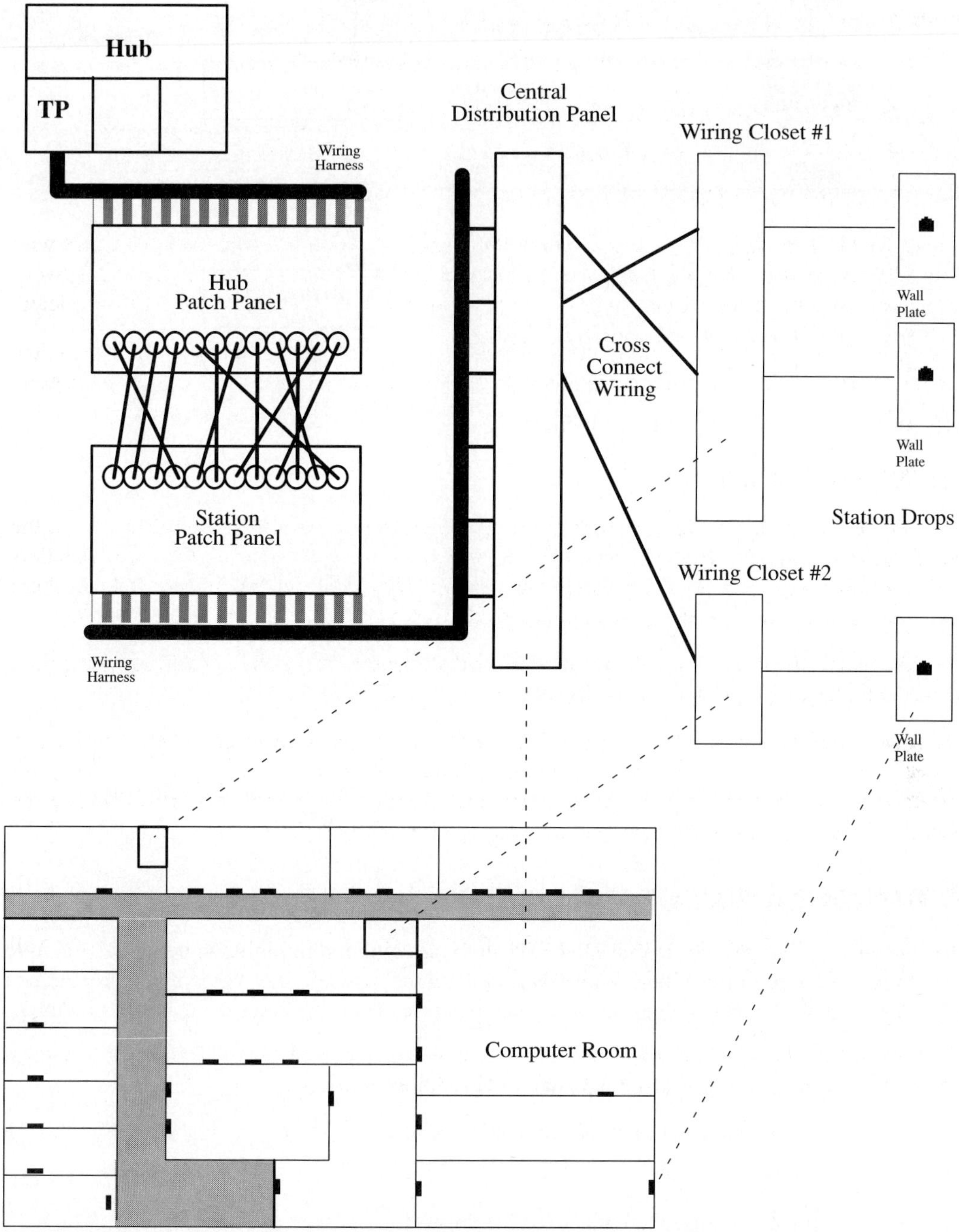

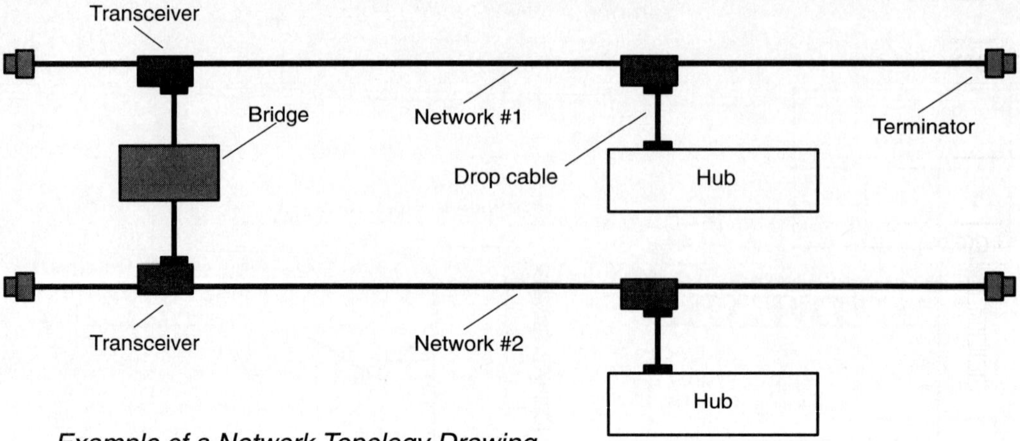

Example of a Network Topology Drawing

When you make a topology drawing include:

- Segment cables
- Bridges
- Repeaters
- Transceivers
- Hubs
- Terminators
- Routers

If you use a network design consultant, you should expect a complete topology drawing as a part of any design.

COMPILING A BILL OF MATERIALS

The bill of materials is nothing more than a list of parts required to build the network. A simple way to develop a complete bill of materials is to draw the network one segment at a time. It also helps to separate the drop cables and office connections from the segment cables and components.

- Draw one network segment at a time (without office drops)
- List parts required to build segment
- Draw office drops
- List parts required to connect office drops

Segment Bill of Materials Worksheet - Part 1

Segment Name	Segment Location

Segment Drawing

- ☐ Thick Ethernet
- ☐ Thin Ethernet
- ☐ Fiberoptic
- ☐ Twisted Pair
- ☐ Other

____

Common Segment Component Symbols

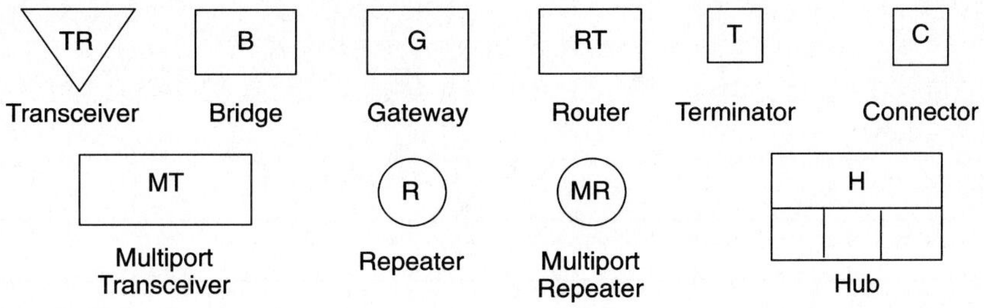

Segment Bill of Materials Worksheet - Part 2

Bill of Materials

	Qty	Description	Cost	Extended Cost
1				
2				
3				
4				
5				
6				
7				
8				
9				
10				
11				
12				
13				
14				
15				
16				
17				
18				
19				
20				

Total	

Notes: ____

____

____

____

____

The process proposed here is just one way to approach the problem. The object is to get a complete list of parts and estimate the component cost. You could do this on the back of a napkin if your network is very small, but if you are dealing with large networks you will need a bit more structure.

Once again, if you are working with a network design consultant, you should expect a complete bill of materials from the consultant as part of any design.

The Segment

The segment drawing should include all cabling and components required to get the network segment extended to the office wall plate in each network node location.

Segment Worksheet

It helps to draw each segment of the network before developing the bill of materials. The segment bill-of-materials worksheet example on page 67 is a simple form that can be used to help create a bill of materials for each network segment. The completed worksheet defines the physical characteristics of a unique segment of the network and lists the parts required to build it.

The worksheet provides a common set of network symbols that can be used to simplify the segment drawing.

The Office Drops

In a typical network design, each x86 system on the network will require a cable or transceiver and cable combination that connects the network adapter card to the wall outlet in the office. It is important to review the connection requirement of each network adapter board to determine the type of interface required.

Standard Drop

A standard drop would be one where the office wall plate connector and the x86 system network adapter have the same type of network media connection. In the example below, UTP is used from the segment distribution panel to the office wall plate. Since the x86 system has a matching UTP interface, a standard RJ-45 cable can be used to make the connection. This is much the same as a phone system and is the easiest type of connection to complete. The cable connecting the workstation to the wall plate is available in a variety of lengths. The bill of materials for this type of drop should indicate the type and length of the cable required.

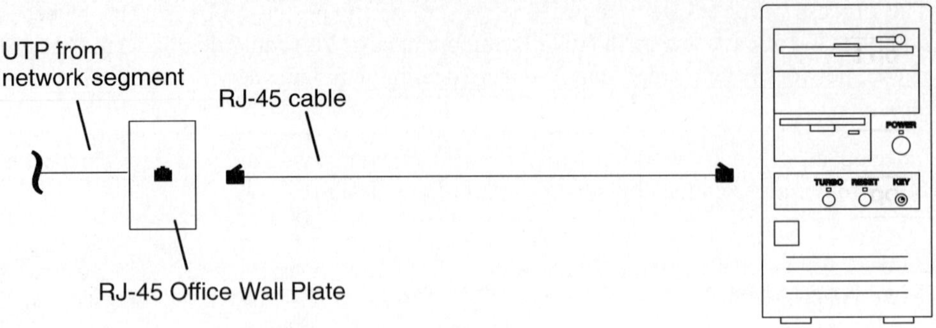

Sample of a Standard Drop

Drop with a Transceiver

It is commonplace to design a network with UTP to all office wall plates and then customize the drop connection to match the type of network media connection on the target workstation. In the example below, the workstation has a thick coax AUI connection that cannot be connected to the RJ-45 wall plate without the use of a transceiver.

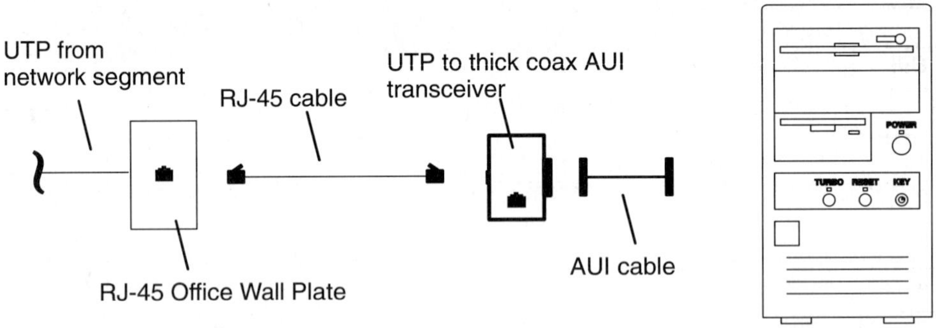

Sample of a Drop with a Transceiver

This type of drop is more expensive because of the added requirement for a transceiver and second cable. This type of drop can be avoided by making sure that the x86 network adapter is properly matched to the type of connection at the wall plate.

The transceiver in the example has both the RJ-45 UTP connector and the AUI connector. The transceiver connects to the workstation using a standard AUI cable, performs the necessary conversion of signal data, and then connects to the wall plate with a standard RJ-45 cable.

There are many variations of this type of drop due to the variety of network connections available on x86 network adapter boards. The bill of materials for the drops must account for the correct cables and transceiver for each workstation.

Office Drop Bill of Materials Worksheet

Drop Location	**Description**

Drop Drawing

Office Drop Bill of Materials Worksheet - Part 2

Bill of Materials

	Qty	Description	Cost	Extended Cost
1				
2				
3				
4				
5				
6				

Total	

Notes: ____

Office Drop Worksheet

The office drop example worksheet on page 71 provides a space to draw and label the components required to complete a network drop to the workstation. You should have a worksheet for each unique drop configuration.

If you have multiple drops that are identical, you can use one worksheet for the group of identical configurations. List the quantity of each part required to complete the bill of materials. When you are done filling out the worksheets, you can add up the parts and get a material cost estimate.

PLANNING CHECKLIST

This checklist is a quick guide for network design. Review this list to see if you have considered the major planning details.

Performance

- ❑ *Number of nodes*
- ❑ *Application requirements*
- ❑ *Gateway traffic*
- ❑ *Printer services*
- ❑ *Diskless clients*

Media

- ❑ *Unshielded twisted pair (UTP)*
- ❑ *Fiberoptic*
- ❑ *Other*
- ❑ *Thin coax*
- ❑ *Thick coax*

Topology

- ❑ *Ethernet*
- ❑ *Other*
- ❑ *Token ring*

Site Survey

- ❑ *Building plans*
- ❑ *Power outlets*
- ❑ *Wiring closets*
- ❑ *Workstation locations*
- ❑ *Electromagnetic interference*
- ❑ *Distance between furthest two nodes*
- ❑ *Other*
- ❑ *Walk the cable path*
- ❑ *Plenums, fire codes*
- ❑ *Printer locations*
- ❑ *Server locations*
- ❑ *Wall plate locations*
- ❑ *Mark locations on plan*

Design

- ❑ *Network topology drawing*
- ❑ *Cable layout drawing*
- ❑ *Consultant required?*

Bill of Materials

- ❑ *Segment drawing*
- ❑ *Material list*
- ❑ *Other*
- ❑ *Standard drop drawings*
- ❑ *Nonstandard drop drawings*

Hard-Disk Partitioning 6

BASIC FACTS ABOUT x86 HARD-DISK PARTITIONS

Hard-disk partitioning is one of the first steps in the x86 hardware configuration process. You have to create at least one partition on the hard disk for each operating system you intend to use. In addition, you may need to create partitions for optional file systems.

Unfortunately, the early stages of configuration and installation are the worst time to make partitioning decisions. Partitioning your hard disk is much like making the final seating arrangements for a wedding reception before you know who will be coming. You will have to get out your crystal ball and gaze into the future of your system. You must decide how much space to allocate to each OS and how much space in each OS partition to allocate for the various file systems. You must anticipate your future needs as best you can.

There are some simple rules of thumb for hard disk partitioning; remember them.

- Every hard disk must have a valid partition table written on it.
- A hard disk can be divided into a maximum of four primary partitions.
- Each primary partition can contain an operating system.
- Only one primary partition can be active at a time.

Rules of thumb are helpful. If you follow them, you can avoid common configuration errors. There are always the rare exceptions to rules, but unless you are an expert in hard-disk partitioning, I would not recommend trying to prove them wrong!

Every Disk Has One

The first rule of thumb is that every PC hard disk must have a valid partition table before it can be used by an operating system. The partition table is created and written onto the hard disk by a program such as the DOS `fdisk` utility.

Once a hard-disk partition is created, it cannot be changed without destroying its contents. Consequently, take all the time needed to ensure that partitioning the disks is done correctly the first time.

The partition table can only be created on hard disk drives that have been formatted with a low-level format. Hard disks are shipped from the factory with a low-level format. You can use utility programs to low-level format SCSI hard disks after they leave the factory, but IDE drives can only be low-level formatted on specialized equipment.

Four Primary Partitions

The second rule is that you can create up to four primary partitions on a hard disk. You can configure a hard disk as one large primary partition, or break it up into two, three, or four smaller partitions. Each primary partition can be used by a different operating system.

Operating Systems on Primary Partitions

The third rule of thumb is that operating systems are loaded onto primary partitions. If you want to setup a hard disk with two operating systems, it is simply done by creating two primary partitions, each with a different operating system. You can switch from one operating system to the other by merely changing the active partition. In fact, one of my test systems was configured with three primary partitions. DOS was installed on the first partition, and Solaris and OS/2 were loaded on the other two partitions.

Note: *Well-behaved operating systems do not modify or manipulate data on inactive partitions. There is, however, the possibility that a hardware or software failure can cause any disk partition to be corrupted. Backup all partitions to protect against accidental loss of data.*

Only One Active Partition at a Time

The fourth rule of disk partitioning is that only one primary partition can be active (bootable) at one time. If you divide a hard disk into four primary partitions and then boot from an active DOS partition, you will only be able to use the space on the DOS partition. The three inactive partitions are still on the disk, but you cannot get access to the data on an inactive partition until it becomes active or unless you have an operating system that can access file systems on inactive partitions. Solaris can access inactive partitions but DOS cannot.

Booting from the Inactive Partition

When the DOS partition is the only partition on the boot disk or when the DOS partition is the active partition on the boot disk, the system will boot DOS directly. DOS does not provide a means to dynamically make another partition active. The only way to boot from the inactive partition is to use `fdisk` to designate another primary partition as the active partition and then reboot the system. This is a cumbersome process.

Operating systems such as OS/2 and Solaris x86 have a multiple-partition boot feature that enables a user with multiple primary partitions to choose which partition to boot from. If a system has multiple primary partitions and the Solaris partition is the active partition, the system boots to a menu that enables a user to choose which primary partition is used for the current session. After five seconds without input from the user, the boot process will continue, and the Solaris operating system will load.

DOS FILE SYSTEM PARTITION

Initially, I spent a lot of my time reconfiguring Solaris systems that were setup without a DOS partition. It is easy to convince yourself that you could do without it, because the need is not apparent. Before you do — consider what it would be like to build your house without insulation because it happens to be a warm summer. Winter will surely come again!

You can use DOS `fdisk` or Solaris installation software to create a valid partition table. It is best to create the initial partition table using the DOS `fdisk` utility to create the DOS partition, and then use the Solaris installation program to create the Solaris partition on the unused portion of the disk. This will enable you to configure and test your system using the DOS operating system before attempting to install Solaris.

Note: *There are rare cases where the DOS partition on an IDE drive should be partitioned by the Solaris installation program — "not" by DOS* `fdisk`. *The logical IDE geometry in CMOS may not match the physical geometry of the drive. Solaris always uses the physical geometry taken from the drive and therefore may not match the logical geometry stored in CMOS. See Appendix C for details on IDE drive configuration.*

Why Do I Need It?

Omitting the DOS partition can make it nearly impossible to troubleshoot or test your x86 hardware. The DOS partition is a necessity. The only real issue is how big to make it!

Here are some reasons why you need a DOS partition:

- Easy access to utility software
- Backup copy of original software
- Easy to execute diagnostic programs
- Utility software extremely difficult to run from diskette

There was a day when you could easily configure and test your system using a single floppy disk drive, but those days are gone. The utility programs provided with option cards and motherboards today are larger in size and work best from the hard disk.

Manufacturers of x86 hardware products have used the DOS operating system as a standard for development. It is the common thread and standard that enables such great product diversity, while at the same time preserving compatibility. Most of today's products are designed to be installed and then run on a DOS partition.

The most compelling argument for creating a DOS partition on your hard disk is that it is always easiest to load all of the DOS utility programs when you first configure the system. Locating diskettes for a system a year after installation is usually difficult, time consuming, and sometimes impossible. If you copy or install all of your x86 utility software on a DOS partition when you initially configure your system, it can be easily accessed and backed up.

How Big?

The size of the DOS partition is based on your application needs. In most cases you will be using Solaris as the primary operating system, so your DOS partition only needs to be large enough to contain the x86 hardware utility software. If you intend to use your DOS operating system and your Solaris operating system equally, you will need a DOS partition that provides space for application programs.

- 5MB minimum DOS partition
- 15MB recommended DOS partition
- 40MB or greater for DOS partition with applications

The absolute minimum DOS partition must be large enough to contain a full installation of the DOS operating system programs. In addition, there should be enough space left over for a minimum complement of basic utility programs for configuring and testing the hardware components. Anything less than 5MB would be of little use.

My recommendation is that you create a primary DOS partition of at least 15MB on your Solaris system. This will almost always provide you with enough space for full installation of the DOS operating system and x86 hardware utilities.

SOLARIS OPERATING-SYSTEM PARTITION

Not a Science

Partitioning a hard disk is probably closer to magic than it is to science. My recommendations are based on my experience and the belief that it is always better to provide a margin of safety when calculating disk-partition-size requirements. An undersize partition can cause an operating system to fail, but an oversize partition simply has extra space. My personal recommendations are based on the assumption that too much disk space is better than too little disk space.

If you must calculate absolute minimum partition sizes, I recommend that you refer to your DOS or Solaris x86 documentation.

Guidelines

The Solaris operating system requires a minimum partition size of 50MB just to load the "core system," but the core system running a computer is just about as useful as a match lighting a ballroom. Creating a minimal 50MB partition for the core system is neither practical nor usable.

Could you imagine a house built with bedrooms just big enough to contain the bed and nothing else? A bedroom that is the same size as the bed is not very functional. A system configured with the Solaris partition just big enough to contain the software is similarly dysfunctional.

For a Solaris partition 250MB is a usable size on a networked system. With a 250MB partition, there is enough space for:

- Local booting
- Local print spooling
- Local mail spooling
- Adequate swap space
- Local home directory

Slicing the Partition

You may be confused when you you hear the terms partition and slice used interchangeably. There is a very big difference. A partition is a contiguous block of disk space that is defined by the partition table written by the `fdisk` utility.

The 265MB hard disk illustrated to the right is divided into two partitions.

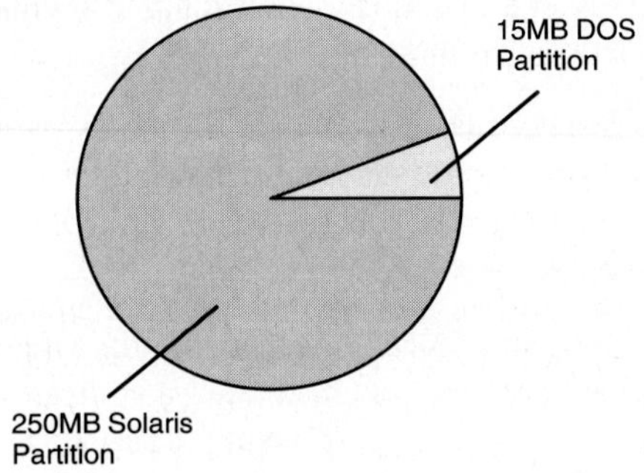

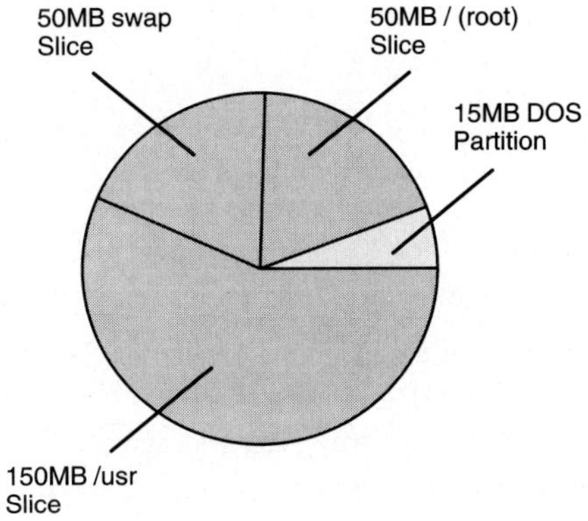

The Solaris operating system further defines the disk partition by dividing it into slices. The 265MB hard disk illustrated on the left has a 15MB DOS partition and a 250MB Solaris partition. The Solaris partition is further divided into three "slices." Each Solaris slice can contain a unique file system. Slicing a Solaris disk partition is very useful for managing file systems.

This partition example is typical of systems that are configured with a minimum of disk space.

What's in a Name?

Keeping track of controllers, hard drives, partitions, and slices is not an easy task. The Solaris operating system uses a device-naming convention that helps to eliminate confusion. A primary partition can be uniquely identified by an eight-character name such as `c0t0d0p1`.

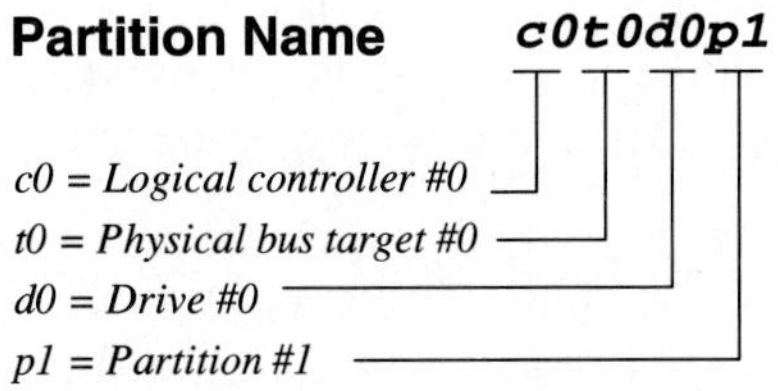

The partition name is rarely used within the operating system. You will more commonly see eight-character slice names used to identify file systems. A Solaris partition slice is uniquely identified by a name such as `c0t0d0s1`.

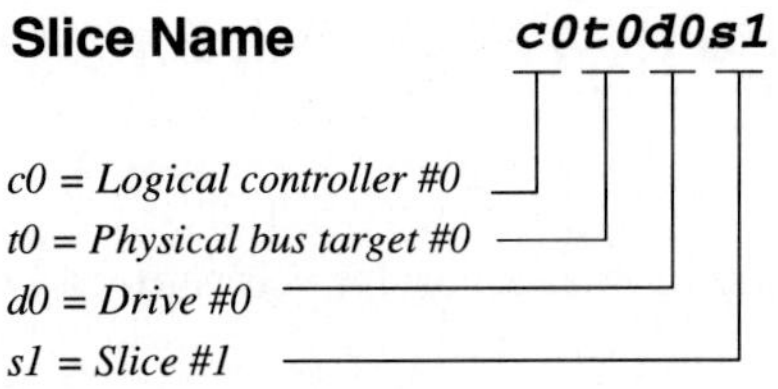

The name can be more than eight characters if one of the valid numbers is larger than nine. While unlikely, it is possible to have a name such as `c0t0d0s10`. For purposes of this discussion it is safe to assume that only eight characters are needed to create a valid name.

The first two characters of the slice or partition name designate the logical controller number. Most Solaris x86 systems are configured with one disk controller and one hard disk. The primary disk controller is designated as controller number 0. A secondary disk controller would be designated as controller #1.

The third and fourth characters of the slice or partition name designate the physical bus target number. The devices attached to a controller are designated as bus target numbers. The primary disk drive (boot disk) is usually designated as target number 0. The target ID numbers on SCSI devices directly correspond to the physical bus target number in the name. IDE drives are designated as target #0 and #1.

Note: *Solaris x86 version 2.4 has changed the naming convention for IDE drives. The target ID is not used.*

IDE partitions are designated using the format `c0d0p1`, where `d0` is the master drive and `d1` is the slave drive; and where `p1` is the first partition and `p2-4` are the other partitions.

IDE slices are designated using the format `c0d0s1`, where `d0` is the master drive and `d1` is the slave drive; and where `s1` is the first slice and `s2-6` are the other slices.

The fifth and sixth characters of the slice or partition name designate the drive number. The drive number is always 0 if the drive has an embedded controller. The IDE drives and SCSI devices are considered to have embedded controllers. The disk number in the name is nearly always "d0". I have never needed to use any disk number other than 0.

The seventh and eighth characters of the name designate the slice or partition number. When used to designate a partition, the characters can be p0 through p4. To specify the whole disk use p0.

When used to designate a slice, the seventh and eighth characters are usually in the range of s0 through s7. When a slice name is used, it is assumed that the slice is on the active Solaris partition on the target hard disk designated by the third and fourth characters of the name. The name `c0t3d0s2`, therefore, would refer to Solaris slice 2 (on controller 0, target ID 3).

What's in a Slice?

Solaris slices contain file systems. Solaris file systems are organized into logical and standard arrangements to match the primary use of the system. Slices can be mounted locally and exported to the network.

So How Big Is Big Enough?

The ideal partition size for any system is determined by its use. If you do not have experience in this area, you may wish to consult an experienced system administrator. Determining the right partition size requires planning, a knowledge of application software, a knowledge of network file system requirements, a knowledge of Solaris operating system requirements, and occasionally, some guesswork.

There are three partition examples in this chapter:

- The boot/network server 800MB and larger
- The networked system 250MB
- The standalone workstation 500MB

In addition to the three partition examples listed above, the diskless client (a server provides all file systems) deserves mention as a reminder that a local hard disk is not required to run the Solaris operating system. A diskless client uses disk space provided for it on a boot server. The boot server, therefore, will require a Solaris partition large enough to contain essential file systems for its diskless clients.

You can actually get by with as little as 200MB for a networked system, but the results would probably disappoint you. This amount of memory (200MB) will not give you the margin you need to accommodate applications that require large swap space, large data space, or large e-mail spool files. Although the networked system example listed above is for 250MB partition, you would be better served to use a partition of 350MB or larger.

Note: *The swap space on a Solaris partition must be equal to or larger than the amount of main memory installed on the motherboard. For instance, a system with 64MB of main memory must have a minimum of 64MB of disk swap space.*

The Network Server

To avoid duplicating space on local disks, the network file server is designated as the system to provide network clients with boot partitions and shared file systems for optional application software, print spools, home directories, and mail files. A small file server with a few diskless boot clients could easily use an 800MB partition.

This partition (800MB) will get you started in the server business, but it is a pretty safe bet that the server will need a second disk to expand the space available for optional software and exported file systems.

It is a good idea to create a slice for the /var file system on a server. Spool files contained in /var can overflow a file system. By creating a separate /var slice, the root file system is protected from overflowing. Overflowing the root file system can be disastrous.

Server Partition Sample			
Directory	**Slice**	**Size MB**	**Description**
/	0	100	The root directory contains essential directories and files required for system operation. It also contains the mount point directories where local and remote file systems can be attached to the file tree.
swap	1	100	Swap is the space setup on the disk for virtual memory.
whole partition	2	800	Slice 2 is the entire partition. It includes all of the other slices.
/export	3	150	File systems and home directories for export.
/var	4	50	Spool directory to keep the root file system from overflowing.
/opt	5	220	Mount point or directory for optional software.
/usr	6	180	Contains system files and directories that can be shared with other users.
	7		

The Networked System

The networked system usually depends on the server for shared-application file systems, but depends on its own local partition space to contain the Solaris file systems. A 250MB partition on a networked system will work well when file system growth space is provided by a server.

Networked System Partition Sample			
Directory	**Slice**	**Size MB**	**Description**
/	0	50	The root directory contains essential directories and files required for system operation. It also contains the mount point directories where local and remote file systems can be attached to the file tree.
swap	1	50	Swap is the space setup on the disk for virtual memory. Swap space must be at least equal to the size of main memory. You can use much smaller swap sizes if you are certain of your application swap requirements. I prefer to have too much swap rather than too little.
whole partition	2	250	Slice 2 is the entire partition. It includes all of the other slices.
	3		
	4		
	5		
/usr	6	150	Contains system files and directories that can be shared with other users.
	7		

The benefit to this configuration is that it is only partly dependent upon the network server and therefore places less of a load on the network. A less costly diskless network node could be used instead of the networked system, but booting and file access performance would be reduced during peak network traffic.

The Standalone Workstation

The standalone workstation needs enough partition space to contain a full installation of Solaris operating system software, and enough additional space for optional application programs and data files. A 500MB partition is big enough to do the job. A standalone workstation, by definition, should be able to perform its primary function with or without a network connection.

A 500MB partition can be easily filled with growing application programs. A larger primary disk drive or a second disk drive should be considered if you anticipate substantial growth in your applications or data files.

OTHER FILE SYSTEM PARTITIONS

It is possible to partition your hard disk for use with other operating systems. Your only limitations are disk space and the four primary partition restriction.

I have a system setup with partitions for the DOS operating system, the OS/2 operating system, and the Solaris operating system. It is only good for testing and training purposes because only one operating system can be used at a time.

Operating systems have installation programs such as `fdisk` to create a partition on the hard disk. Follow the same process for installing any operating system.

- Create a primary partition using some available hard-disk space
- Leave enough space for use by other operating systems
- Load the operating system
- Backup the operating system

One thing to watch for if you are creating partitions for several operating systems on the same disk is not to allow any operating system to use the entire disk when partitioning is done. Most operating system installation programs will give you the option to use the entire disk and thereby delete any existing partitions. Make certain you read the partitioning dialog carefully.

MULTIPLE DISKS

If you plan to use more than one disk, it is easiest to install the Solaris operating system with all of the disk drives installed. Trying to add a hard disk drive after installing Solaris x86 Version 2.1 is extremely difficult and might require assistance from an experienced system administrator.

The example shown for slicing multiple disks takes advantage of the increased disk capacity by moving the /export and /opt file systems to the secondary disk drive. This example is just a possible solution — not the only solution. You will have to plan your partition slices to fit your needs.

Note: *Solaris Version 2.4 procedure for adding a disk after installation is much more user friendly than the Solaris Version 2.1 procedure. Any user should be able to do it without assistance. It is, however, much easier to let the installation program do it for you.*

Network Server Partition Example (2 disks)			
Directory	**Slice**	**Size MB**	**Description**
			Disk target 0 (800MB)
/	0	150	The root directory contains essential directories and files required for system operation. It also contains the mount point directories where local and remote file systems can be attached to the file tree.
swap	1	200	Swap is the space setup on the disk for virtual memory.
whole partition	2	800	Slice 2 is the entire partition. It includes all of the other slices.
	3		
/var	4	70	Spool directory to keep the root file system from overflowing.
/extra	5	200	Extra space reserved for future use.
/usr	6	180	Contains system files and directories that can be shared with other users.
	7		
			Disk target 1 (800MB)
	0		
	1		
whole partition	2	800	Slice 2 is the entire partition. It includes all of the other slices.
/export	3	400	File systems and home directories for export.
	4		
/opt	5	400	Directory for optional software.
	6		
	7		

PLANNING CHECKLIST

This checklist is a quick guide for hard-disk partitioning. Review this list to see if you have considered the major planning details.

Space Needed

Go through this checklist early in the planning phase of your installation.

Things to consider .... ***Space Required***

- ❑ *Solaris Operating System (300MB recommended)* .... ____________
- ❑ *Solaris, Exported Client File Systems (/export)* .... ____________
- ❑ *Solaris, Home Directories (/export)* .... ____________
- ❑ *Solaris, Application Software (/opt)* .... ____________
- ❑ *Solaris, Answerbook - Online Documentation (/opt)* ...... ____________
- ❑ *Solaris, Spool and Mail Files (/var)* .... ____________
- ❑ *Solaris, Swap* .... ____________

- ❑ *DOS Operating System (20MB recommended)* .... ____________
- ❑ *DOS Applications* .... ____________
- ❑ *Other Operating Systems (optional)* .... ____________
- ❑ *Other OS Applications* .... ____________

- ❑ *Other*____________ .... ____________
- ❑ *Other*____________ .... ____________
- ❑ *Other*____________ .... ____________

Total Disk Space Required .... ____________

Partition Map

Drive 1

Partition	*Active*	*Type*	*Size*
1	❑	________	________
2	❑	________	________
3	❑	________	________
4	❑	________	________

Drive 2

Partition	*Active*	*Type*	*Size*
1	❑	________	________
2	❑	________	________
3	❑	________	________
4	❑	________	________

MCA Installation 7

The following Micro Channel Architecture (MCA) installation procedure contains a moderate level of component-specific detail. For more detailed information refer to the Appendices.

Caution:

- *Throughout the installation procedure you will be required to connect or disconnect boards and cables. Turn power off whenever performing any activity that involves connecting or disconnecting hardware.*
- *Do not remove or replace screws while power is on. A screw can fall into the system and cause damage to the motherboard.*
- *Static electricity can be a serious problem, especially in cold winter climates where heating systems remove moisture from the air. Take precautions to prevent static electricity from building up in your workplace.*

If you invested your money in a PC system with an MCA bus, you are about to receive a substantial dividend payment. Configuring a system based on MCA bus technology is quick, easy to do, and usually without hardware conflicts.

MCA systems are rarely sold as component parts to be assembled, but are preconfigured with power supply, motherboard, hard disks, and video display already installed. Optional boards such as network cards, video accelerators, or SCSI controllers can be added to a baseline system with very little effort. Lucky you!

PHASE 1: SETUP THE BASELINE SYSTEM

- ✓ **Gather components in a clean, safe workplace.**
- ✓ **Install options.**
- ✓ **Install keyboard and mouse.**
- ✓ **Install video adapter and monitor.**
- ✓ **Test baseline configuration.**

Step 1: Gather Components in a Clean, Safe Workplace

A complete standalone installation will take from two to four hours, depending on your level of experience. Make sure you have plenty of space for tools, documentation, components, and refreshments! When everything is gathered in one place, you are ready to begin.

Step 2: Installation Options

All optional hardware and software should be in front of you or otherwise easily accessible. You will also need the documentation for each option.

- ✓ **Install memory**
- ✓ **Install optional boards**
- ✓ **Configure peripheral devices**
- ✓ **Install floppy/hard drive devices into case**
- ✓ **Install peripheral devices into case**
- ✓ **Connect power cables to devices**
- ✓ **Connect external SCSI bus devices**
- ✓ **Connect data cables to all devices**
- ✓ **Check your work**

Install Memory

New installations and upgrades usually require additional memory to meet the 12MB minimum requirement. Add memory to the motherboard at this time. Verify all memory to ensure proper match for speed and size. Refer to the motherboard documentation to verify proper position of memory. Memory is usually installed in numbered banks of four and in sequential order.

Install Optional Boards

Just plug and play! Optional boards require no manual configuration before installation into an MCA bus slot. Configuration is done automatically but can be edited or fine tuned through software control.

Configure Peripheral Devices

Peripheral devices such as SCSI disks will require manual configuration before they can be installed. If you are adding new devices to your system, configure them now.

Assign each SCSI device a target ID address and configure each device with its unique address. Use the following sample SCSI target ID's as a guide. If you do not use the sample provided, you should pick a consistent scheme to meet your needs. The object is to configure systems in the same way each time, and not create random patterns which can be hard to support.

Refer to your hardware documentation for target ID jumper settings.

Sample SCSI Target ID Map for MCA Configuration		
Device	**ID**	**Comments**
CD-ROM	0	You could set the address to any available ID. If you are configuring many systems, it helps to be consistent with your ID selection.
Unassigned	1	This target ID is not assigned to any device. It can be used when a SCSI device is added to the configuration.
Unassigned	2	This target ID is not assigned to any device. It can be used when a SCSI device is added to the configuration.
Magnetic Tape Unit (MTU)	3	You could set the address to any available ID. If you are configuring many systems, it helps to be consistent with your ID selection. Always setting the MTU to ID 3 could be helpful when maintaining many systems. The MCA system used for this chart used ID 3, but ISA and EISA systems generally use ID 5. Once you decide on a scheme, be consistent.
Hard Disk	4	Add additional hard disks in sequence (recommendation).
Hard Disk	5	Add additional hard disks in sequence (recommendation).
Hard Disk	6	Most SCSI controllers require the first hard disk to be set to address 0, but the MCA system used for this chart required the system boot disk at target address 6.
SCSI Controller	7	This target ID is reserved for the SCSI controller.

Note: *The MCA system I used for testing required specific address assignments for the bootable SCSI disk (target ID 6). Be sure to read your system documentation and review the SCSI target address assignments before installing additional devices.*

Install Floppy/Hard Drive Devices into Case

This procedure will vary in difficulty depending on the type of case you have. Keep in mind that you will have to route the power and signal cables to the drives after they are mounted. Check your cables for proper length.

Install Peripheral Devices into Case

If you have CD-ROM, magnetic tape, or other peripherals, install them now.

Connect Power Cables to Devices

Connect power to each internal device. If you do not have enough power connectors, you can purchase power cable splitters at most computer supply stores.

Connect External SCSI Bus Devices

If you are using external devices, connect them to the SCSI controller external bus connector.

Connect Data Cables to All Devices

Connect the SCSI bus cable to the internal SCSI devices and SCSI controller. You should already have terminators at the appropriate points. Refer to Appendix C for termination details.

Check Your Work

Before proceeding to the next step, check your work to make sure that all cables are on tight, all switches are still set correctly, all screws are snug, and all boards are plugged into the bus correctly. I recently spent hours troubleshooting a problem because I had inserted a SCSI controller and changed a switch setting by handling the board carelessly.

Step 3: Install Keyboard and Mouse

This is probably the easiest part of the installation process. Plug it in!

- ✓ **Install the keyboard**
- ✓ **Install mouse and keyboard**

Step 4: Install Video Adapter and Monitor

Note: *If your system has a proprietary motherboard with a compatible video chip, you will not need to install a video adapter.*

- ✓ **Install video adapter board**
- ✓ **Connect monitor to power and video connector**

Install Video Adapter Board on Motherboard

Install your video adapter if necessary. If you are installing a video accelerator on a motherboard with embedded video support, be sure to read your system documentation to review special requirements for multiple video adapters. You may need to disable on-board video if adding a video adapter board.

Software is used to configure most adapters and motherboard video chips. You will perform software setup in another phase of this procedure.

Connect Monitor to Power and Video Connector

Note: *Most power supplies on system units provide a switched power outlet for a monitor power connection. If your power supply can handle the AC power required by your monitor, you can connect your monitor power cable to the system and use the system power switch to turn on your system and monitor. AC power adapter cables are available for this purpose.*

Step 5: Test Baseline Configuration

- ✔ **Connect to power source**
- ✔ **Turn on monitor power (allow a minute for warmup)**
- ✔ **Turn on computer power**
- ✔ **Verify POST completes OK**
- ✔ **Disconnect power**

Connect to Power Source

At this point you should be able to connect the system to your power source and begin testing your work. A switchable power strip is helpful. If all of the power cords are plugged into the same strip, it will be easier to power the test configuration on and off.

Turn on Monitor Power (Allow a Minute for Warm-up)

Power on the monitor first and give it time to warm up before turning on power to the system. Remember to use caution whenever power is applied to your system. A warm-up period is required so that the monitor will be able to display the BIOS messages.

Turn on Computer Power

Turn on the system power and observe the messages that appear on the screen and listen for any beeps that may come from the speaker. If you get no display or hear no sound, refer to Chapter 11 on troubleshooting and isolate the failure. If the messages appear too fast or if you were not looking, use the reset button on the front of the case to restart the process as many times as necessary to view the message.

Note: *Many systems are not equipped with a reset button. You may have to restart the system with the power switch if no other means is provided.*

It is always recommended that you wait 20 seconds after turning the power off before turning it on again. Rapid cycling of the power switch can cause the power supply to stop working temporarily because of thermal reset. If this happens, wait a few minutes and allow the power supply thermal sensor to cool before retrying the power switch. This is a normal safety feature of most power supplies. No harm is done.

Verify POST Completes OK

Power on self test (POST) should run as soon as system power is turned on. You should see some information displayed on the screen to indicate the test status as POST executes. If an error is reported during execution of POST, record the message and refer to your system documentation for further information.

MCA systems use a Programmable Option Select (POS) feature to autoconfigure option board settings such as IRQ, DMA level, and I/O port addresses. Each option board is set during POST from information stored on the motherboard in nonvolatile RAM.

Option boards added to an existing MCA bus may not be completely configured until the appropriate configuration file is loaded from the floppy disk. You will be prompted by the configuration program when the configuration file is needed. The POST program is robust enough to inform you when a board has been changed, removed, or added.

If you have completed a pass through the POST, you have established that:

1. The monitor is displaying data correctly.
2. The motherboard has completed power on self test.
3. The keyboard is working.

If you cannot get through the POST because of a fatal error, you must troubleshoot and fix the problem before proceeding.

PHASE 2: SETUP

MCA systems with hard disks will reserve a special area on the hard disk known as the system partition. This small system partition (~3MB) is protected from being overwritten by any software other than MCA system utility programs. The system partition contains the configuration information that is used by POST at boot time.

The partition is created and maintained through the use of special programs that are provided on a bootable floppy disk called a reference disk. The system partition is not created by `fdisk` and is not related to other partitions on the hard disks. The reference disk should come with the MCA system. Do not lose your reference disk — bad things will happen.

- ✓ **Boot the system using the reference disk**
- ✓ **Create system partition if required**
- ✓ **Run automatic configuration**
- ✓ **Load optional configuration files**
- ✓ **Set options**

If you are working with a system that is already configured properly, you can skip ahead to creating a DOS partition (phase 3 of this procedure). MCA systems are not usually sold as components to be assembled, and generally are ready for disk partitioning. If your system already boots from the hard disk, it is a sure sign that you can safely skip this phase.

Step 1: Boot the System Using the Reference Disk

Place the reference diskette in floppy drive A and turn on the system. The system should go through the normal power-on sequence, and then the reference program will display a menu of options.

Step 2: Create System Partition if Required

You may have to go through a complete setup of the system partition on the hard disk if you are installing on a new hard disk. Follow the instructions provided with your MCA reference disk.

MCA setup programs are very easy to use because they provide excellent on-line help to prompt you through the setup process.

Step 3: Run Automatic Configuration

You will probably have the option to select automatic configuration. This makes setup much easier. Use autoconfiguration if it is available on your system reference diskette option menu.

Step 4: Load Optional Configuration Files

During setup it is not unusual to be prompted for optional diskettes that are provided with optional adapter boards. If you have optional configuration files, the setup program will prompt you to insert the option diskette.

Step 5: Set Options

The reference disk programs allow you to set some options such as date, time, and adapter settings. This feature is available to customize your configuration. Customizing adapter configuration is usually unnecessary. Review the documentation provided with your optional adapters for more information about custom configuration.

PHASE 3: CREATE A DOS PARTITION

This is a necessary procedure. Do not attempt to partition the disk without creating a DOS partition. The DOS partition will be used to store setup utilities, diagnostic programs, and other programs that are included with your hardware. System troubleshooting depends heavily on DOS utility programs. Some hardware components cannot be configured without DOS!

This procedure is based on MS–DOS 6.x. Versions of DOS prior to 6.x do not include the full range of useful setup features such as:

- Automatic Installation
- System Information Utility (`msd.exe`)
- Backup Utility
- Antivirus Utility
- Automatic Memory Configuration

Overview

- ✓ **Boot from DOS floppy disk**
- ✓ **Perform low-level format (hard disk)**
- ✓ **Create primary DOS partition (`fdisk.exe`)**

- ✓ **Format DOS partition (`format.exe`)**
- ✓ **Load DOS files (`c:\dos`)**
- ✓ **Verify DOS partition**

Step 1: Boot from DOS Floppy Disk

Boot from Floppy

The purpose of this step is to verify that the floppy-drive interface works. If the DOS installation starts normally, it verifies that the floppy drive and floppy-drive controller are functioning properly. DOS cannot be installed on the hard disk until the hard disk is partitioned and formatted.

Put the DOS install diskette in Drive A and boot (power cycle or reset button) the system. If the floppy drive and controller are properly connected, the DOS installation program will display a message. If you do not see the install message, do not proceed until you troubleshoot the failure.

A diagnostic boot diskette is a valuable tool for configuring or testing a system. You can easily create your own DOS boot diskette. Refer to the procedure on page 165.

Step 2: Perform Low–Level Format (Hard Disk)

Decide whether You Need Low-Level Format

Warning: *IDE drives do not use low level-format. Any attempt to low-level format IDE drives will destroy the low level format done at the factory!*

This step is optional for SCSI drives. Low-level format is a good test of the controller and drives, but most drives are properly formatted at the factory and usually never require formatting before installation. I strongly recommend you perform this step if you are installing a used disk drive, or if you are not sure about the state of the disk drive.

Any valuable data on the disk should be backed up before installation began. Do not try to preserve data on the disk. Restore the data from your backup media after the installation process is complete.

Low-level format each SCSI drive. This will ensure you are starting the install process with a clean disk. Low-level format will delete unwanted old partition maps.

Accessing Low-Level Format via BIOS Hot-key

Some SCSI controllers allow access to the low-level format utility through the use of a "hot-key" sequence during the boot process. Each time the system boots, the SCSI controller BIOS will display a message indicating the hot-key (such as, Control-A) sequence to enter the format utility. Use the hot-key sequence to start the format utility.

If the drive format utility completes normally, it is a strong indication that your SCSI controller and drives are working normally. If the format did not work or if your SCSI controller does not display a list of available SCSI devices when the system boots, do not proceed until you troubleshoot the failure.

Accessing Low-Level Format via DOS

Some SCSI controllers only allow access to the BIOS low-level format utility through DOS. If you have a controller that requires debug.exe or another utility program, you must boot from a DOS floppy disk and run the program that gives you access to low-level format.

To access low level format in DOS use the debug command. Boot from the DOS install diskette, exit from install, and then type:

```
debug
```

at the DOS prompt. Your SCSI controller documentation should give you specific instructions on how to start the low level format utility. You may have to use a utility program from the installation diskette provided with your controller.

Low-level format will wipe the hard disk clean, mark any bad blocks, update the bad block table, and verify the disk surface. This is all quite painless and takes about two to fifteen minutes depending on disk size.

Reboot

When the low-level format utility exits, the system will reboot itself. Make sure you put the DOS diskette back in Drive A to continue with the installation. If your system does not reboot — reboot it yourself.

Step 3: Create Primary DOS Partition (`fdisk.exe`)

Start the `fdisk` Utility Program

Boot from the DOS installation diskette. The DOS installation program will guide you through the installation process. The easiest way to partition, format, and load the hard disk, is to let the DOS install program do it for you. There is, however, a danger in allowing the DOS installation program to partition your disk — DOS will partition the entire disk for itself! To be on the safe side, use `fdisk` to manually partition the hard disk.

If you let the DOS installation program partition the disk, no harm will be done. You can let it partition and format the disk as a test and then repartition it manually after DOS installation is done.

If you wish to use `fdisk` to manually create or delete partitions, you can exit the installation program and type **`fdisk`** at the DOS prompt.

```
A:\>fdisk
```

Delete Old Partition Maps (using `fdisk`)

If your disk drives already have partition maps, do not use them. It is important that you delete any old partitions and start with new partition maps. This condition should only occur if you are using a drives that were previously partitioned and used with DOS.

If you low level formatted your SCSI drives (as recommended), there will be no old partition maps. IDE drives cannot be low level formatted, but you can use the `fdisk` utility to delete old partitions on IDE drives.

Create DOS Partition (using `fdisk`)

Create a primary DOS partition with a minimum size of 15MB. Make the partition you created the "active" partition. This small 15MB partition is only for test and configuration purposes. If you intend to have a working DOS partition, a larger partition size would be appropriate.

Exit the `fdisk` Utility Program

While you are in `fdisk`, feel free to experiment with the menu options. If you make a mistake, no harm will be done at this stage of the installation. When you exit `fdisk`, the system will reboot. Make sure you still have your DOS diskette in drive A.

Step 4: Format DOS Partition (`format.exe`)

This format is not the same as low-level format. The low-level format created the underlying disk address structure used by all operating systems. This step uses the DOS operating system format.exe program to create a file system structure that is unique to DOS. This step only formats the 15MB DOS partition created in the previous step.

Start the Format Utility Program

The DOS installation program can automatically format the unformatted 15MB DOS partition after partitioning is done. If you wish to use format.exe to manually format a DOS partition, you can exit the installation program and type **`format c: /s`** at the DOS prompt.

```
A:\>format c: /s
```

Formatting a 15MB partition only takes a minute.

Step 5: Load DOS Files (`c:\dos`)

Allow the DOS Installation Program to Load DOS Files

Allow the DOS installation program to copy DOS files into the c:\dos directory. The DOS files are in compressed format and must be uncompressed by the installation program as they are copied to the c:\dos directory.

Step 6: Verify DOS Partition

When the DOS installation program is done, you should be able to remove any diskettes from the floppy drives and reboot the system from the primary hard disk. If you cannot boot DOS from the hard disk, do not proceed with the installation until you troubleshoot the failure. If your system boots normally, you can begin loading your optional hardware files from floppy disks.

Power Off

Remove power from the system before proceeding to the next step.

PHASE 4: SOFTWARE CONFIGURATION UTILITIES

- ✓ **Load hardware specific files**
- ✓ **Install printer**
- ✓ **Check video adapter**
- ✓ **Boot from Solaris Diskette**

Load Hardware Specific Files

Some of your adapter boards may include utility software on floppy diskettes. Now is a good time to go through your hardware and install the software onto the DOS partition. Follow the instructions provided with your hardware.

You may perform this step in stages as you add your optional hardware components. Some software, such as the mouse drivers, require the hardware to be installed before the software can be loaded.

Most x86 hardware installation instructions are written for a DOS environment. Install and test your optional hardware using DOS. This is the easiest way to ensure that everything works properly before attempting to load the Solaris operating system.

Install Printer

Connect the printer to the appropriate serial or parallel port. You can use DOS to send text to the printer. A simple command such as **`dir >lpt1`** will direct the standard output of the directory command to the first parallel printer port.

```
C:>dir >lpt1
```

Using a serial COM port for your printer requires an additional DOS setup step to assign the printer serial COM port to an LPT port. Refer to your DOS user manual or your printer manual.

Check Video Adapter

Your video adapter software should be loaded on the DOS partition and then used to test the display modes. Verify that the monitor and video adapter work in the resolution you intend to use with your applications.

Boot from Solaris Diskette

Chapter 10, Here I Come!

Chapter 10 provides a detailed guide through the Solaris installation program. You have completed the hardware portion of the installation. Turn to Chapter 10 to complete the software portion of the installation.

MCA CONFIGURATION CHECKLIST

Some steps may not be required if your system already has the motherboard and peripheral devices installed. Use this checklist to verify that each step in the process is completed in sequence.

Phase 1: Build the Baseline System

- ☐ Collect components, software, and documentation in a clean, sake work area
- ☐ Install options and verify SCSI configuration
- ☐ Install memory into motherboard
- ☐ Install keyboard and mouse
- ☐ Install video adapter and monitor
- ☐ Apply power, verify memory test, and check system BIOS defaults

Phase 2: Setup

- ☐ Boot the system using the reference diskette
- ☐ Create system partition if required
- ☐ Run automatic configuration
- ☐ Load optional MCA configuration files
- ☐ Set MCA options

Phase 3: Building a DOS Partition

- ☐ Configure DOS partition with fdisk command
- ☐ Format DOS partition with format command
- ☐ Copy DOS files to hard disk

Phase 4: Software Configuration Utilities

- ☐ Load hardware specific files
- ☐ Install printer
- ☐ Check video adapter

ISA Installation 8

The following Industry Standard Architecture (ISA) installation procedure contains a moderate level of component specific detail. For more detailed information refer to the Appendices.

Caution:

- *Throughout the installation procedure you will be required to connect or disconnect boards and cables. Turn power off whenever performing any activity that involves connecting or disconnecting hardware.*
- *Do not remove or replace screws while power is on. A screw can fall into the system and cause damage to the motherboard.*
- *Static electricity can be a serious problem, especially in cold winter climates where heating systems remove moisture from the air. Take precautions to prevent static electricity from building up in your workplace.*

If you are configuring a motherboard with both ISA and EISA bus slots, use the EISA configuration and installation procedure (Chapter 9).

PHASE 1: BUILDING THE BASELINE SYSTEM

- ✓ **Gather components in a clean, safe workplace**
- ✓ **Set jumpers and switches on all boards**
- ✓ **Install motherboard, power supply, and memory**
- ✓ **Install keyboard**
- ✓ **Install video adapter and monitor**
- ✓ **Test baseline configuration**

Note: *The floppy drives are usually connected to the primary disk controller. Omitting them from the baseline system eliminates the SCSI or IDE drives as a potential problem source. This is done intentionally. The floppy drives will be added in Phase 2.*

Step 1: Gather Components in a Clean, Safe Workplace

A complete standalone installation will take from three to eight hours depending on your level of experience. Make sure you have plenty of space for tools, documentation, components, and refreshments! When everything is gathered in one place, you are ready to begin.

Step 2: Set Jumpers and Switches on All Boards

The adapter boards should all be in front of you or otherwise easily accessible. You will also need the documentation for each board. Set all switches and jumpers now! This is the appropriate time to reconcile all configuration conflicts.

- Configure SCSI disk controller
- Configure network adapter
- Configure audio board
- Configure I/O board
- Configure FAX/modem board

Preconfigured Systems and Upgrades

If your system is already assembled with components, you probably think your work is all done. Wrong! The system was probably assembled and tested to run DOS, but not UNIX. The first thing you must do is to remove any boards that are installed in your case (except the motherboard). Every board configuration should be checked, and the boards must be reinstalled and tested in the proper sequence.

Every installation should be treated as an upgrade. Strip the components from the system and reconfigure the system to match your configuration worksheet. The temptation to start with the hardware already installed will be great. Don't make that mistake! Use of an existing configuration is the primary source of installation problems.

Remove any previously installed peripheral device cables and adapter boards from the motherboard. After removing the cables, you can leave preinstalled peripheral devices mounted in the case (floppy disk, hard disk, tape, and CD–ROM), provided you already verified the correctness of each device address and termination setting.

Floppy drives seldom cause conflicts during configuration if the cable is connected properly, but SCSI hard disks are another story. Termination and SCSI target ID are very important. If you are not sure about the SCSI device settings, you must remove the devices and verify each one before reinstalling it.

It is very important to disable or remove all components from your system except the ones being tested.

Proprietary Motherboards

Many preconfigured systems have floppy or IDE drive connections embedded on the proprietary motherboard. In this case, it is acceptable to leave the floppy drives and IDE hard disk drives connected. It is reasonable to assume that the factory tested the configuration before shipping the system.

Configure SCSI Disk Controller

Some controllers require software configuration, which cannot be done at this time. Software configuration will be done when the DOS partition is created.

Configure the jumpers and switches appropriate for your controller. VESA local bus SCSI adapters may not require DMA setting.

There is only one floppy controller required per system. If you are installing multiple SCSI controllers with floppy controllers or if you are installing IDE drives and a SCSI controller on the same system, you must disable all floppy controllers except the one you connect to the floppy drive.

In systems with IDE and SCSI, the IDE controller can be considered the "primary" controller. If you install IDE drives using an IDE adapter with a floppy controller, enable the IDE adapter floppy controller and disable all others. If you follow this rule you can easily avoid conflicts between IDE and SCSI adapters. If you decide to enable the floppy controller on the SCSI adapter, make sure your that the floppy controller on the IDE interface adapter can be disabled.

Note: *Proprietary system designs often have the IDE interface and floppy interface embedded on the motherboard. If a SCSI controller is added to this type of motherboard, it should be designated as the secondary controller, and the floppy controller on the SCSI board should be disabled (if present).*

On multiple SCSI controller systems with no IDE adapter, one of the SCSI controllers must be installed as the primary controller and any others must be installed as secondary controllers. This is important because it will determine which drive is the primary boot disk. Refer to the appendices for details on configuring multiple SCSI controllers.

The example SCSI settings given below are for a standalone system with no IDE drives and only one SCSI controller for hard disks and floppy drives.

✓ **Set BIOS address**	**C8000**
✓ **Set IRQ**	**11**
✓ **Set I/O port address**	**330**
✓ **Set DMA**	**5**

Recommended Configuration Settings

Follow the recommendations given below as closely as possible. Each system is different and may require slight variations from the recommended settings. The *SCSI Adapter Configuration Recommendations for ISA Bus* table on page 100 illustrates settings for common system configurations.

- SCSI controller only
- IDE controller only
- Two SCSI controllers
- Both IDE and SCSI controllers

SCSI Adapter Configuration Recommendations for ISA Bus

Controller Configuration		BIOS Address	IRQ	I/O Port Address	DMA	Floppy
1	Primary Controller - SCSI	C8000	11,6	330	5	Enable
	No other controllers					
2	IDE Primary Disk Controller	N/A	14,6	1F0-1F8	N/A	Enable
	No other controllers					
3	Primary Controller - SCSI	C8000	11,6	330	5	Enable
	Second Controller - SCSI	CC000	15	230	6	Disable
4	Primary Controller - IDE	N/A	14,6	1F0-1F8	N/A	Enable
	Second Controller - SCSI	C8000	11	330	5	Disable
	Third Controller - SCSI	CC000	15	230	6	Disable

Notes:

1. VESA local bus controllers do not require DMA transfers because they are located directly on the memory bus.
2. IDE uses program I/O and does not require DMA setting.
3. Standard IDE does not require BIOS address setting.
4. IRQ 6 is always used for floppy drive controller.

Set SCSI BIOS Memory Address Configuration

C8000 is a good choice for the BIOS memory address setting on the primary controller. It is the beginning of the usable memory space that begins after the space used by the video adapter. The best BIOS address choice for the secondary SCSI controller is CC000.

There is 16K of space between C8000 and CC000. This is enough space for most SCSI BIOS requirements. I have not yet seen a SCSI BIOS that uses more than 16K.

Since IDE implementations do not require a BIOS memory address (support is already present in the system BIOS), C8000 can also be assigned to the first SCSI controller on a system that uses IDE as the primary controller. Case #4 on the *SCSI Adapter Configuration Recommendations for ISA Bus* table on page 100 is an example of this.

Set SCSI I/O Memory Port Address Configuration

Floppy drive controllers always use I/O port address 1F0-1F8. Secondary floppy port addresses are sometimes provided as options on some controllers, but I see no need to actually use them.

Refer to the *I/O Port Address* table on page 31 for a list of common port assignments.

Set SCSI IRQ Configuration

IRQ 14 is the standard PC interrupt for the primary hard-disk controller. The IDE drive interface (if present) will default to use IRQ 14. The first SCSI controller should use IRQ 11, but it can also use IRQ 14 if there is no IDE interface installed.

If you have multiple SCSI controllers, each one must have a unique IRQ setting.

Note: *Many SCSI adapters are set at the factory to IRQ 11. Using IRQ 11 for your first SCSI adapter can simplify the configuration process. Some adapters, such as the Adaptec 1542B, are difficult to reconfigure from the factory settings. It is wise to use the default factory settings on your SCSI adapter whenever possible.*

Refer to the IRQ table on page 32 for more details.

Set SCSI DMA Configuration

The IDE interface uses programmed I/O and does not require a DMA channel assignment. VESA local bus implementations of SCSI controllers also do not require DMA settings. Check the documentation on your controller to confirm DMA requirements.

Refer to the *DMA* table on page 33 for more details.

Configure Network Adapter

The network adapter may not require RAM, DMA, or BIOS settings. Check your documentation to confirm the adapter requirements. Some older network adapters will not provide optional settings. Now is the time to reconcile conflicts with older cards.

✔ **Set RAM address**	**CC000**
✔ **Set BIOS address (optional)**	**D0000**
✔ **Set IRQ**	**10**
✔ **Set I/O port address**	**300**
✔ **Set DMA**	**6**

Configure Audio Board

Always setup your audio board to the settings listed below, unless there is a conflict with another adapter.

✔ **Set IRQ**	**5**
✔ **Set I/O port address**	**220**
✔ **Set DMA**	**1**
✔ **Enable game port**	

Configure I/O Board

I/O boards come in a limitless combination of configurations. The potential conflicts are with the network card, internal FAX/modem, and the audio board.

✓ **Set COM1 IRQ (serial mouse)**	**4**
✓ **Set COM2 IRQ (external modem)**	**3**
✓ **Set LPT1 IRQ (printer #1)**	**7**
✓ **Set COM1 I/O port address**	**3F8**
✓ **Set COM2 I/O port address**	**2F8**
✓ **Set LPT 1 I/O port address**	**378**

- ✓ **Disable any other I/O ports that are not in use**
- ✓ **Disable game port if audio board has a game port**

The audio board is set to IRQ 5 which is normally assigned to printer port LPT2. If your system must use LPT2, then reassign the audio board IRQ or do not use a audio board. The audio board also has a game port. You can enable the game port on the I/O board or on the audio board, but not both.

If you use an internal FAX/modem and wish to set it to use COM2 IRQ 3, disable the COM2 port on the I/O board that will conflict with the internal modem board.

Some older network boards can only be set to IRQ 3. If you must use a network board that cannot be reconfigured, consider a FAX/modem that can be configured to IRQ 10, 11, or 12. The best solution is to get a newer network card.

Configure FAX/Modem Board

If you are using an internal FAX/modem adapter board, it will have a COM port IRQ and port address to configure. Use the COM2 setting on your modem and set the port address if your modem requires it.

✓ **Set COM2 IRQ (internal modem)**	**3**
✓ **Set COM2 I/O port address**	**2F8**

You cannot have COM2 enabled on the I/O board if you are using an internal modem at the same COM port. Disable the I/O board COM port if you have not already done so.

Step 3: Install Motherboard, Power Supply, and Memory

Note: *If your system is preconfigured, your motherboard, memory, and power supply are already installed and configured. Check the connections and proceed to the next step.*

- ✓ **Install motherboard (if not previously installed)**

- **Install memory on motherboard (if not previously installed)**
- **Connect power supply to motherboard**

Install the Motherboard

If your motherboard is already mounted in the case, leave it there. If you are upgrading or building your system from scratch, mount the motherboard in the case. There are several small wires that connect the motherboard to the control panel of the case. For proper connection, follow the installation instructions provided with your motherboard and case.

The control panel indicators are handy but optional. The motherboard is designed to function properly if the wires are not connected.

Install the Memory

New installations and upgrades usually require additional memory to meet the 12MB minimum requirement. Add memory to the motherboard at this time. Verify all memory to ensure proper match for speed and size. Refer to the motherboard documentation to verify proper position of memory. Memory is usually installed in numbered banks of 4 and in a sequential order.

Connect the Power Supply

Connect the power supply to the motherboard and connect the battery if one was provided.

Step 4: Install Keyboard

This is probably the easiest part of the installation process. Plug it in!

- **Install the keyboard**

Step 5: Install Video Adapter and Monitor

Note: *If your system has a proprietary motherboard with a compatible video chip, you will not need to install a video adapter.*

- **Install video adapter board**
- **Check video adapter board and monitor**
- **Connect monitor to power and video connector**

Install Video Adapter Board on Motherboard

The first board that you will install on your motherboard is the video display adapter.

Check Video Adapter Board and Monitor

Check the board settings if you have not done so previously. The board should be properly set to match the monitor specifications.

Software is used to configure most adapters and motherboard video chips. You will perform software setup in another phase of this procedure.

Connect Monitor to Power and Video Connector

Note: *Most power supplies on system units provide a switched power outlet for a monitor power connection. If your power supply can handle the AC power required by your monitor, you can connect your monitor power cable to the system and use the system power switch to turn on your system and monitor. AC power adapter cables are available for this purpose.*

Step 6: Test Baseline Configuration

- ✓ **Connect to power source**
- ✓ **Turn on monitor power (allow a minute for warm up)**
- ✓ **Turn on computer power**
- ✓ **Verify memory test completes OK**
- ✓ **Setup BIOS CMOS to defaults**
- ✓ **Set CMOS date and time**
- ✓ **Disconnect power**

Connect to Power Source

At this point, you should be able to connect the system to your power source and begin testing your work. A switchable power strip is helpful. If all of the power cords are plugged into the same strip, it will be easier to power the test configuration on and off.

Turn on Monitor Power (allow a minute for warm up)

Power on the monitor first and give it time to warm up before turning on power to the system. Remember to use caution whenever power is applied to your system. A warm-up period is required so the monitor can display the BIOS messages.

Turn on Computer Power

Turn on the system power and observe the messages that are displayed on the screen and listen for any beeps that may come from the speaker. If you get no display or hear no sound, refer to Chapter 11 on troubleshooting to determine the failure. If the messages are displayed too fast or you were not looking, use the reset button on the front of the case to restart the process as many times as necessary to view the message.

Verify Memory Test Completes OK

Power on self test (POST) should run as soon as you turn the power on. The first messages to display (within 10 seconds of power on) should be a banner with the type and version of video display adapter BIOS, and then a memory test indicator that displays the memory count in kilobytes (Kbytes) as each memory location is tested. Observe the memory test display output to verify that all memory is accounted for.

Setup BIOS CMOS to Defaults

The system BIOS will usually display an error message indicating that the memory size is mismatched or that the CMOS is not configured correctly. This is normal when the motherboard is first installed. The error occurs because the BIOS CMOS must be initialized to the new configuration.

You may see a message asking you to hit F1 (or some other key) to continue. This may vary from one BIOS to another. Hit the key indicated on your display and continue booting. If there is a memory mismatch or a checksum error, the setup program may start automatically when you hit F1.

The information displayed should also indicate which key (usually the delete or insert key) should be pressed to start the BIOS CMOS "setup" program manually. You must press the key at the time indicated or the BIOS program will continue without giving you another opportunity. The time to depress the BIOS setup key is usually while the memory is being tested. If you miss your opportunity, use the reset key/button to restart the process.

Note: *If you cannot access your BIOS setup program using the methods listed above, try booting the system with an unformatted floppy diskette in Drive A. This may activate the BIOS setup program on some systems.*

Once you access the setup utility, the first thing to do is to reset the BIOS to the default settings. Refer to your motherboard documentation for the proper procedure. Usually it is only a matter of selecting the "reset defaults" option from the BIOS setup menu. Resetting the BIOS will ensure that you begin the setup process from a known state. This is just the first of several times you will get an opportunity to change the CMOS settings. You cannot hurt anything at this stage, so do not be bashful about resetting the system and saving your changes. Feel free to browse the BIOS setup options.

You are not doing a final setting of the CMOS at this stage. The purpose of setting CMOS now is to verify normal system functionality. At this stage of the installation:

1. The monitor is displaying data correctly.
2. The motherboard has completed power on self test.
3. The keyboard is working.
4. You have set the CMOS to a default state.

Set CMOS Date and Time

After resetting the BIOS defaults, use the BIOS standard CMOS setup program to:

1. Set the date and time.
2. Save BIOS changes.

Disconnect Power

The purpose of this first phase was to establish a known, working baseline system. If you have completed this baseline configuration, you have established a good foundation on which to build. Now we can go to the next phase in the process and install the floppy disk, hard disk, and SCSI subsystem.

PHASE 2: HARD-DISK AND FLOPPY-DRIVE INSTALLATION

Now is the time to collect and install all floppy disks, hard disks, and SCSI devices. All cables and connectors should have been prepared in advance with the proper length and the appropriate number of connectors.

- **Set and verify IDE master/slave drives and adapter**
- **Set and verify SCSI device target IDs**
- **Set and verify SCSI termination**
- **Install all SCSI/IDE devices and cables**
- **Set BIOS floppy-disk and hard-disk parameters**
- **Save BIOS changes**

This process takes a lot of time and requires a steady and cautious approach. If you did not plan ahead, this is where you will begin to feel the pain!

If you are mounting devices in the case, you must have screws of the proper size. Hard-disk drives and CD–ROM drives are notorious for their tendency to malfunction because of long mounting screws!

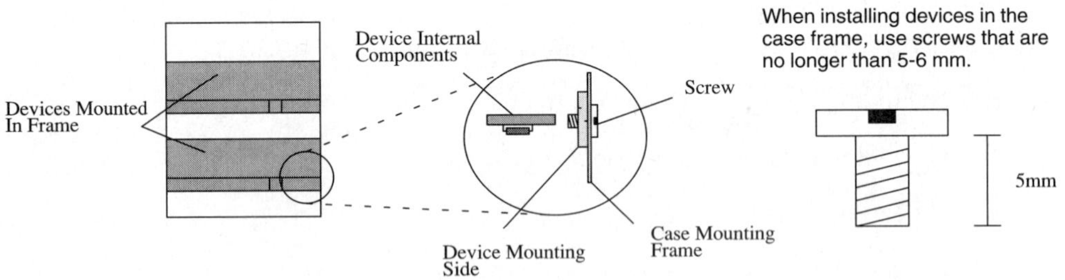

Most cases have metal frames that hold the hard disks and other peripherals. Screws are inserted through the frame and into the side of the device. The proper screw thread length is 5 to 6

millimeters. Screws with threads that extend 7 millimeters or more may cause the device to fail because the screws will extend through the side of the device and make contact with the internal printed circuit board or its components. When this happens, it can be your worst nightmare. This is the kind of thing you usually have to learn the hard way.

Step 1: Set and Verify IDE Master/Slave Drives and Adapter

If you are not installing IDE drives, skip this step.

Many IDE adapters provide the added features of a multifunction I/O board. It is not uncommon to find an IDE board with a game port, parallel port, and two serial ports. If you have such a board, configure the optional features before installing the adapter. Refer to your configuration worksheet (page 55).

- ✓ **Verify that the first IDE drive is set to "master"**
- ✓ **Verify that the second IDE drive is set to "slave"**
- ✓ **Install floppy/IDE drives and cables with caution (red stripe to pin 1)**

Verify First IDE Drive Is Set to "Master"

The first IDE drive should be set to "master." Most IDE drives come from the factory set as master. If the drive is already installed in a preconfigured system, it is probably configured properly. The only possible settings on the drive are master or slave. You have a 50-50 chance of being correct. If the drive is not set correctly, it will not work.

Verify that the Second IDE Drive Is Set to "Slave"

The second IDE drive should be set to "slave."

Install Floppy/IDE Drives and Cables with Caution (red stripe to pin 1)

The floppy cable can be installed backward on many systems. Make sure you connect the cable with the striped side of the cable on pin 1. Connect the cable to the floppy drives and to the floppy drive controller. The controller connection could be on the IDE interface board or on the motherboard. Check your hardware for the correct location.

Note: *Pin 1 is usually designated on cable connectors, devices, and adapters by a triangle, arrow, dot, square, numeral 1, or other such mark. Look closely at your cables, devices, and adapters to locate pin 1.*

Step 2: Set and Verify SCSI Device Target IDs

Skip steps 2 and 3 if you are not installing SCSI devices.

Assign a target ID address to each SCSI device, and configure each device with its unique address. Use the following sample SCSI target ID map as a guide. If you do not use the sample provided, you should pick a consistent scheme that meets your needs. The object is to configure systems in the same way each time, so as not to create random configurations that can prove hard to support.

Refer to your hardware documentation for target ID jumper settings.

Sample SCSI Target ID Map for ISA Configuration		
Device	**ID**	**Comments**
Hard Disk	0	Most SCSI controllers require the first hard disk to be set to target ID 0. Always set your primary boot disk to this ID.
Hard Disk	1	Add additional hard disks in sequence (recommendation).
Hard Disk	2	Add additional hard disks in sequence (recommendation).
Unassigned	3	This target ID is not assigned to any device. It can be used when a SCSI device is added to the configuration.
Unassigned	4	This target ID is not assigned to any device. It can be used when a SCSI device is added to the configuration.
Magnetic Tape Unit (MTU)	5	You could set the address to any available ID. If you are configuring many systems, it helps to be consistent with your ID selection. Always setting the MTU to ID 5 could be helpful when maintaining many systems.
CD–ROM	6	You could set the address to any available ID. If you are configuring many systems, it helps to be consistent with your ID selection. Always setting the CD–ROM to ID 6 could be helpful when maintaining many systems.
SCSI Controller	7	This target ID is reserved for the SCSI controller.

Set Primary Disk Controller

If you install IDE drives, your SCSI controller is the secondary controller and should have the floppy controller disabled. If your SCSI controller is the primary disk controller, enable the floppy controller and connect the front panel hard disk LED cable to the controller. Refer to the configuration worksheet (page 55) for recommended settings.

Step 3: Set and Verify SCSI Termination

Terminate the SCSI bus at each physical end. This process will vary according to the combination of internal and external devices installed on the bus. Refer to Appendix C for termination details.

Step 4: Install all SCSI/IDE Devices and Cables

- ✓ **Install floppy/hard drive devices into case (if not already done)**
- ✓ **Install peripheral devices into case (if not already done)**
- ✓ **Install controller boards into motherboard slots**

- ✓ **Connect power cables to devices**
- ✓ **Connect external SCSI bus devices**
- ✓ **Connect data cables to all devices**

Install Floppy/Hard Drive Devices into Case

This procedure will vary in difficulty depending on your type of case. Keep in mind that you will have to route the power and signal cables to the drives after they are mounted. Check your cables for proper length.

Install Peripheral Devices into Case

If you have CD–ROM, magnetic tape, or other peripherals, install them now.

Install Adapter Board into Motherboard Slots

Insert the SCSI controller into the appropriate slot on the motherboard. Connect the control panel hard disk LED cable to the SCSI controller. Do not forget to attach the adapter mounting bracket to the case with the appropriate screw.

Connect Power Cables to Devices

Connect power to each internal device. If you do not have enough power connectors, you can purchase power cable splitters at most computer supply stores.

Connect External SCSI Bus Devices

If you are using external devices, connect them to the SCSI controller external bus connector.

Connect Data Cables to All Devices

Connect the SCSI bus cable to the internal SCSI devices and SCSI controller. You should already have terminators at the appropriate points.

Check Your Work

Before proceeding to the next step, check your work to make sure that all cables are on tight, all switches are still set correctly, all screws are snug, and all boards are plugged into the bus correctly. I recently spent hours troubleshooting a problem because I inserted a SCSI controller and changed a switch setting by handling the board carelessly.

You are about to apply power to the system again. Remove all those screws you dropped when you were fastening the boards and devices in your case!

Step 5: Set BIOS Floppy-Disk and Hard-Disk Parameters

The majority of the physical work is done. The next step is to setup the system CMOS to include the floppy and hard disk devices.

Power On

Turn on the power, first to the monitor and then to any external peripheral devices on the SCSI bus, and finally to the case.

It is absolutely necessary to reset the system CMOS to the default values. You cannot troubleshoot problems on any system where the CMOS values are not set to a known state. Start out at the default settings, and if changes become necessary, document each change so you can re-create the conditions on demand.

Set Time and Date

The time and date were set in a previous step. Verify the setting and reset them if necessary.

Set IDE Drives

If you have IDE drives, you must manually set the CMOS drive type to match your drive geometry. The hard-disk value should be set to "none" if you are not installing IDE disk drives.

Your CMOS setup may have an auto-drive detection feature. Use auto-drive detection to set the drive type (when available).

Note: *BIOS auto-detect routines create a logical drive geometry that is not the same as the actual physical geometry of the drive. Setting CMOS with a logical IDE drive geometry may cause a conflict with Solaris disk partitioning. Refer to Appendix C for more information concerning IDE drive geometry.*

Set Floppy Drives

Select the floppy type for drives A and B.

Step 6: Save BIOS Changes

Choose the save changes option and exit the CMOS setup program. Remove the diskettes from the floppy drives to prevent the system from booting.

Test Disk Drives

When the CMOS setup program exits, the system will try to boot from floppy drive A or from hard disk C. Observe the boot process and verify that the floppy drive lights blink. If the hard disk is not preformatted with a bootable partition, you should get an error message indicating there is no valid boot device. If there is a bootable partition on the hard disk, the system will attempt to boot.

PHASE 3: CREATE A DOS PARTITION

This is a necessary procedure. Do not attempt to partition the disk without DOS. The DOS partition will be used to store setup utilities, diagnostic programs, and other programs that are included with your hardware. System troubleshooting depends heavily on DOS utility programs. Some hardware components cannot be configured without DOS!

This procedure is based on MSDOS 6.0. Versions of DOS prior to 6.0 do not include the full range of useful setup features such as:

- Automatic Installation
- System Information Utility (msd.exe)
- Backup Utility
- Antivirus Utility
- Automatic Memory Configuration

Overview

- ✓ **Boot from DOS floppy disk**
- ✓ **Perform low-level format (hard disk)**
- ✓ **Create primary DOS partition (`fdisk.exe`)**
- ✓ **Format DOS partition (`format.exe`)**
- ✓ **Load DOS files (`C:\DOS`)**
- ✓ **Verify DOS partition**
- ✓ **Load hardware specific files**

Step 1: Boot from DOS Floppy Disk

The purpose of this step is to verify that the floppy drive interface works. If the DOS installation starts normally, it verifies that the floppy drive and floppy drive controller are functioning properly. DOS cannot be installed on the hard disk until the hard disk is partitioned and formatted.

Put the DOS install disk in drive A and boot (power cycle or reset button) the system. If the floppy drive and controller are properly connected, the DOS installation program will display a message. If you do not see the install message, do not proceed until you troubleshoot the failure.

A diagnostic boot diskette is a valuable tool for configuring or testing a system. You can easily create your own DOS boot diskette. Refer to the procedure on page 165.

Step 2: Perform Low-Level Format (Hard Disk)

Decide if You Need Low-Level Format

Warning: *IDE drives do not use low-level format. Any attempt to low-level format IDE drives will destroy the low-level format performed at the factory !*

This step is optional for SCSI drives. Low-level format is a good test of the controller and drives, but most drives are properly formatted at the factory and usually never require formatting before installation. I strongly recommend you perform this step if you are installing a used disk drive or if you are not sure about the state of the disk drive.

Low-level format each SCSI drive. This will ensure that you are starting the installation process with a clean disk. Low-level format will delete unwanted old partition maps.

Any valuable data on the disk should have been backed up before installation began. Do not try to preserve data on the disk. Restore the data from your backup media after the installation process is complete.

Accessing Low-Level Format via BIOS Hot-key

Some SCSI controllers, such as the Adaptec 1542C, allow access to the low-level format utility through the use of a "hot-key" sequence during the boot process. Each time the system boots, the SCSI controller BIOS will display a message indicating the hot-key sequence (such as, Control-A) to enter the format utility. Use the hot-key sequence to start the format utility.

If the drive format utility completes normally, it is a strong indication that your SCSI controller and drives are working normally. If the format did not work or your SCSI controller does not display a list of available SCSI devices when the system boots, do not proceed until you troubleshoot the failure.

Accessing Low-Level Format via DOS

Some SCSI controllers only allow access to the BIOS low-level format utility through DOS. If you have a controller that requires `debug.exe` or another utility program to access the format utility, you must boot from a DOS floppy diskette and run the program that gives you access to low-level format.

To use DOS debug, boot from the DOS install diskette, exit from install, and then type:

```
debug
```

at the DOS prompt. Your SCSI controller documentation should give you specific instructions on how to start the low-level format utility. You may have to use a utility program from the installation diskette provided with your controller.

Low-level format will wipe the hard disk clean (erase all data), mark any bad blocks, update the bad block table, and verify the disk surface. This is all quite painless and takes about two to fifteen minutes depending on disk size.

Reboot

When the low-level format utility exits, the system will reboot itself. Make sure you put the DOS diskette back in Drive A to continue with the installation. If your system does not reboot, reboot it yourself.

Step 3: Create Primary DOS Partition (`fdisk.exe`)

Start the `fdisk` Utility Program

Boot from the DOS installation diskette. The DOS installation program will guide you through the installation process. The easiest way to partition, format, and load the disk is to let the DOS install program do it for you. There is, however, a danger in allowing the DOS installation program to partition your disk — DOS will partition the entire disk for itself! To be on the safe side, use `fdisk.exe` to manually partition the hard disk.

If you let the DOS installation program partition the disk, no harm will be done. You can let it partition and format the disk as a test and then repartition it manually after DOS installation is done.

If you wish to use `fdisk.exe` to manually create or delete partitions, you can exit the installation program and type **`fdisk`** at the DOS prompt as follows:

```
A:\>fdisk
```

Delete Old Partition Maps (using `fdisk`)

If your disk drives already have partition maps, do not use them. It is important that you delete any old partitions and start with new partition maps. This condition should only occur if you are using drives that were previously partitioned and used with DOS.

If you low-level formatted your SCSI drives (as recommended), there will be no old partition maps. IDE drives cannot be low-level formatted, but you can use the `fdisk` utility to delete old partitions on IDE drives.

Create DOS Partition (using `fdisk`)

Create a primary DOS partition with a minimum size of 15MB. Make the partition you created the “active” partition. This small 15MB partition is only for test and configuration purposes. If you intend to have a working DOS partition, a larger partition size would be appropriate.

Exit the `fdisk` Utility Program

While you are in `fdisk`, feel free to experiment with the menu options. If you make a mistake, no harm will be done at this stage of the installation. When you exit `fdisk`, the system will reboot. Make sure you still have your DOS diskette in Drive A.

Step 4: Format DOS Partition (`format.exe`)

This format is not the same as low-level format. The low-level format created the underlying disk address structure used by all operating systems. This step uses the DOS operating system `format.exe` program to create a file system structure that is unique to DOS. This step only formats the 15MB DOS partition created in the previous step.

Start the `format` Utility Program

The DOS installation program can automatically format the unformatted 15MB DOS partition after partitioning is done. If you wish to use `format.exe` to manually format a DOS partition, you can exit the installation program and type **`format c: /s`** at the DOS prompt.

```
A:\>format c: /s
```

Formatting a 15MB partition only takes a minute.

Step 5: Load DOS Files (c:\dos)

Allow the DOS Installation Program to Load DOS Files

Allow the DOS installation program to copy DOS files into the `c:\dos` directory. The DOS files are in compressed format and must be uncompressed by the installation program as they are copied to the `c:\dos` directory.

Step 6: Verify DOS Partition

When the DOS installation program is done, you should be able to remove any diskettes from the floppy drives and reboot the system from the primary hard disk. If you cannot boot DOS from the hard disk, do not proceed with the installation until you troubleshoot the failure. If your system boots normally, you can begin loading your optional hardware files from floppy disk.

Power Off

Turn off the system power before proceeding to the next step.

PHASE 4: SOFTWARE CONFIGURATION UTILITIES

- ✓ **Install audio board**
- ✓ **Install multi-I/O adapter**
- ✓ **Install mouse**
- ✓ **Install other board options (except network card)**
- ✓ **Install printer**
- ✓ **Check video adapter**
- ✓ **Load hardware specific files**

Install Audio Board

Install the audio board using the recommended settings from your configuration worksheet. Use the DOS utilities included with your board to verify the functions of your audio board. Do not forget the speakers or headsets!

Install Multi-I/O Adapter

Almost all x86 configurations include a multi-I/O card with both a parallel and a serial port. The printer is usually connected to the first parallel port, and the mouse is usually connected to the first serial port.

Check your configuration worksheet and verify the IRQ and I/O port assignments before you install the adapter. Remember to disable functions, such as the joystick, if you have duplicate functionality on another adapter such as the audio board.

Install Mouse

There are many types of mice, but they usually all require some software driver to work with DOS. They also usually have a test utility you can run under DOS to verify each mouse function. Install and test your mouse. Use the software provided with the mouse.

If your mouse is connected to your video adapter, use the video adapter setup utility to configure the mouse IRQ and I/O port address.

Install Other Board Options

You may have other optional devices to install or test. This is the time to integrate optional hardware, such as a modem or a scanner. Install your optional devices and test them under DOS.

It is NOT yet time to install the network card. Before introducing network problems to the installation, you will boot the system in a standalone mode. The network connection will come last.

Note: *Performing a Solaris test installation without a network adapter is recommended for first time installations. If you do not wish to perform a test installation, you can install the network adapter now.*

Install Printer

Connect the printer to the appropriate serial or parallel port. You can use DOS to send text to the printer. A simple command such as **`dir >lpt1`** will direct the standard output of the directory command to the first parallel printer port.

```
C:>dir >lpt1
```

Using a serial port for your printer requires some additional DOS setup if you want to test your printer. Refer to your DOS user manual or your printer manual.

Check Video Adapter

Your video adapter software should be loaded on the DOS partition and then used to test the display modes. Verify that the monitor and video adapter work in the highest resolution intended for use with DOS or Solaris.

Load Hardware Specific Files

Some of your adapter boards may include utility software on floppy diskettes. Now is a good time to go through your hardware and install the software onto the DOS partition. Follow the instructions provided with your hardware.

You may perform this step in stages as you add your optional hardware components. Some software such as the mouse drivers require the hardware to be installed before the software can be loaded.

Most x86 hardware installation instructions are written for a DOS environment. Install and test your optional hardware using DOS. This is the easiest way to ensure everything works properly before attempting to load the Solaris operating system.

Install your hardware one board at a time. Verify that each component works before going on to the next component. Do not forget to power off before connecting components.

Boot from the Solaris Diskette

Chapter 10, Here I Come!

Chapter 10 provides a detailed guide through the Solaris installation program. You have completed the *hardware* portion of the installation. Turn to Chapter 10 to complete the *software* portion of the installation.

Install the Network Card

After the test installation is completed in Chapter 10, install your network card and perform the final installation on your network.

NOTE: *A test installation is done without the network adapter to verify complete system functionality before introducing the added complexity that comes with network connections. Performing a quick test installation without a network will simplify the troubleshooting process if the installation fails.*

If you plan to bypass the test installation, it is critical to install the network card before attempting to install Solaris x86. The network card must be installed or the network drivers will not be enabled.

ISA CONFIGURATION CHECKLIST

Some steps may not be required if your system already has the motherboard and peripheral devices installed. Use this checklist to verify that each step in the process is completed in sequence.

Phase 1: Build the Baseline System

- ☐ Collect components, software, and documentation in a clean, safe work area
- ☐ Take all boards out of the system except the motherboard
- ☐ Install memory into motherboard
- ☐ Connect battery and power supply to motherboard (if required)
- ☐ Install floppy disk drives and other peripherals into the case (without cables)
- ☐ Install keyboard
- ☐ Install video monitor and adapter
- ☐ Apply power, verify memory test, and check system BIOS defaults

Phase 2: Floppy and Hard-Disk Configuration

- ☐ Configure and cable floppy disk drives
- ☐ Configure and cable hard disk drives (configure all SCSI devices now)
- ☐ Configure and install disk drive controller and cables
- ☐ Set system CMOS for floppy drives and IDE drives
- ☐ Boot from floppy with DOS diskette and confirm normal operating system behavior

Phase 3: Building a DOS Partition

- ☐ Configure DOS partition with fdisk command
- ☐ Format DOS partition with format command
- ☐ Copy hardware setup software to the DOS partition

Phase 4: Software Configuration Utilities

- ☐ Add optional boards (configure each to avoid conflicts)
- ☐ Test peripherals and options
- ☐ Install and test mouse
- ☐ Do not install network card until network is functional and you are ready to connect to it

EISA Installation 9

The following Extended Industry Standard Architecture (EISA) installation procedure contains a moderate level of component specific detail. For more detailed information, refer to the appendices. This procedure is based on a proprietary motherboard and system design.

Caution:

- *Throughout the installation procedure you will be required to connect or disconnect boards and cables. Turn power off whenever performing any activity that involves connecting or disconnecting hardware.*
- *Do not remove or replace screws while power is on. A screw can fall into the system and cause damage to the motherboard.*
- *Static electricity can be a serious problem, especially in cold winter climates where heating systems remove moisture from the air. Take precautions to prevent static electricity from building up in your workplace.*

PHASE 1: BUILDING THE BASELINE SYSTEM

Overview

- ✓ **Gather components in a clean, safe workplace**
- ✓ **Set jumpers and switches on all boards**
- ✓ **Check or install motherboard, power supply, and memory**
- ✓ **Install keyboard**
- ✓ **Install video adapter and monitor**
- ✓ **Test baseline configuration**

Step 1: Gather Components in a Clean, Safe Workplace

A complete standalone installation will take from three to eight hours depending on your level of experience. Make sure you have plenty of space for tools, documentation, components, and refreshments! When everything is gathered in one place, you are ready to begin.

Step 2: Set Jumpers and Switches on all Boards

The adapter boards should all be in front of you or otherwise easily accessible. You will also need the documentation for each board. EISA boards do not use jumpers or switches, but most EISA systems have at least one ISA board installed. ISA boards are configured in the same way, regardless of the type of system.

Set all ISA board switches and jumpers now! This is the appropriate time to reconcile all ISA board configuration conflicts.

- Configure SCSI disk controller
- Configure network adapter
- Configure audio board
- Configure I/O board
- Configure FAX/modem board

Preconfigured Systems and Upgrades

If your system is already assembled with components, you probably think your work is all done. Wrong! The first thing you must do is to remove any boards that are installed in your case (except the motherboard). Every board configuration should be checked, and the boards must be reinstalled and tested in the proper sequence.

Every installation should be treated as an upgrade. Strip the components from the system and reconfigure the system to match your configuration worksheet. The temptation to start with the hardware already installed will be great. Do not make that mistake! Using an existing configuration is the primary source of installation problems.

Remove any previously installed peripheral device cables and adapter boards from the motherboard. After removing the cables, you can leave preinstalled peripheral devices mounted in the case (floppy disk, hard disk, tape, and CD–ROM), provided you already verified thc correctness of each device address and termination setting.

Floppy drives seldom cause conflicts during configuration if the cable is connected properly, but SCSI hard disks are another story. Termination and SCSI target IDs are very important. If you are not sure about the SCSI device settings, you must remove the devices and verify each one before reinstalling it.

It is very important to disable or remove all components from your system except the ones being tested.

Proprietary Motherboards

Many preconfigured systems have floppy or IDE drive connections embedded on the proprietary motherboard. In this case, it is acceptable to leave the floppy drives and IDE hard disk drives connected. It is reasonable to assume that the factory tested the configuration before shipping the system.

Configure SCSI Disk Controller

Check the SCSI adapter terminators while the board is in front of you. If you plan to connect external SCSI devices, you may have to remove or disable the terminators on the SCSI controller. Check the documentation that came with your SCSI controller.

If you are installing a ISA bus SCSI controller, refer to the SCSI disk controller configuration section of the ISA configuration and installation procedure (page 98). ISA controllers are not recommended, but if you have one set properly, it should work fine.

On multiple SCSI controller systems with no IDE adapter, one of the SCSI controllers must be installed as the primary controller and any others must be installed as secondary controllers. This is important, as it will determine which drive is the primary boot disk. Refer to Appendix C for details on configuring multiple SCSI controllers.

Floppy Controller Settings

You may have to change the floppy controller enable/disable function on the SCSI controller or motherboard. There can only be one floppy controller enabled on a system. If you are installing multiple SCSI controllers with floppy controllers or are installing IDE drives and a SCSI controller on the same system, you must disable all floppy controllers except the one you connect to the floppy drive.

In systems with IDE and SCSI, the IDE controller can be considered the "primary" controller. If you install IDE drives using an IDE adapter with a floppy controller, enable the IDE adapter floppy controller and disable all others. If you follow this rule, you can easily avoid conflicts between IDE and SCSI adapters. If you decide to enable the floppy controller on the SCSI adapter, make sure your that the floppy controller on the IDE interface adapter can be disabled.

Note: *Proprietary system designs often have the IDE interface and floppy interface embedded on the motherboard. If a SCSI controller is added to this type of motherboard, it should be designated as the secondary controller, and the floppy controller on the SCSI board should be disabled (if present).*

The example SCSI settings given below are for a standalone system with no IDE drives and only one SCSI controller for hard disks and floppy drives.

- **Set BIOS address** **C8000**
- **Set IRQ** **11**
- **Set I/O port address** **330**
- **Set DMA** **5**

Note: *EISA SCSI controllers will default to settings that may not match the recommended settings. The default settings cannot be changed until the EISA configuration program is executed. Because of this EISA bus quirk, it is necessary to delay installation of option boards until after the SCSI controller has been configured.*

Recommended Configuration Settings

The *SCSI Adapter Configuration Recommendations for ISA Bus* table on page 100 illustrates settings for common system configurations. Use it as a guideline.

Configure Network Adapter

The network adapter may not require RAM, DMA, or BIOS settings. Check your documentation to confirm the adapter requirements. Some older network adapters will not provide optional settings. Now is the time to reconcile conflicts with older cards.

✓ **Set RAM address**	**CC000**
✓ **Set BIOS address (optional)**	**D0000**
✓ **Set IRQ**	**10**
✓ **Set I/O port address**	**300**
✓ **Set DMA**	**6**

Configure Audio Board

Always setup your audio board to the settings listed below unless there is a conflict.

✓ **Set IRQ**	**5**
✓ **Set I/O port address**	**220**
✓ **Set DMA**	**1**
✓ **Enable game port**	

Configure I/O Board

I/O boards come in a unlimited combination of configurations. The potential conflicts are with the network card, internal FAX/modem, and the audio board.

✓ **Set COM1 IRQ (serial mouse)**	**4**
✓ **Set COM2 IRQ (external modem)**	**3**
✓ **Set LPT1 IRQ (printer #1)**	**7**
✓ **Set COM1 I/O port address**	**3F8**
✓ **Set COM2 I/O port address**	**2F8**
✓ **Set LPT 1 I/O port address**	**378**
✓ **Disable any other I/O ports that are not in use**	
✓ **Disable game port if audio board has a game port**	

The audio board is set to IRQ 5, which is normally assigned to printer port LPT2. If your system must use LPT2, then reassign the audio board IRQ or do not use a audio board. The audio board also has a game port. You can enable the game port on the I/O board or on the audio board, but not both.

If you use an internal FAX/modem, it should be set to COM2 IRQ 3. Disable the COM2 port on the I/O board that will conflict with the internal modem board.

Some older network boards can only be set to IRQ 3. If you must use a network board that cannot be reconfigured, consider a FAX/modem that can be configured to IRQ 10, 11, or 12. The best solution is to get a newer network card.

Configure FAX/Modem Board

If you are using an internal FAX/modem adapter board, it will have a com port IRQ and port address to configure. Use the COM2 setting on your modem and set the port address if your modem requires it.

- ✓ **Set COM2 IRQ (internal modem)** **3**
- ✓ **Set COM2 I/O port address** **2F8**

You cannot have com2 enabled on the I/O board if you are using an internal modem at the same com port. Disable the I/O board com port if you have not already done so.

Step 3: Check or Install Motherboard, Power Supply, and Memory

Note: *If your system is preconfigured, your motherboard, memory, and power supply are already installed and configured. Check the connections and proceed to the next step.*

- ✓ **Install the motherboard (if not previously installed)**
- ✓ **Install the memory in motherboard (if not previously installed)**
- ✓ **Connect the power supply to the motherboard**

Install the Motherboard

If your motherboard is already mounted in the case, leave it there. If you are upgrading or building your system from scratch, mount the motherboard in the case. There are several small wires that connect the motherboard to the control panel of the case. For proper connection, follow the installation instructions provided with your motherboard and case.

The control panel indicators are handy but optional. The motherboard is designed to function properly even if the wires are not connected.

Install the Memory

New installations and upgrades usually require additional memory to meet the 12MB minimum requirement. Add memory to the motherboard at this time. Verify all memory to ensure proper match for speed and size. Refer to the motherboard documentation to verify proper position of memory. Memory is usually installed in numbered banks of four and in sequential order.

Connect the Power Supply

Connect the power supply to the motherboard and connect the battery if one was provided.

Step 4: Install Keyboard

This is probably the easiest part of the installation process. Plug it in!

- ✓ **Install the keyboard**

Step 5: Install Video Adapter and Monitor

Note: *If your system has a proprietary motherboard with a compatible video chip, you will not need to install a video adapter. If you want to install an adapter, you will need to disable the on-board video.*

- ✓ **Install video adapter board on the motherboard**
- ✓ **Check video adapter board and monitor**
- ✓ **Connect monitor to power and video connector**

Install Video Adapter Board on Motherboard

The first board that you will install on your motherboard is the video display adapter.

Check Video Adapter Board and Monitor

Check the board settings if you have not done so previously. The board should be properly set to match the monitor.

Software is used to configure most adapters and motherboard video chips. You will perform software setup in another phase of this procedure.

Connect Monitor to Power and Video Connector

Note: *Most power supplies on system units provide a switched power outlet for a monitor power connection. If your power supply can handle the AC power required by your monitor, connect your monitor power cable to the system and use the system power switch to turn on your system and monitor. AC power adapter cables are available for this purpose.*

Step 6: Test Baseline Configuration

- ✓ **Connect to power source**
- ✓ **Turn on monitor power (allow a minute for warmup)**
- ✓ **Turn on computer power**
- ✓ **Verify memory test completes OK**
- ✓ **Setup BIOS CMOS to defaults**
- ✓ **Set CMOS date and time**
- ✓ **Disconnect power**

Connect to Power Source

At this point, you should be able to connect the system to your power source and begin testing your work. A switchable power strip is helpful. If all of the power cords are plugged into the same strip, it will be easier to power the test configuration on and off.

Turn on Monitor Power (allow a minute for warm up)

Power on the monitor first and give it time to warm up before turning on power to the system. Remember to use caution whenever power is applied to your system. A warm up period is required so the monitor can display the BIOS messages.

Turn on Computer Power

Turn on the system power and observe the messages that display on the screen and listen for any beeps that may come from the speaker. If you get no display or hear no sound, refer to Chapter 11 on troubleshooting and isolate the failure. If the messages display too fast or you were not looking, use the reset button on the front of the case to restart the process as many times as necessary to view the message.

Verify Memory Test Completes OK

Power on self test (POST) should run as soon as you turn the power on. The first messages to display (within 10 seconds of power on) should be a banner with the type and version of video display adapter BIOS, and then a memory test indicator that displays the memory count in kilobytes (Kbytes) as each memory location is tested. Observe the memory test display output to verify that all memory is accounted for.

Setup BIOS CMOS to Defaults

The system BIOS will usually display an error message, indicating that the memory size is mismatched or the CMOS is not configured correctly. This is normal when the motherboard is first installed. The error occurs because the BIOS CMOS must be initialized to the new configuration.

You may see a message asking you to hit F1 (or some other key) to continue. This may vary from one BIOS to another. Hit the key indicated on your display and continue booting. If there is a memory mismatch or a checksum error, the setup program may start automatically when you hit F1.

The information displayed should also indicate which key (usually the delete or insert key) should be pressed to start the BIOS CMOS "setup" program manually. You must press the key at the time indicated, or the BIOS program will continue without giving you another opportunity. The time to depress the BIOS setup key is usually while the memory is being tested. If you miss your opportunity, use the reset key/button to restart the process.

Once you access the setup utility, the first thing to do is to reset the BIOS to the default settings. Refer to your motherboard documentation for the proper procedure. Usually it is only a matter of selecting the "reset defaults" option from the BIOS setup menu. Resetting the BIOS will ensure that you begin the setup process from a known state. This is just the first of several times that you will get an opportunity to change the CMOS settings. You cannot hurt anything at this stage, so do not be bashful about resetting the system and saving your changes. Feel free to browse through the BIOS setup options.

You are not doing a final setting of the CMOS at this stage. The purpose of setting CMOS now is to verify normal system functionality. At this stage of the installation:

1. The monitor is displaying data correctly.
2. The motherboard has completed power on self test.
3. The keyboard is working.
4. You have set the CMOS to a default state.

Set CMOS Date and Time

After resetting the BIOS defaults, use the BIOS standard CMOS setup program to:

1. Set the date and time.
2. Save BIOS changes.

Disconnect Power

The purpose of this first phase was to establish a known working baseline system. If you have completed this baseline configuration, you have established a good foundation on which to build. Now we can go to the next phase in the process and install the floppy disk, hard disk, and SCSI subsystem.

PHASE 2: HARD-DISK AND FLOPPY-DRIVE INSTALLATION

Now is the time to collect and install all floppy disks, hard disks, and SCSI devices. All cables and connectors should have been prepared in advance with the proper length and the appropriate number of connectors.

Overview

- ✓ **Set and verify IDE master/slave drives and adapter**
- ✓ **Set and verify SCSI device target IDs**
- ✓ **Set and verify SCSI termination**
- ✓ **Install all SCSI/IDE devices and cables**

- **Set BIOS floppy and hard disk parameters**
- **Save BIOS changes**
- **EISA SCSI configuration**

This process takes considerable time and requires a steady and cautious approach. If you did not plan ahead, this is where you will begin to feel the pain!

If you are mounting devices in the case, you must have screws of the proper size. Hard-disk drives and CD–ROM drives are especially notorious for their tendency to malfunction because of long mounting screws!

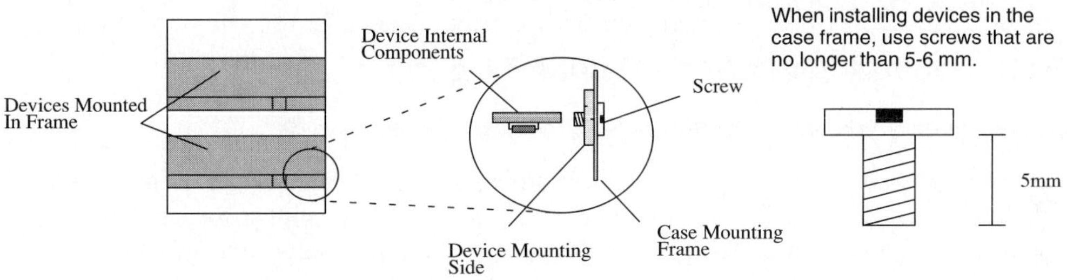

Most cases have metal frames that hold the hard disks and other peripherals. Screws are inserted through the frame and into the side of the device. The proper screw thread length is 5 to 6 millimeters. Screws with threads that extend 7 millimeters or more may cause the device to fail because the screws will extend through the side of the device and make contact with the internal printed circuit board or its components. When this happens, it can be your worst nightmare. This is the kind of thing you usually have to learn the hard way.

Step 1: Set and Verify IDE Master/Slave Drives and Adapter

If you are not installing IDE drives, skip this section of the procedure. Go to step 2.

Many IDE adapters provide the added features of a multifunction I/O board. It is not uncommon to find an IDE board with a game port, a parallel port, and two serial ports. If you have such a board, configure the optional features before installing the adapter. Refer to your configuration worksheet (page 55).

- **Verify that first IDE drive is set to "master"**
- **Verify that second IDE drive is set to "slave"**
- **Install floppy and IDE drives and cables caution (colored stripe to pin 1)**

Verify That First IDE Drive Is Set to "Master"

The first IDE drive should be set to "master." Most IDE drives come from the factory set as master. If the drive is already installed in a preconfigured system, it is probably configured properly. The only possible settings on the drive are master and slave. You have at least a 50-50 chance of being correct. If the drive is not set correctly, it will not work.

Verify Second IDE drive Is Set to "Slave"

The second IDE drive should be set to "slave."

Install Floppy/IDE Drives and Cables with Caution (red stripe to pin 1)

The floppy cable can be installed backward on many systems. Make sure you connect the cable with the striped side of the cable on pin 1. Connect the cable to the floppy drives and to the floppy drive controller. The controller connection could be on the IDE interface board or on the motherboard. Check your hardware for the correct location.

Step 2: Set and Verify SCSI Device Target IDs

Skip this section if you are not installing SCSI devices. Go to step 3.

Assign a target ID address to each SCSI device and configure each device with its unique address. Use the following sample SCSI target ID map as a guide. If you do not use the sample provided, you should pick a consistent scheme that meets your needs. The object is to configure systems in the same way each time, and not create random configurations which can prove difficult to support.

Refer to your hardware documentation for target ID jumper settings.

Sample SCSI Target ID Map for EISA Configuration		
Device	**ID**	**Comments**
Hard Disk	0	Most SCSI controllers require the first hard disk to be set to target ID 0. Always set your primary boot disk to this target ID.
Hard Disk	1	Add additional hard disks in sequence (recommendation).
Hard Disk	2	Add additional hard disks in sequence (recommendation).
Unassigned	3	This target ID is not assigned to any device. It can be used when a SCSI device is added to the configuration.
Unassigned	4	This target ID is not assigned to any device. It can be used when a SCSI device is added to the configuration.
Magnetic Tape Unit (MTU)	5	You could set the address to any available ID. If you are configuring many systems, it helps to be consistent with your ID selection. Always setting the MTU to ID 5 could be helpful when maintaining many systems.
CD–ROM	6	You could set the address to any available ID. If you are configuring many systems, it helps to be consistent with your ID selection. Always setting the CD–ROM to ID 6 could be helpful when maintaining many systems.
SCSI Controller	7	This target ID is reserved for the SCSI controller.

Set Primary Disk Controller

If you install IDE drives, your SCSI controller is the secondary controller and should have the floppy controller disabled. If your SCSI controller is the primary disk controller, enable the floppy controller and connect the front panel hard disk LED cable to the controller. Refer to the configuration worksheet (page 55) for recommended settings.

Step 3: Set and Verify SCSI Termination

Terminate the SCSI bus at each end. This process will vary according to the combination of internal and external devices installed on the bus. Refer to Appendix C for termination details.

Step 4: Install All SCSI/IDE Devices and Cables

- ✓ **Install floppy/hard drive devices into case (if not already done)**
- ✓ **Install peripheral devices into case (if not already done)**
- ✓ **Install controller boards into motherboard slots**
- ✓ **Connect power cables to devices**
- ✓ **Connect external SCSI bus devices**
- ✓ **Connect data cables to all devices**

Install Floppy/Hard Drive Devices into Case (if required)

This procedure will vary in difficulty depending on the type of case you have. Keep in mind that you will have to route the power and signal cables to the drives after they are mounted. Check your cables for proper length.

Install Peripheral Devices into Case (if required)

If you have CD–ROM, magnetic tape, or other peripherals, install them now.

Install Controller Boards into Motherboard Slots (if required)

Insert the SCSI controller into the appropriate slot on the motherboard. Connect the control panel hard-disk LED cable to the SCSI controller. Do not forget to attach the board to the case with the appropriate screw.

Connect Power Cables to Devices

Connect power to each internal device. If you do not have enough power connectors, you can purchase power cable splitters at most computer supply stores.

Connect External SCSI Bus Devices

If you are using external devices, connect them to the SCSI controller external bus connector.

Connect Data Cables to All Devices

Connect the SCSI bus cable to the internal SCSI devices and SCSI controller. You should already have terminators at the appropriate points.

Check Your Work

Before proceeding to the next step, check your work to make sure that all cables are on tight, all switches are still set correctly, all screws are snug, and all boards are plugged into the bus correctly. I recently spent hours troubleshooting a problem because I inserted a SCSI controller and changed a switch setting by handling the board carelessly.

You are about to apply power to the system again. Remove all those screws you dropped when you were fastening the boards and devices in your case!

Step 5: Set BIOS Floppy-Disk and Hard-Disk Parameters

The majority of the physical work is done. The next step is to setup the system CMOS to include the floppy and hard disk devices.

Power On

Turn on the power first to the monitor and then to any external peripheral devices on the SCSI bus, and finally to the case.

It is absolutely necessary to reset the system CMOS to the default values. You cannot troubleshoot problems on any system where the CMOS values are not set to a known state. Start out at the default settings, and if changes become necessary, document each change so you can recreate the conditions on demand.

Set Time and Date

The time and date were set in a previous step. Verify the setting and reset them if necessary.

Set IDE Drives

If you have IDE drives, you must manually set the CMOS drive type to match your drive geometry. The hard disk value should be set to "none" if you are not installing IDE disk drives.

Your CMOS setup may have an auto-drive detection feature. Use auto–drive detection to set the drive type (when available).

Set Floppy Drives

Select the floppy type for drives A and B.

Step 6: Save BIOS Changes

Choose the "save changes" option and exit the CMOS setup program. Remove diskettes from floppy drives to prevent the system from booting.

Test Disk Drives

When the CMOS setup program exits, the system will try to boot from floppy drive A or from hard disk C. Observe the boot process and verify that the floppy drive lights blink.

Step 7: EISA SCSI Configuration

The Trouble with EISA

Consider yourself fortunate if you are installing on a system with a SCSI adapter that has already been configured by the EISA configuration program. The initial installation of a SCSI adapter can be very difficult, and the EISA SCSI adapter will not work until the EISA configuration program adds it to the system configuration profile stored in nonvolatile RAM on the EISA motherboard.

If your SCSI adapter is already correctly configured on the EISA bus, you can skip this step.

Diskette Type

The first obstacle to face is *floppy diskette type*. To configure the SCSI adapter for use on the EISA bus you must use a floppy drive to boot from a DOS diskette, to load and execute the EISA configuration program from diskette, and to copy the SCSI adapter configuration files from a diskette. If you only have one type of floppy drive (i.e., 3.5 inch), you must make sure that your DOS diskette, your EISA configuration utility diskette, and your SCSI adapter configuration diskette match your floppy drive type.

Boot DOS from Diskette

The EISA configuration program is a DOS utility. Use your DOS diskette to boot the system. Once you are at the DOS prompt (`A:\>`) you can insert your EISA configuration diskette and run the EISA configuration utility. Refer to your EISA configuration utility documentation for specific instructions on loading and executing the program from the DOS prompt.

Run EISA Configuration Utility

EISA configuration programs vary from system to system, but they all have one thing in common. Each optional EISA adapter board comes with a configuration file on a floppy disk. The configuration file is required by the EISA setup program. There is also a configuration file for the motherboard. ISA boards do not have configuration files. To configure the SCSI adapter you must:

- Copy adapter configuration files to the configuration disk or directory
- Run the configuration program
- Configure the adapter in the correct slot
- Save changes to CMOS (save to a file for backup)

Some EISA configuration programs allow you to define ISA board configurations manually and to save the information along with the EISA board configurations. This step is optional.

Set SCSI Configuration

If your SCSI adapter can operate in enhanced mode, use the EISA configuration program to setup the enhanced mode operation.

Now is the time to use the EISA configuration program to set the SCSI configuration parameters.

- BIOS address C8000
- I/O port address 330
- IRQ 11
- DMA (if required) 5

Set SCSI BIOS Address

C8000 is a good choice for the BIOS memory address setting on the primary controller. It is the beginning of the usable memory space that begins after the space used by the video adapter. The best BIOS address choice for the secondary SCSI controller is CC000.

There is 16Kbytes of space between C8000 and CC000. This is enough space for most SCSI BIOS requirements. I have yet to see a SCSI BIOS that uses more than 16Kbytes.

Since IDE implementations do not require a BIOS memory address (support is already present in the system BIOS), C8000 can also be assigned to the first SCSI controller on a system that uses IDE as the primary controller. Case #4 on the *SCSI Adapter Configuration Recommendations for ISA Bus* table on page 100 is an example of this.

Set SCSI I/O Memory Port Address Configuration

The floppy drives always use I/O port address 1F0-1F8 for the primary floppy drives. Secondary floppy port addresses are sometimes provided as options on some controllers, but I see no need to actually use them.

Refer to the *I/O Port Address* table on page 31 for a list of common port assignments.

Set SCSI IRQ Configuration

IRQ 14 is the standard PC interrupt for the primary hard-disk controller. The IDE drive interface (if present) will default to use IRQ 14. The first SCSI controller should use IRQ 11, but it can also use IRQ 14 if there is no IDE interface installed.

If you have multiple SCSI controllers, each one must have a unique IRQ setting.

Note: *Many SCSI adapters are set at the factory to IRQ 11. Using IRQ 11 for your first SCSI adapter can simplify the configuration process. Some adapters, such as the Adaptec 1542B, are difficult to reconfigure from the factory settings. It is wise to use the default factory settings on your SCSI adapter whenever possible.*

Refer to the IRQ table on page 32 for more details.

Set SCSI DMA Configuration

If you can set enhanced mode for your SCSI controller, you may not have to set the DMA channel. EISA enhanced mode will allow the SCSI controller to use enhanced high speed 32-bit DMA modes on the EISA bus.

Refer to the *DMA* table on page 33 for more details.

PHASE 3: CREATE A DOS PARTITION

This is a necessary procedure. Do not attempt to partition the disk without DOS. The DOS partition will be used to store setup utilities, diagnostic programs, and other programs that are included with your hardware. System troubleshooting depends heavily on DOS utility programs. Some hardware components cannot be configured without DOS!

This procedure is based on MS-DOS 6.0. Versions of DOS prior to 6.0 do not include the full range of useful setup features such as:

- Automatic Installation
- System Information Utility (msd.exe)
- Backup Utility
- Antivirus Utility
- Automatic Memory Configuration

Overview

- **Boot from DOS floppy disk**
- **Perform low-level format (Hard Disk)**
- **Create primary DOS partition (`fdisk.exe`)**
- **Format DOS partition (`format.exe`)**
- **Load DOS files (`C:\DOS`)**
- **Run EISA configuration utility**

Step 1: Boot from DOS Floppy Disk

The purpose of this step is to verify that the floppy drive interface works. If the DOS installation starts normally, it is verification that the floppy drive and floppy-drive controller are functioning properly. DOS cannot be installed on the hard disk until the hard disk is partitioned and formatted.

Put the DOS install disk in drive A and boot (power cycle or reset button) the system. If the floppy drive and controller are properly connected, the DOS installation program will display a message. If you do not see the install message, do not proceed until you troubleshoot the failure.

A diagnostic boot diskette is a valuable tool for configuring or testing a system. You can easily create your own DOS boot diskette. Refer to the procedure on page 165.

Step 2: Perform Low-Level Format (Optional)

Decide if You Need Low-Level Format

Warning: *IDE drives do not use low-level format. Any attempt to low-level format IDE drives will destroy the low-level format performed at the factory!*

This step is optional for SCSI drives. Low-level format is a good test of the controller and drives, but most drives are properly formatted at the factory and usually never require formatting before installation. I strongly recommend you perform this step if you are installing a used disk drive or if you are not sure about the state of the disk drive.

Low-level format each SCSI drive. This will ensure that you are starting the install process with a clean disk. Low-level format will delete unwanted old partition maps.

Any valuable data on the disk should have been backed up before installation began. Do not try to preserve data on the disk. Restore the data from your backup media after the installation process is complete.

Accessing Low-Level Format via BIOS Hot-Key

Some SCSI controllers such as the Adaptec 1542C allow access to the low-level format utility through the use of a "hot-key" sequence during the boot process. Each time the system boots, the SCSI controller BIOS will display a message indicating the hot-key sequence (such as Control-A) to enter the format utility. Use the hot-key sequence to start the format utility.

If the drive format utility completes normally, it is a strong indication that your SCSI controller and drives are working normally. If the format did not work or your SCSI controller does not display a list of available SCSI devices when the system boots, do not proceed until you troubleshoot the failure.

Accessing Low-Level Format via DOS

Some SCSI controllers only allow access to the BIOS low-level format utility through DOS. If you have a controller that requires debug.exe or another utility program, you must boot from a DOS floppy disk and run the program that gives you access to low-level format.

To use DOS debug, boot from the DOS install diskette, exit from install, and then type:

```
A:\>debug
```

at the DOS prompt. Your SCSI controller documentation should give you specific instructions on how to start the low-level format utility. You may have to use a utility program from the installation diskette provided with your controller.

Low-level format will wipe the hard disk clean (erase all data), mark any bad blocks, update the bad block table, and verify the disk surface. This is all quite painless and takes about two to fifteen minutes depending on disk size.

Reboot

When the low-level format utility exits, the system will reboot itself. Make sure that you put the DOS diskette back in Drive A to continue with the installation. If your system does not reboot, reboot it yourself.

Step 3: Create Primary DOS Partition (fdisk.exe)

Start the `fdisk` Utility Program

Boot from the DOS installation diskette. The DOS installation program will guide you through the installation process. The easiest way to partition, format, and load the disk, is to let the DOS install program do it for you. There is however a danger in allowing the DOS installation program to partition your disk — DOS will partition the entire disk for itself! To be on the safe side, use `fdisk.exe` to manually partition the hard disk.

If you let the DOS installation program partition the disk, no harm will be done. You can let it partition and format the disk as a test and then repartition it manually after DOS installation is done.

If you wish to use `fdisk.exe` to manually create or delete partitions, you can exit the installation program and type **`fdisk`** at the DOS prompt as follows:

```
A:\>fdisk
```

Delete Old Partition Maps (using `fdisk`)

If your disk drives already have partition maps, do not use them. It is important that you delete any old partitions and start with new partition maps. This condition should only occur if you are using drives that were previously partitioned and used with DOS.

If you low-level formatted your SCSI drives (as recommended), there will be no old partition maps. IDE drives cannot be low-level formatted, but you can use the `fdisk` utility to delete old partitions on IDE drives.

Create DOS Partition (using `fdisk`)

Create a primary DOS partition with a minimum size of 15MB. Make the partition you created the "active" partition. This small 15MB partition is only for test and configuration purposes. If you intend to have a working DOS partition, a larger partition size would be appropriate.

Exit the `fdisk` Utility Program

While you are in `fdisk`, feel free to experiment with the menu options. If you make a mistake, no harm will be done at this stage of the installation. When you exit `fdisk`, the system will reboot. Make sure you still have your DOS diskette in Drive A.

Step 4: Format DOS Partition (`format.exe`)

This `format` is not the same as low-level format. The low-level format created the underlying disk address structure used by all operating systems. This step uses the DOS operating system `format.exe` program to create a file system structure that is unique to DOS. This step only formats the 15MB DOS partition created in the previous step.

Start the `format` Utility Program

The DOS installation program can automatically format the unformatted 15MB DOS partition after partitioning is done. If you wish to use `format.exe` to manually format a DOS partition, you can exit the installation program and type **`format c: /s`** at the DOS prompt.

```
A:\>format c: /s
```

Formatting a 15MB partition only takes a minute.

Step 5: Load DOS Files

Allow the DOS Installation Program to Load DOS Files

Allow the DOS installation program to copy DOS files into the `c:\dos` directory. The DOS files are in compressed format and must be uncompressed by the installation program as they are copied to the `c:\dos` directory.

When the DOS installation program has completed, you should be able to remove any diskettes from the floppy drives and reboot the system from the primary hard disk. If you cannot boot DOS from the hard disk, do not proceed with the installation until you troubleshoot the failure. If your system boots normally, you can begin loading your optional hardware files from floppy disk.

Step 6: Run EISA Configuration Utility

- Copy adapter configuration files to the configuration disk or directory
- Run the configuration program
- Configure each EISA adapter board in the proper bus slot
- Save changes to CMOS (save to a file for backup)

Skip this step if you do not have EISA boards to configure.

Setup EISA Utility Directory

It was necessary to configure the SCSI controller before creating the DOS partition. Now that the DOS partition is formatted, you can create a directory for your EISA configuration utility and copy the files from your EISA diskette to the EISA directory. This will eliminate any future need to run the EISA utility from diskette.

Example:

```
C:\>mkdir c:\eisa
C:\>xcopy a:\ c:\eisa /s
```

In the example above, a directory called "`eisa`" is created on drive C and then all of the contents of drive A are copied to it. The `xcopy` command is used with the `/s` switch, thus copying the root directory and all subdirectories of drive A.

Copy Configuration Files to EISA Directory

Once the EISA directory is created, you can copy all EISA adapter configuration files from floppy diskettes to the EISA directory. Each EISA adapter should have documentation explaining which configuration files are to be copied.

The EISA configuration program usually has built-in support to copy configuration files (you are prompted to insert the diskette with the configuration files).

Run the EISA Configuration Utility

It may not be necessary to manually copy files to the EISA directory if the EISA utility does it for you. Check your documentation on this point. Load your EISA utility as in the example below, and check all of your boards for correct configuration.

Example:

```
C:\>chdir c:\eisa
C:\>cfg
```

In the example above `cfg` was used as the name of the EISA configuration utility. Substitute your utility name where `cfg` appears.

Check SCSI Configuration

Review the SCSI adapter setting to ensure that your previous configuration was correctly transferred to the hard disk.

Save Configuration Changes

Save your configuration changes before exiting the EISA configuration utility.

PHASE 4: SOFTWARE CONFIGURATION UTILITIES

- ✓ **Install audio board**
- ✓ **Install multi-I/O adapter**
- ✓ **Install mouse**
- ✓ **Install other board options (except network card)**
- ✓ **Install printer**
- ✓ **Check video adapter**
- ✓ **Load hardware specific files**

Install Audio Board

Install the audio board using the recommended settings from your configuration worksheet. Use the DOS utilities included with your board to verify the functions of your audio board. Do not forget the speakers or headsets!

Install Multi-I/O Adapter

Almost all x86 configurations include a multi-I/O card with both parallel and serial ports. The printer is usually connected to the first parallel port, and the mouse is usually connected to the first serial port.

Check your configuration worksheet and verify the IRQ and I/O port assignments before you install the adapter. Remember to disable functions, such as the joystick, if you have duplicate functionality on another adapter such as the audio board.

Install Mouse

There are many types of mice, but they usually all require some software driver to work with DOS. They also usually have a test utility you can run under DOS to verify each mouse function. Install and test your mouse. Use the software provided with the mouse.

If your mouse is connected to your video adapter, use the video adapter setup utility to configure the mouse IRQ and I/O port address.

Install Other Board Options

You may have other optional devices to install or test. This is the time to integrate optional hardware, such as a modem or a scanner. Install your optional devices and test them under DOS. If you have an EISA adapter, you must use the EISA configuration utility to configure the adapter.

It is NOT yet time to install the network card. Before introducing network problems to the installation, you will boot the system in a standalone mode. The network connection will come last.

Note: *Performing a Solaris test installation without a network adapter is recommended for first time installations. If you do not wish to perform a test installation, you can install the network adapter now.*

Install Printer

Connect the printer to the appropriate serial or parallel port. You can use DOS to send text to the printer. A simple command such as **`dir >lpt1`** will direct the standard output of the directory command to the first parallel printer port.

```
C:>dir >lpt1
```

Using a serial port for your printer requires some additional DOS setup if you want to test your printer. Refer to your DOS user manual or your printer manual.

Check Video Adapter

Your video adapter software should be loaded on the DOS partition and then used to test the display modes. Verify that the monitor and video adapter work in 1024×768 resolution.

Load Hardware Specific Files

Some of your adapter boards may include utility software on floppy diskettes. Now is a good time to go through your hardware and install the software onto the DOS partition. Follow the instructions provided with your hardware.

You may perform this step in stages as you add your optional hardware components. Some software, such as the mouse drivers, require the hardware to be installed before the software can be loaded.

Most x86 hardware installation instructions are written for a DOS environment. Install and test your optional hardware using DOS. This is the easiest way to ensure everything works properly before attempting to load the Solaris operating system.

Install your hardware one board at a time. Verify that each component works before going on to the next component. Do not forget to power off the machine before connecting components.

Boot from Solaris Diskette

Chapter 10, Here I Come!

Chapter 10 provides a detailed guide for the Solaris installation program. You have completed the *hardware* portion of the installation. Turn to Chapter 10 to complete the *software* portion of the installation.

Install the Network Card

After the test installation is completed in Chapter 10, install your network card and perform the final installation on your network.

Note: *A test installation is done without the network adapter to verify complete system functionality before introducing the added complexity that comes with network connections. Performing a quick test installation without a network will simplify the troubleshooting process if the installation fails.*

If you plan to bypass the test installation, it is critical to install the network card before attempting to install Solaris x86. The network card must be installed or the network drivers will not be enabled.

EISA CONFIGURATION CHECKLIST

Some steps may not be required if your system already has the motherboard and peripheral devices installed. Use this checklist to verify that each step in the process is completed in sequence.

Phase 1: Build the Baseline System

- ☐ Collect components, software, and documentation in a clean, safe work place
- ☐ Take all boards except the motherboard out of the system
- ☐ Install memory into motherboard
- ☐ Connect battery and power supply to motherboard (if required)
- ☐ Install floppy disk drives and other peripherals into case
- ☐ Install keyboard
- ☐ Install video adapter and monitor
- ☐ Apply power, verify memory test, and check system BIOS defaults

Phase 2: Floppy-Disk and Hard-Disk Configuration

- ☐ Configure and cable floppy-disk drives
- ☐ Configure and cable hard-disk drives (configure all SCSI devices now)
- ☐ Configure and install disk drive controller and cables
- ☐ Set system CMOS for floppy drives and IDE drives
- ☐ Boot from floppy with DOS diskette and confirm normal operating system behavior
- ☐ Configure EISA SCSI adapter

Phase 3: Building a DOS Partition

- ☐ Configure DOS partition with fdisk and format
- ☐ Run EISA configuration utility
- ☐ Copy hardware setup software to the DOS partition

Phase 4: Software Configuration Utilities

- ☐ Add optional boards (configure each to avoid conflicts)
- ☐ Test peripherals and options
- ☐ Install and test mouse
- ☐ Do not install network card until network is functional and you are ready to connect to it

Solaris x86 Installation 10

THE DRESS REHEARSAL

This chapter contains procedures for performing a test installation. The plan is to perform a quick default installation of the user software set and then verify that OpenWindows is functional. If you have installed Solaris before, this step is unnecessary, unless you want a quick check of the system before committing to a major installation effort. If you have not installed Solaris for x86 before, do it now!

You cannot perform this part of the installation if you do not have disk drives and a SCSI controller with a CD–ROM device. If you are configuring a network client without CD–ROM and hard disk, install your network card and proceed to the final installation step with the network card as the boot device. Follow the network installation instructions in your Solaris x86 installation documentation.

Note: *If you have not recorded your system configuration on a worksheet you will not be able to answer the questions posed by the installation program. Chapter 4 explains how to record your configuration on a worksheet.*

The installation process will vary according to the version of software you are installing. This chapter has procedures for installing two different versions of Solaris x86 and a section on the use of driver update diskettes.

- Solaris x86 Version 2.1
- Solaris x86 Version 2.4
- Driver update diskettes

Solaris x86 version 2.1 installation uses a nongraphic user interface. The installation strategy is to enter all of the user supplied installation information via a simple character-based interface. The OpenWindows graphic user interface is not invoked and tested until after the operating system software is booted from the hard disk.

Starting with Solaris x86 version 2.4, the installation uses OpenWindows. Because of this major difference, both versions of the installation process are covered in this chapter.

DRIVER UPDATE DISKETTES

SunSoft releases periodic Solaris x86 driver updates on diskette. The updates are made available as new products and drivers are released. The updates are distributed via CompuServe, SunSoft BBS, and the Internet. For details on accessing these driver updates, refer to Appendix A.

Solaris x86 Installation Using the Driver Update Diskettes

If you are performing the installation using the update boot diskette, just substitute the updated diskette for the standard Solaris x86 boot diskette and proceed with the standard installation process.

Installation using the *driver update boot* diskette is much like installation with the Solaris 2.1 for x86 boot diskette. There will be many times during the early booting process when the system will read data from the diskette, but the sequence of interaction with the user remains the same. Early in the boot process there will also be warning messages for each new driver whose device is not on the system being installed. The warning messages will look like the following:

```
Warning: forceload of drv/xxx failed.
```

Such warning messages are expected and can be ignored.

Late in the installation process, after all the standard packages have been installed, new driver packages will be installed from the *driver update distribution* diskettes. At the start of that phase of the installation, one of the install scripts will ask you to insert the first *driver update distribution* diskette into the drive. After reading the contents of each distribution diskette, the script will ask you to insert the next one. When the new driver packages have all been added, the script will ask you to remove the last diskette from the drive. In each case, it will wait for you to perform the requested action and then to press Enter.

After this is accomplished, the system will reboot as usual. When the system comes up, the new device drivers should be completely installed and functional.

The driver updates can also be added to a system after installation. The driver diskette comes with detailed instructions for installing drivers, PMI files, and patches.

CHECK THIS OUT

As you go through the installation procedures, you will notice that each activity requiring your intervention is marked with a ✔. Each check mark represents a step for you to perform.

✔ **Things that you must do**

Each step is explained in some detail for the techno-peasant, but if you are a techno-wizard you can just follow the ✔s and skip the text.

SOLARIS X86 VERSION 2.1 INSTALLATION

The Solaris x86 Version 2.1 installation program uses a text display for the user interface. Selecting options on each menu may vary slightly. The arrow keys, tab key, and return key are used to choose and then confirm options. Each menu has information displayed on the screen explaining which keys to use.

Step 1: Initial Boot

Launch the Probe!

✔ **Boot from Solaris x86 boot diskette (with Solaris x86 disc in CD–ROM)**

Place the Solaris x86 boot diskette in floppy drive A and place the Solaris x86 CD in the CD–ROM drive b:efore booting the system. Turn on the power, press the system reset button, or use "Control-Alt-Delete" key sequence to initiate a boot sequence. As the system boots, a device probe is launched to determine the type of bootable devices available. The probe can identify:

1. SCSI CD–ROM drives
2. Network adapters
3. SCSI devices (hard disk, tape)
4. SCSI controllers

As the probe works to find known hardware types, it will scroll a list of results on the screen. When the probe has finished, it will display the menu. The probe takes about 30 seconds to complete.

If no boot devices are found, an error message will be displayed and the installation will halt. The most likely failure at this point is the SCSI controller. Refer to Chapter 11 for troubleshooting information.

Note: *IDE drives will not appear on the MDB list of bootable devices. If a functional IDE drive is present on the system, it will be recognized and configured when the Solaris installation program prepares the disk partitions.*

The Menu Display

✔ **Verify list of bootable devices**

The multiple device boot (MDB) menu is displayed when the probe has finished and found at least one bootable device. Check the list of devices and verify that your CD–ROM, hard disk, and network devices are all found by the probe. A missing device is a symptom of incompatibility or configuration error.

The menu will only be displayed for 30 seconds before the installation program attempts to boot from the default boot device. In most cases the default boot device is the hard disk. To stop the menu from timing out after 30 seconds, you can touch the space bar on the keyboard. The menu will then remain on the screen until you are ready to select the boot device.

✔ **Select the CD–ROM boot device**

Each boot device is listed with a corresponding number. To begin the installation process, select the number that corresponds to the CD–ROM drive containing the Solaris x86 CD.

Selecting the Type of Installation

✔ **Select interactive installation**

The installation begins with the display of a menu with two choices:

1. Interactive
2. automatic (non-interactive)

Select the interactive option, which is the default selection. As in the previous menu display, the system will time out and continue installation with the default value. The screen timeout can be stopped using the space bar.

The automatic option is for network installations automatically controlled by installation servers. This is an advanced feature that enables system administrators to create installation profiles on servers to automate the client installation process. Do not select the automatic option.

Step 2: Configuration Choices

✔ **Wait for Solaris x86 kernel to load**

Waiting for the kernel to boot is much like watching grass grow. The UNIX kernel is large and the the CD–ROM is a relatively slow input device. Be patient. There is an especially long pause after the `Configuring the /dev directory` message is displayed and before the Solaris installation program screen is displayed.

Keyboard Language

Solaris x86 is a multilanguage operating system. The keyboard language selection screen displays a menu of choices to select from. I selected US English for my keyboard — how about you? Select the language that matches your keyboard and then hit "return" to continue.

✔ **Choose a language using the arrow keys**

✔ **Hit "return" to continue**

Host Name

Think of a name for your computer and enter it into the text input box. If you cannot think of a name, call it "nameless."

✔ **Type your host name in the input box (i.e., "nameless")**

✔ **Hit "return" to continue**

Network Connectivity

Your first installation is without network connection. Do not be tempted to select "yes!" After making the correct choice, confirm it.

- **Select "no" for network connection**
- **Hit "return" to continue**
- **Select "Yes, continue" to confirm your choices**
- **Hit "return" to continue**

The system will load additional software in preparation for the next step. A few messages will be displayed on the bottom of the screen before the next menu is displayed.

Geographic Region

Since most UNIX networks communicate with systems worldwide, it is necessary to configure your software for your local geography and time zone. My selections are always U.S. region and Pacific time zone.

- **Select geographic region (i.e., United States)**
- **Hit "return" to continue**
- **Select time zone (i.e., Pacific)**
- **Hit "return" to continue**

Date and Time

Set the correct date and time in the spaces provided. Confirm your changes when the confirm information dialog box appears.

- **Set year, month, day, hour, and minute**
- **Hit "return" after each entry**
- **Select "Yes, continue" to confirm your choices**
- **Hit "return" to continue**

There is another pause while data is loaded from the CD–ROM into memory.

Remove Floppy Diskette

You will be prompted to remove the floppy diskette before proceeding with the installation.

- **Remove floppy diskette**
- **Hit "return" to continue**

Installation Introduction

Information is displayed for your perusal. Continue with the installation when you are done reading.

- **Select "Continue Install" (hit "return" to continue)**

Device Configuration

The multiple-device boot probe locates and identifies your network adapter, communication ports, parallel printer ports, and SCSI host adapter. This part of the installation provides you with the means to identify the system components that were not identified by the multiple-device boot probe. The devices you can add to the installation profile are:

- Keyboards
- Pointing devices
- Audio interface cards
- Video display adaptors

Use the tab key and then the return key to select and start the "add" option on the device configuration menu. You will have to go through the add process once for each device you want to configure.

Note: *If you configure a device incorrectly during the following device configuration procedure, you can select the incorrect device from the configured devices list, hit return and select "unconfigure" to remove the device. You can reconfigure the device using the "add" procedure below.*

✓ **Select "add" option (use tab and return keys)**

After choosing to "add" a device you will be prompted to select the type of device to configure. Start with the video display adapter.

Video Display Adapter

✓ **Select video display adapter (use tab, arrow, and return keys)**

✓ **Choose your adapter (use arrow and return keys)**

The screen will display a list of compatible graphic boards. Choose the board entry that matches your video adapter and monitor. Refer to Appendix D for more information on video adapter choices.

If you do not find a compatible graphic board on the display list, refer to Appendix A for compatibility information.

Screen Size and Resolution

It is unnecessary to change the default screen size and resolution. Just use the tab key to skip the options and select "apply" to move to the next step.

After selecting your adapter type you will be given a choice of screen sizes and resolutions, depending on the graphic card chosen. The screen size options roughly correspond to 15-, 17-, and 19-inch monitor sizes. Use the arrow keys and the return key to change the default screen size and resolution.

Make sure your monitor is capable of working with the resolution you choose.

- **Choose screen size, optional (use arrow and return keys)**
- **Choose resolution, optional (use arrow and return keys)**
- **Select "Apply" to continue (use tab and return keys)**

When you have completed the selection of your video adapter, you will have to begin the add process again for the next device to be configured. Notice the list of configured devices now includes your video display adaptor.

Device Configuration Continued

- **Select "add" option (use tab and return keys)**

After choosing to add a device, you will be prompted to select the type of device to configure. Select the pointing device.

Pointing Device

- **Select "pointing devices" (use arrow and return keys))**

A list of pointing devices (mice) will be displayed. Choose the one that matches your mouse. The choices are:

PS/2 style built in mouse
Logitech bus mouse
Logitech C7 or C5 mouse
Logitech MouseMan serial mouse
Mouse Systems Corp. serial mouse
Microsoft bus mouse
Microsoft serial mouse

- **Choose pointing device type**

If your mouse is not on the display list, check your mouse documentation to determine if it is compatible with one of the types listed. Most clone mice are compatible with a Microsoft bus or serial mouse.

Device and Buttons

You may be required to select the device connection and number of buttons on your mouse. The serial mouse should be connected to either COM1 `/dev/tty00` or COM2 `/dev/tty01`.

- **Choose the device connection if required (use arrow and return keys)**
- **Choose number of buttons if required (use arrow and return keys)**
- **Select "Apply" to continue (use tab and return keys)**

Device Configuration Continued

If you have a sound card, use the "Add" option again to configure the audio interface card option. If you do not have a sound card, select the "Continue Install" option.

- **Select "Add" option if you have a sound card (use tab and return keys)**
- **Select "Continue Install" option if you do not have a sound card. Move on to the next step (use tab and return keys)**

Sound Card

After choosing to add a device, you will be prompted to select the type of device to configure. Select the audio interface card option. If you do not have a sound card, you can skip to the next step of the installation.

- **Select "audio interface cards" (from the list of available devices)**
- **Select "SoundBlaster/PRO" (hit return)**

The audio interface card has DMA, IRQ, and I/O port address settings that must be verified. Make sure your sound card setting matches your configuration choices. The sound board default IRQ is 5. You may have to change the system configuration because the installation default setting for the SoundBlaster/PRO board is IRQ 7.

The DMA and I/O addresses rarely need to be changed. If you setup your audio interface board, use the settings recommended in Appendix E.

- **Configure DMA (use arrow and return keys)**
- **Configure IRQ (use arrow and return keys)**
- **Configure I/O address (use arrow and return keys)**
- **Select "Apply" to continue (use tab and return keys)**

Device Configuration Continued

When you are finished adding devices, you can move ahead to the next step of the installation.

- **Select "Continue Install" option on the device configuration menu**

Step 3: Disk Preparation

This step of the installation provides you with the opportunity to create a Solaris and DOS partition on your hard disk. If you have more than one hard disk, you will be able to partition each one individually.

If you used the installation procedures in Chapters 7, 8, or 9, you have already created a DOS partition on the primary boot disk. Now you will add the Solaris partition and create slices within each Solaris partition.

Although the Solaris disk preparation utility provides for disk analysis, it is best to use the low-level format utility provided with your SCSI controller. This procedure does not use the analysis option.

Disk-Preparation Utility

The disk-preparation utility will present you with a list of disks to choose from. Choose the disk by using the arrow keys (if you have more than one disk). If you have only one disk, use the return key to select the boot disk.

- ✓ **Select disk (use arrow keys or hit return)**
- ✓ **Select "Run FDISK" (use arrow and return keys)**

The disk-preparation utility will check the disk-partition map and display the partition table. The DOS partition should be shown as partition #1. The object of this step of the procedure is to create a Solaris-type partition as partition #2, using the unused space on the boot disk.

Use the tab key to move about the fields in the partition table. This may seem awkward at first, but it will not do any harm to hit the tab key many times to see how it works. Do not select the "Apply" option on the hard-drive partitioning menu until you are sure the partition is correct.

If you have more than one DOS partition or other partitions on the disk, select the first available free partition for Solaris. This procedure assumes that Solaris will be placed in partition #2.

Before you leave the hard-drive partitioning menu, activate the Solaris partition. The system boot will then default to the Solaris partition.

Note: *In order for Solaris or any other PC operating system to boot, it must be within the first 1024 cylinders of the hard disk. This is a PC BIOS restriction.*

- ✓ **Leave the DOS partition alone**
- ✓ **Select the "Type" field for partition #2 (use the tab and return keys)**
- ✓ **Select "Solaris" from the list (use arrow and return keys)**
- ✓ **Set "Length" to use all unused space on the disk if necessary (use tab, numeric, and return keys)**
- ✓ **Make DOS partition "Not Active" (use tab and space bar keys)**
- ✓ **Make Solaris "Active" (use tab and space bar keys)**
- ✓ **Select "Apply" (use the tab and return keys)**

There may be a slight delay before the new partition information is displayed. The partition-table information update process takes a few seconds.

Use the disk-preparation utility to partition multiple disks if you wish, but it is only necessary to make one Solaris partition of about 210MB for this test installation.

When you are done with the partitioning, select the "Continue Install" option and move on to the next step.

✓ **Select "Continue Install" option (use tab and return keys)**

Step 4: Solaris Installation

After creating a Solaris partition on the disk, you can begin the process of choosing the software to be installed. To make the process easier, you can select the "Quick Install" option from the Solaris Installation menu and let the installation program do most of the work. There is also a "Custom Install" option, but we will not be using it in this installation.

✓ **Select "Quick Install" option (use tab and return keys)**

Quick Install: Software Configurations

You will have four options on the quick install menu:

- Entire Distribution
- Developer System Support
- End User System Support
- Core System Support

"End User System Support" is the default. Select the "Apply" option to accept the default.

✓ **Select "Apply" to accept end user system support**

Quick Install Configuration

The quick install option automatically slices the Solaris partition. This is what you want for testing, but it is not very practical when you go to setup your system for actual use. When you select "Custom Install," you will have the option of customizing the partition slices to suit your needs.

✓ **Select "Begin Install" to accept quick install configuration**

The installation program begins the software installation by building the file systems on the hard disk and then loading the end-user system support files.

Take a Break!

It will take as long as 1 hour to load the software, depending on the speed of your system and CD–ROM device.

Note: *Taking a break has many important benefits. Fatigue can impair your ability to think and act clearly when you work on computers or other complex equipment. Taking a break can relieve frustration, and will provide your brain with the time required to process and assimilate new information. Very often, walking away from a difficult computer problem is all that is necessary to discover the solution. If you are tired or at an impasse — always take a break.*

As luck would have it, I am working at home today on this installation procedure and my wife has just presented me with a delicious-looking shrimp cocktail and a glass of an exceptional California Chardonnay. She has informed me we are having lunch on the patio today. It is 80 degrees Fahrenheit and there is a beautiful meal waiting for me in the back yard. I will return after taking advantage of this perfectly timed opportunity.

Root Password

After the system reboots from the hard disk, you can remove the CD–ROM. The operating system will prompt you to enter a root password twice. Hitting the return key twice will setup the root login without a password. Since this is a test installation, a password is not required.

- ✓ **Set root password or hit return**

Login

The first thing you do after entering the root password is to login.

- ✓ **Enter `root` at the login prompt**
- ✓ **Enter the root password if you have one or hit "return" for no password**

OpenWindows

If all went well you can start up OpenWindows now. This concludes the installation confidence test.

- ✓ **Enter `/usr/openwin/bin/openwin` at the # prompt**

This concludes the installation confidence test. When you are through experimenting with the test installation, you should reinstall your system using the instructions in your Solaris x86 installation guide.

If you are planning to connect to a network, do not forget to install your network adapter and connect to your network before you start the final installation.

Devconfig

Solaris x86 2.1 provides a utility program named `devconfig` that enables the user to manually edit the driver configuration for the keyboard, pointing device, audio-interface cards, and video-display adapters. You may need to use this program to modify your configuration after installation is complete.

The following description of `devconfig` is taken from the Solaris x86 manual pages:

Name

`devconfig`   Configure device attributes.

Description

`devconfig` is an interactive editor for device driver hardware configuration files and the OpenWindows configuration file.

Devices that are not self-identifying require that correct information be supplied in the hardware configuration file in order for the device to be recognized. `Devconfig` is designed to ease the task of maintaining correct device information in the configuration files.

Prototype configuration information files stored in `/usr/lib/devconfig` are used to check user input to ensure that the values provided for each attribute are of the correct type and fall within legal bounds.

After making changes to a hardware configuration file that has a driver associated with it, an attempt is made to reload the driver to verify the attributes. Some drivers may not be unloadable. In this case, a system reboot must be initiated before the new attributes can take effect. If necessary, `devconfig` also updates the OpenWindows configuration file, `and OWconfig`. `devconfig` makes a backup copy of a modified file in a `.bak` file. In addition, the first version of OWconfig is saved in `OWconfig.save`. This is because the original version of `OWconfig` contains helpful prototype information that may be referred to in case `OWconfig` needs to be edited manually.

If the default location for configuration files is not writable (as is the case during installation), `devconfig` writes the updated files in the same location relative to the directory `/tmp/root`. No attempt is made to reload the driver in this case.

`devconfig` is controlled by a simple menu system. The up/down arrow keys move the cursor to different items in a menu. The left/right arrow keys move the cursor to different items in a field. The enter key selects an item. (Note that the enter key may be labeled return on some keyboards.).

Operation

`devconfig` first displays a list of configured devices in the system. Selecting a configured device allows you to view its attributes or unconfigure it. Self-identifying devices cannot be unconfigured by devconfig.

When you add a new device, `devconfig` displays the supported device categories. After choosing a device category, `devconfig` displays the devices supported in that category. Self-identifying devices cannot be added with `devconfig` and they are not displayed in the list of the devices. After you have selected the device to be added, `devconfig` displays the list of the device attributes. Once you have chosen the proper values for the attributes and applied them by using the Apply button, the device is added to the list of configured devices. You may cancel an operation by using the Cancel button.

SOLARIS x86 VERSION 2.4 INSTALLATION

Solaris x86 version 2.4 installation uses a graphic user interface.

Step 1: Selecting the Boot Device

✓ **Boot from Solaris x86 boot diskette**

Launch the Probe!

Place the Solaris x86 boot diskette in floppy drive A and place the Solaris x86 CD in the CD–ROM drive before booting the system. Turn on the power, press the system reset button, or use "Control-Alt-Delete" key sequence to initiate a boot sequence. As the system boots, a device probe is launched to determine the type of bootable devices available. The probe should find:

1. SCSI CD–ROM drives
2. Network adapters
3. Bootable SCSI hard-disk drive
4. SCSI controllers

As the probe works to find known hardware types, it will scroll a list of results on the display. When the probe has finished, it will display the menu. The probe takes about 30 seconds to complete.

If no boot devices are found, an error message will be displayed and the installation will halt. The most likely failure at this point is the SCSI controller. Refer to Chapter 11 for troubleshooting information.

Note: *IDE drives will not appear on the MDB list of bootable devices. If a functional IDE drive is present on the system, it will be recognized and configured when the Solaris installation program prepares the disk partitions.*

The Menu Display

✓ **Verify list of bootable devices**

The multiple-device boot (MDB) menu is displayed when the probe has finished and found at least one bootable device. Check the list of devices and verify that your CD–ROM, hard disk, and network devices are all found by the probe. A missing device is a symptom of incompatibility or configuration error.

The menu will only be displayed for 30 seconds before the installation program attempts to boot from the default boot device. In most cases the default boot device is the hard disk. To stop the menu from timing out after 30 seconds, touch the space bar on the keyboard. The menu will then remain on the screen until you are ready to select the boot device.

✓ **Select the CD–ROM boot device**

Each boot device is listed with a corresponding number. To begin the installation process, select the number that corresponds to the CD–ROM drive containing the Solaris x86 CD.

Step 2: Selecting the Type of Installation

The installation begins with the display of a menu with two choices:

1. Interactive
2. Custom jumpstart

Select the interactive option, which is is the default selection. As in the previous menu display, the system will time out and continue installing with the default value. The screen time out can be stopped using the space bar.

The custom jumpstart option is for network installations that are automatically controlled by installation servers. This is an advanced feature that enables system administrators to create installation profiles on servers to automate the client installation process. Do not select the custom jumpstart option.

✔ **Select interactive installation**

Step 3: Solaris x86 Kernel Loads

The kernel software is large and the the CD–ROM is a slow device. Waiting for the kernel to boot is much like watching grass grow. Be patient. There is an especially long pause after the `Configuring the /dev directory` message is displayed and before the Solaris installation program screen is displayed.

✔ **Wait for Solaris x86 kernel to load**

The Solaris Installation Program

The first installation program display is informational only. You can read it and then hit the F2 function key to continue.

✔ **Hit F2 to continue**

Step 4: Initial Software Choices

Keyboard Language

Solaris x86 is a multilanguage operating system. The keyboard language selection screen displays a menu of choices to select from. I select US English for my keyboard — how about you? Select the language that matches your keyboard and then hit F2 to continue.

✔ **Choose a language**

✔ **Hit F2 to continue**

Identify Graphics Device

A screen will display information about the selection of a graphics device. You can hit F2 and continue to the next menu after reading the message.

- ✓ **Hit F2 to continue**

Graphics Card (video adaptor)

A screen will display with a list of compatible graphics boards. Choose the entry that matches your video adapter and monitor. Refer to Appendix D for more information on video adapter choices.

- ✓ **Choose a graphics board**
- ✓ **Hit F2 to continue**

If you do not find a compatible graphics board on the display list, refer to Appendix A for compatibility information.

Resolution (optional)

You may be given a choice of resolutions, depending on the graphics card chosen. Make sure your monitor is capable of working with the resolution you choose.

- ✓ **Choose resolution (optional)**
- ✓ **Hit F2 to continue**

Screen Size

The size of screen is important because of display font readability. The combination of resolution and screen size will determine the font size used by OpenWindows.

- ✓ **Choose screen size**
- ✓ **Hit F2 to continue**

Pointing Device

A list of pointing devices (mice) will be displayed. Choose the one that matches your mouse. The choices are:

Logitech bus mouse
Logitech C7 or C5 serial mouse
Logitech MouseMan serial mouse
Microsoft bus mouse
Microsoft serial mouse
PS/2 style built in mouse

- **Choose pointing device type**
- **Hit F2 to continue**

If your mouse is not on the display list, check your mouse documentation to determine if it is compatible with one of the types listed. Most clone mice are compatible with a Microsoft bus or serial mouse.

Serial Communications Port (optional)

If you have a serial mouse, you will need to identify its serial port connection. This procedure assumes a serial mouse connection at COM1 `/dev/tty00`. Your installation process will vary slightly if you have a bus mouse.

- **Choose serial port**
- **Hit F2 to continue**

Number of Mouse Buttons (optional)

You may also be required to select the number of buttons on your mouse.

- **Choose number of buttons**
- **Hit F2 to continue**

Confirm Information

After selecting your mouse type you will be presented with a confirmation screen. If you have completed the previous steps correctly, you should see your choices displayed for confirmation.

- **Check your choices**
- **Hit F2 to continue**

The installation program can now proceed to the OpenWindows interface portion of the installation. Now that the mouse, keyboard, and display are properly identified, OpenWindows can be started. There is a long pause while the OpenWindows software is loaded from CD–ROM.

Step 5: Defining the System

If OpenWindows fails to start or the mouse docs not function, you probably have a compatibility or configuration problem. You may have to check your mouse and graphics card again and reinstall new settings.

The first OpenWindows dialog box identifies some of the system information that needs to be defined. The mouse can be used to point and click on the dialog box buttons. The mouse can also be used to change focus to a text input box by pointing and clicking with the left button. When you have read the information in the "Identify the System" dialog box, you can move on to the next step by clicking with the left mouse button while at the same time pointing to the continue button. If you are already a mouse master, please forgive this lengthy introduction!

When you are ready to proceed use the mouse to select "continue."

- **Select "continue"**

Host Name

Think of a name for your computer and enter it into the text input box. If you cannot think of a name, call it "nameless."

- **Type your host name in the input box**
- **Select "continue" (the return key also works)**

Network Connectivity

Your first installation is without network connection. Do not select "yes"! After making the correct choice, confirm it.

- **Select "no" for network connection**
- **Select "continue"**
- **Select "continue" again when the "Confirm Information" box appears**

The system will load additional software in preparation for the next step. This will take a few minutes.

Time Zone and Geographic Region

When the time zone dialog box appears, select the geographic region option.

- **Select geographic region**
- **Select the set button**

When the geographic region dialog box appears select the geographic region and time zone for your location. My selections are always "U.S." region, and "Pacific" time zone.

- **Select your region**
- **Select your time zone**
- **Select "continue"**

Date and Time

Make sure that the date and time are correct in the date and time dialog box. Make changes as required. Confirm your changes when the confirm information dialog box appears.

- **Set date and time**
- **Select "continue"**
- **Select "continue" to confirm information**

The installation program will pause for a minute as it loads more data from the CD–ROM.

STEP 6: INSTALLING SOLARIS SOFTWARE

This is the final step of the installation before the installation program builds your file system and loads the selected software. The "Install Solaris Software - Initial" dialog box informs you that you will be:

- Selecting a system type
- Selecting Solaris software
- Selecting disks to hold selected software
- Specifying how software is to be laid out on disks

After you have read the dialog box, select "continue".

✓ **Select "continue"**

System Type

Select "standalone" for this test installation.

✓ **Select "standalone"**

✓ **Select "continue"**

Software

Select "end user system" for this test installation.

✓ **Select "end user system"**

✓ **Select "continue"**

Disks

The "disks" dialog box will present you with a list of disks on the left side of the display. Choose the disk by using the left mouse button to point and click. When the disk is highlighted, use the left mouse button to point and click on the dialog box add button. The selected disk will appear on the right side of the display. To edit the `fdisk` partition on a disk, select it with the mouse and then click on the edit button.

Remember not to change the DOS partition that you created when you configured your system. Using the `fdisk` partition edit function performs the same function as the DOS `fdisk` program.

If you have multiple disks, you can use the selection and `fdisk` partition editing functions on each disk, but it is only necessary to make one Solaris partition of at least 210MB on a single disk for this test installation.

- ✔ **Select disk to add from the left side of dialog box**
- ✔ **Select dialog box "add" button to add disk**
- ✔ **Select disk to be partitioned from the right side of dialog box**
- ✔ **Select "edit" to customize Solaris fdisk partition size**
- ✔ **Enter size of Solaris partition (portion not used by DOS)**
- ✔ **Do not change DOS partition!!!**
- ✔ **Select "OK"**
- ✔ **Select "continue"**

Preserve Data

- ✔ **Select "continue" (Do not try to preserve data)**

Automatically Layout File Systems

The easiest method to layout file systems for this test installation is to let the installation program do it for you.

- ✔ **Select auto-layout**

File System and Disk Layout

You can use the custom option but it is unnecessary for this installation. If you do use it, you may have a problem seeing the bottom of the custom dialog box because it is quite long. If your screen is too small, you can use the mouse to drag the dialog box window and make the lower part visible. Moving a window on the screen is done by pointing the mouse at the window top bar or one of the edges and holding down the left mouse button while dragging the mouse.

Auto-layout displays the file systems it has created. After reviewing the information about file systems you can move ahead by selecting "continue."

- ✔ **Select "continue"**
- ✔ **Select "continue" again to confirm the auto-layout choices**

Mount Remote File Systems

Do not attempt to mount remote file systems. There are none on this installation.

- ✔ **Select "continue"**

Profile

The time has come to begin the creation of the file system and loading of the software. Review the profile displayed in the dialog box, and select the begin installation button to continue.

- **Select "begin installation"**
- **Select "Reboot" to boot after installation**

Take a Break!

It will take as long as one hour to load the software, depending on the speed of your system and CD–ROM device. Take a break!

Root Password

After the system reboots from the hard disk, you can remove the floppy diskette and CD–ROM. The operating system will prompt you twice to enter a root password. Hitting the return key twice will setup the root login without a password. Since this is a test installation, a password is not required.

- **Set root password or hit "return" twice**

The system continues to reboot after asking to set the password. Then the login prompt appears.

Login

The first thing you do after entering the root password is to login.

- **Enter `root` at the login prompt**
- **Enter the root password if you have one or hit "return" for no password**

OpenWindows

- **Enter `/usr/openwin/bin/openwin` at the # prompt**

You should be running OpenWindows now. This concludes the installation confidence test. When you are through experimenting with the test installation, you should reinstall your system using the instructions in your Solaris x86 installation guide.

If you are planning to connect to a network, do not forget to install your network adapter and connect to your network before you start the final installation .

Kdmconfig

Solaris x86 2.4 provides a utility program named `kdmconfig` that enables the user to manually edit the driver configuration for the keyboard, pointing device, and video display adapters. You may need to use this program to modify your configuration after installation.

The following description of `kdmconfig` is taken from the Solaris x86 manual pages:

Name

`kdmconfig` Configure or unconfigure keyboard, display, and mouse options for OpenWindows and internationalization.

Synopsis

```
kdmconfig -c | -u [ -s host ] [ -v ] [ -f ]
```

Description

The `kdmconfig` program configures or unconfigures the `/etc/defaultkb` and `/etc/openwin/server/etc/OWconfig` files with the keyboard, display and mouse information relevant to a client's machine. It can also be used to set up the display, pointer, and keyboard entries in the bootparams database on a server machine.

The `kdmconfig` program is not normally run from a shell prompt, except when run with the `-s` option. When configuring a client during an initial installation or reconfigure reboot, the `sysidconfig` program will invoke `kdmconfig` with the `-c` option, and when the user executes the `sysunconfig` program, `kdmconfig` will be executed with the `-u` option.

Options

`-c` Run the program in the configuration mode. This mode is used to create or update the `defaultkb` and `OWconfig` files. When invoked in this way, `kdmconfig` first looks for the relevant configuration information in the bootparams databases. The bootparams databases available to the client are all of the `/etc/bootparams` files on servers on the same subnet as the client, provided the server machine is running the bootparamd daemon. `kdmconfig` is invoked with the `-c` option when called by `sysidconfig`.

`-u` Unconfigure the system, returning it to an "out-of-the-box" state. In this state, the factory default keyboard, mouse, and display are selected as a result of removing the `/etc/openwin/server/etc/OWconfig` and `/etc/defaultkb` files.

`-s client` Set up the bootparams database on this machine for the specified client. This option presents the same screens as it does when run on a client, but instead writes the resulting information to the `/etc/bootparams` file. Either the `-c` or the `-u` option must be used in conjunction with the `-s` option. Also, `-s` implies the use of the `-f` option. That is, the program will always present the screens to the user when invoked this way. This option will reconfigure the `nsswitch.conf` file to look for a bootparams database on a local server. This option is only available to the superuser.

`-v` Enable verbose mode. Normally, `kdmconfig` will not produce any output. This option is helpful for debugging, as it records the different actions taken by `kdmconfig` on stderr

`-f` Force screens mode. When invoked with `-f`, no network probing will be performed. This is helpful when debugging the client's configuration environment. Note that the `-s` option implies the use of `-f` bypassing network probing when setting up a server.

Troubleshooting 11

BEFORE YOU BEGIN

This chapter addresses the most common configuration problems that you may encounter. If you are like most people, the problems you are trying to heal are self-inflicted. We have a tendency to be our own worst enemies in situations like this. If you are reading this chapter because you have encountered a problem, the first thing I have to say to you is, before going any further, make sure you followed the installation sequence and configuration recommendations in this book — please!

Troubleshooting flowcharts are provided to simplify the troubleshooting process. If you wish to skip ahead, the charts begin on page 166.

Troubleshooting Basics

- Do not ever think you are mistake-proof
- Cables appear to be correct even when backward
- Unplug power when handling hardware
- Keep everything as simple as possible (verify basic functionality)
- Do not jump to conclusions
- Ask someone who knows

New Systems

Before you get too deep into any troubleshooting project, check the system components to make sure they are the right parts and that they are configured correctly. This is especially important if you are building a system from the ground up.

The top five problems with new system installations are caused by:

1. Incompatible components
2. Incorrect jumper and switch settings (conflicts)
3. Loose or backward cables
4. Incorrect CMOS setup
5. Improperly seated adapters or memory modules

If you cannot boot the system, start troubleshooting with the minimum configuration possible. Remove or disconnect all nonessential components, and verify basic functionality before testing fully loaded system configurations.

Component failure can cause trouble, but more often than not component failure on new systems is the result of improper handling or installation. Carelessness can easily damage memory modules, adapter boards, and motherboards.

Upgraded Systems

Troubleshoot upgraded systems in the same way you would troubleshoot a new system.

Existing Systems

If you are troubleshooting a system that was working properly at one time, you do not have to verify that all of the components are correctly configured. This assumes you are absolutely sure no one has tampered in any way with the hardware or software. It is not uncommon to ignore recent hardware or software changes because they seemed insignificant or unimportant.

The most common causes of problems with existing systems are:

- Corrupt or incorrect data on hard disk
- Configuration changes when new hardware or software is added
- Incompatible software or hardware
- Software or hardware bugs (design failure)
- Cables, adapters, or connectors that are loose
- Component failure

If you cannot boot the system, start troubleshooting with the minimum configuration possible. Remove or disconnect all nonessential components, and verify basic functionality before testing fully loaded system configurations.

Diagnostics (DOS)

DOS provides the best environment for testing system functionality. Since most diagnostic and test software is written for use with DOS, it makes sense to use what is readily available. If you configured your system with a DOS partition and loaded your utility programs as recommended in Chapters 7-9, you should have no trouble using the diagnostic programs.

If you cannot access the hard disk for any reason, then you must boot DOS from a floppy diskette and use the utility diskettes provided with your hardware. Major hardware components are usually shipped with software utilities on diskettes. If your system is like most, you should have:

- Mouse drivers and setup tests
- Network adapter driver, setup utilities, and diagnostics
- SCSI controller drivers, low-level format, and diagnostic utilities
- Sound adapter drivers, sound demos, and test utilities

Diagnostic Boot Diskette

A diagnostic boot diskette is a valuable tool for troubleshooting systems that are not bootable from hard disk. You can easily create your own DOS 6.x diagnostic boot diskette as follows:

- Format a diskette using `format a: /s`
- Copy DOS format, `fdisk`, `debug`, and `edit` utilities to the diskette
- Copy mouse utility to the diskette
- Copy network diagnostic utility to diskette
- Copy SCSI controller utility to diskette
- Copy video adapter utility to diskette
- For EISA, copy EISA configuration program and configuration (`.cfg`) files

The utilities vary from product to product, but the general process is the same in most cases. Read your component documentation to find the name of the appropriate utility. Only copy the utility that allows you to test or configure the product.

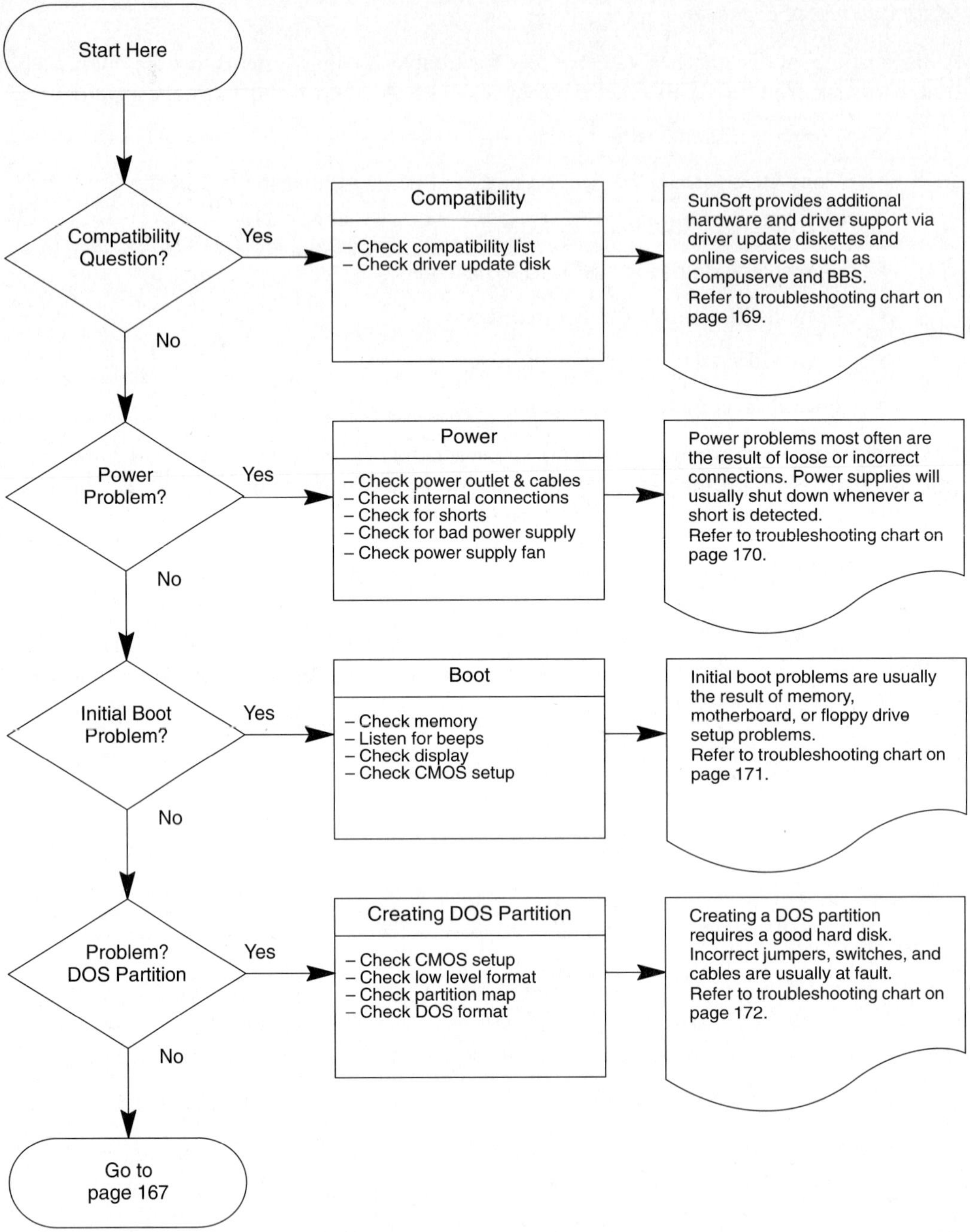
Start Here
Compatibility Question?
Yes
No
Compatibility
– Check compatibility list
– Check driver update disk
SunSoft provides additional hardware and driver support via driver update diskettes and online services such as Compuserve and BBS.
Refer to troubleshooting chart on page 169.
Power Problem?
Yes
No
Power
– Check power outlet & cables
– Check internal connections
– Check for shorts
– Check for bad power supply
– Check power supply fan
Power problems most often are the result of loose or incorrect connections. Power supplies will usually shut down whenever a short is detected.
Refer to troubleshooting chart on page 170.
Initial Boot Problem?
Yes
No
Boot
– Check memory
– Listen for beeps
– Check display
– Check CMOS setup
Initial boot problems are usually the result of memory, motherboard, or floppy drive setup problems.
Refer to troubleshooting chart on page 171.
Problem? DOS Partition
Yes
No
Creating DOS Partition
– Check CMOS setup
– Check low level format
– Check partition map
– Check DOS format
Creating a DOS partition requires a good hard disk. Incorrect jumpers, switches, and cables are usually at fault.
Refer to troubleshooting chart on page 172.
Go to page 167

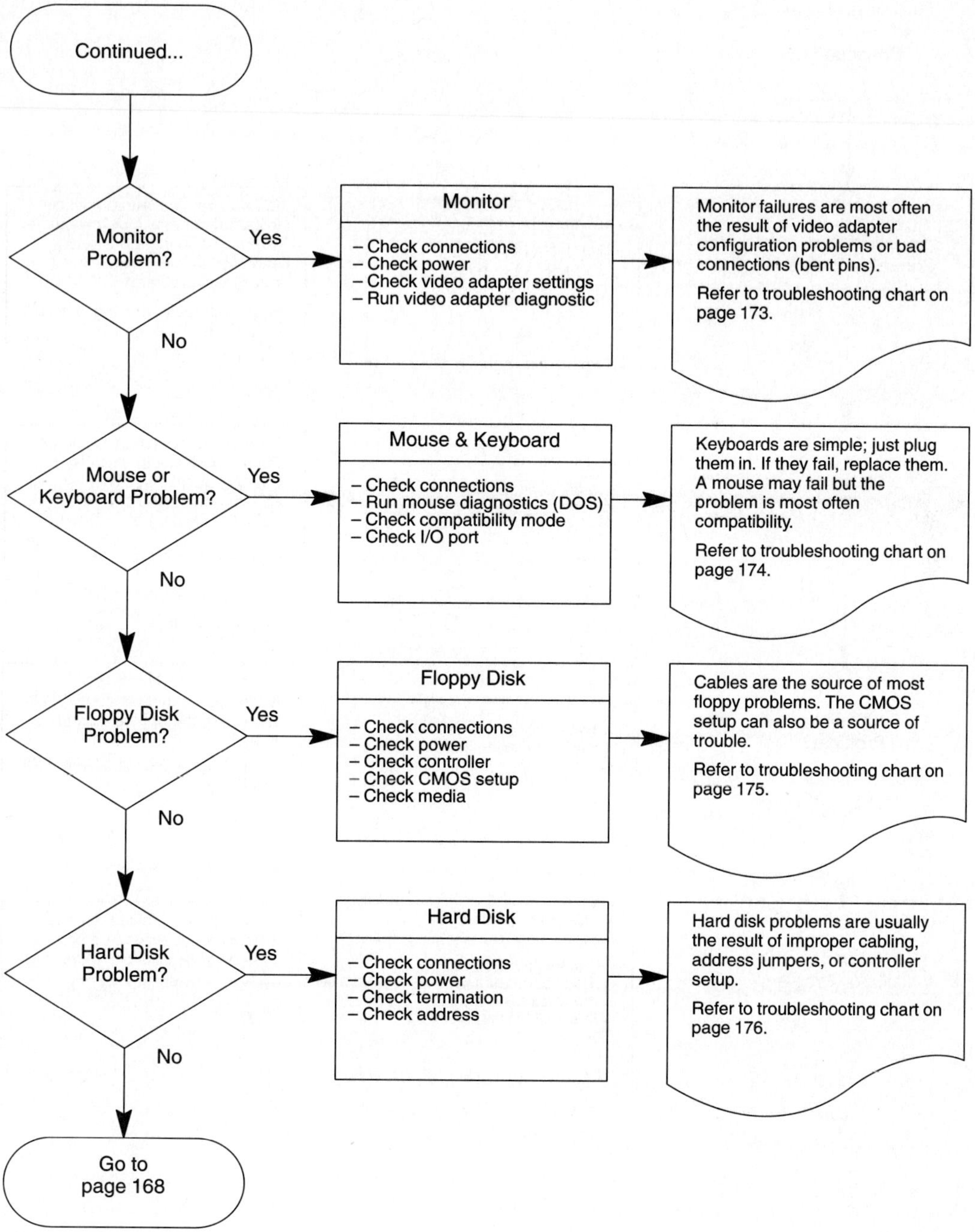
Continued...
Monitor Problem?
Yes
No
Monitor
– Check connections
– Check power
– Check video adapter settings
– Run video adapter diagnostic
Monitor failures are most often the result of video adapter configuration problems or bad connections (bent pins).
Refer to troubleshooting chart on page 173.
Mouse or Keyboard Problem?
Yes
No
Mouse & Keyboard
– Check connections
– Run mouse diagnostics (DOS)
– Check compatibility mode
– Check I/O port
Keyboards are simple; just plug them in. If they fail, replace them. A mouse may fail but the problem is most often compatibility.
Refer to troubleshooting chart on page 174.
Floppy Disk Problem?
Yes
No
Floppy Disk
– Check connections
– Check power
– Check controller
– Check CMOS setup
– Check media
Cables are the source of most floppy problems. The CMOS setup can also be a source of trouble.
Refer to troubleshooting chart on page 175.
Hard Disk Problem?
Yes
No
Hard Disk
– Check connections
– Check power
– Check termination
– Check address
Hard disk problems are usually the result of improper cabling, address jumpers, or controller setup.
Refer to troubleshooting chart on page 176.
Go to page 168

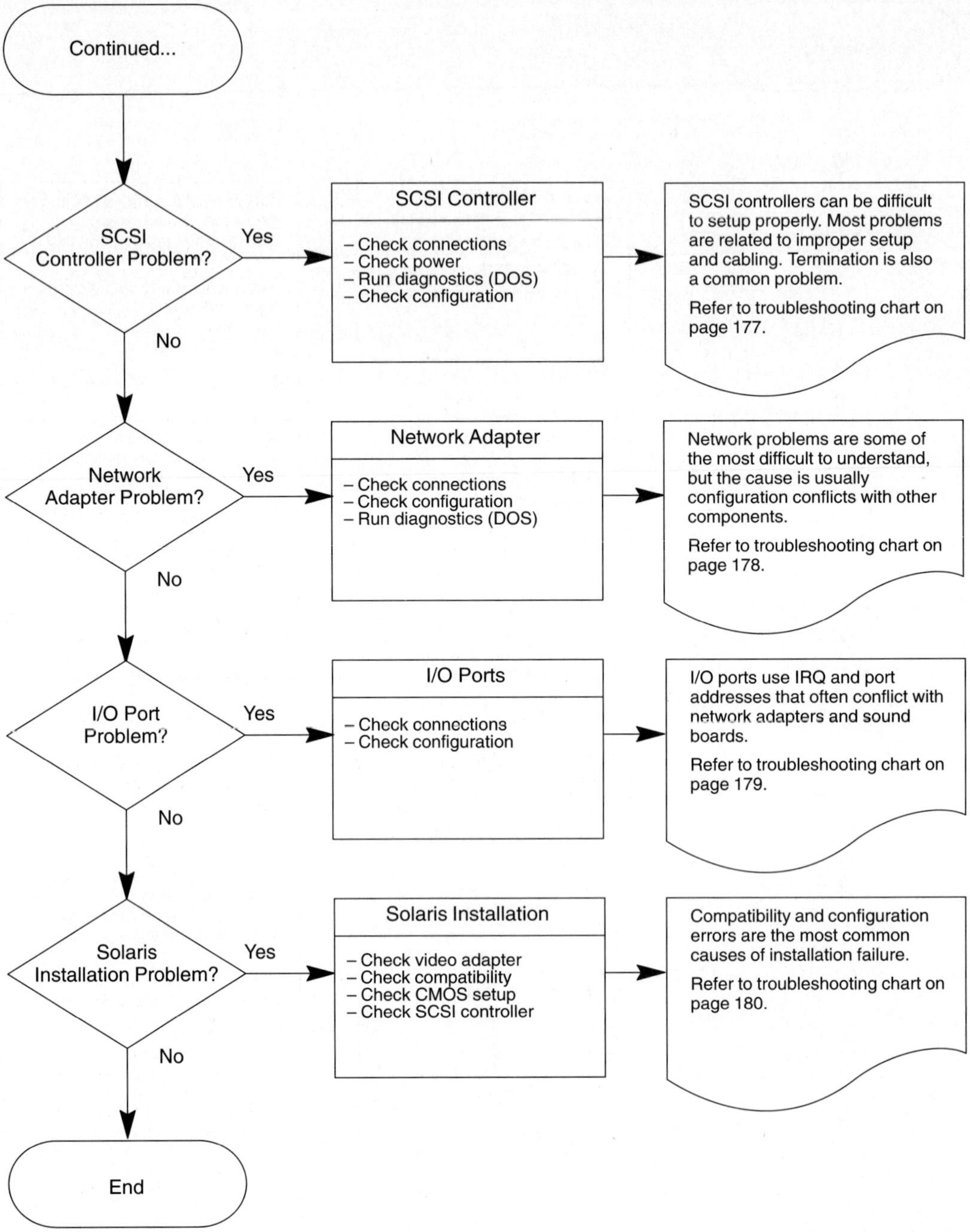
Continued...
SCSI Controller Problem?
Yes
No
SCSI Controller
– Check connections
– Check power
– Run diagnostics (DOS)
– Check configuration
SCSI controllers can be difficult to setup properly. Most problems are related to improper setup and cabling. Termination is also a common problem.
Refer to troubleshooting chart on page 177.
Network Adapter Problem?
Yes
No
Network Adapter
– Check connections
– Check configuration
– Run diagnostics (DOS)
Network problems are some of the most difficult to understand, but the cause is usually configuration conflicts with other components.
Refer to troubleshooting chart on page 178.
I/O Port Problem?
Yes
No
I/O Ports
– Check connections
– Check configuration
I/O ports use IRQ and port addresses that often conflict with network adapters and sound boards.
Refer to troubleshooting chart on page 179.
Solaris Installation Problem?
Yes
No
Solaris Installation
– Check video adapter
– Check compatibility
– Check CMOS setup
– Check SCSI controller
Compatibility and configuration errors are the most common causes of installation failure.
Refer to troubleshooting chart on page 180.
End

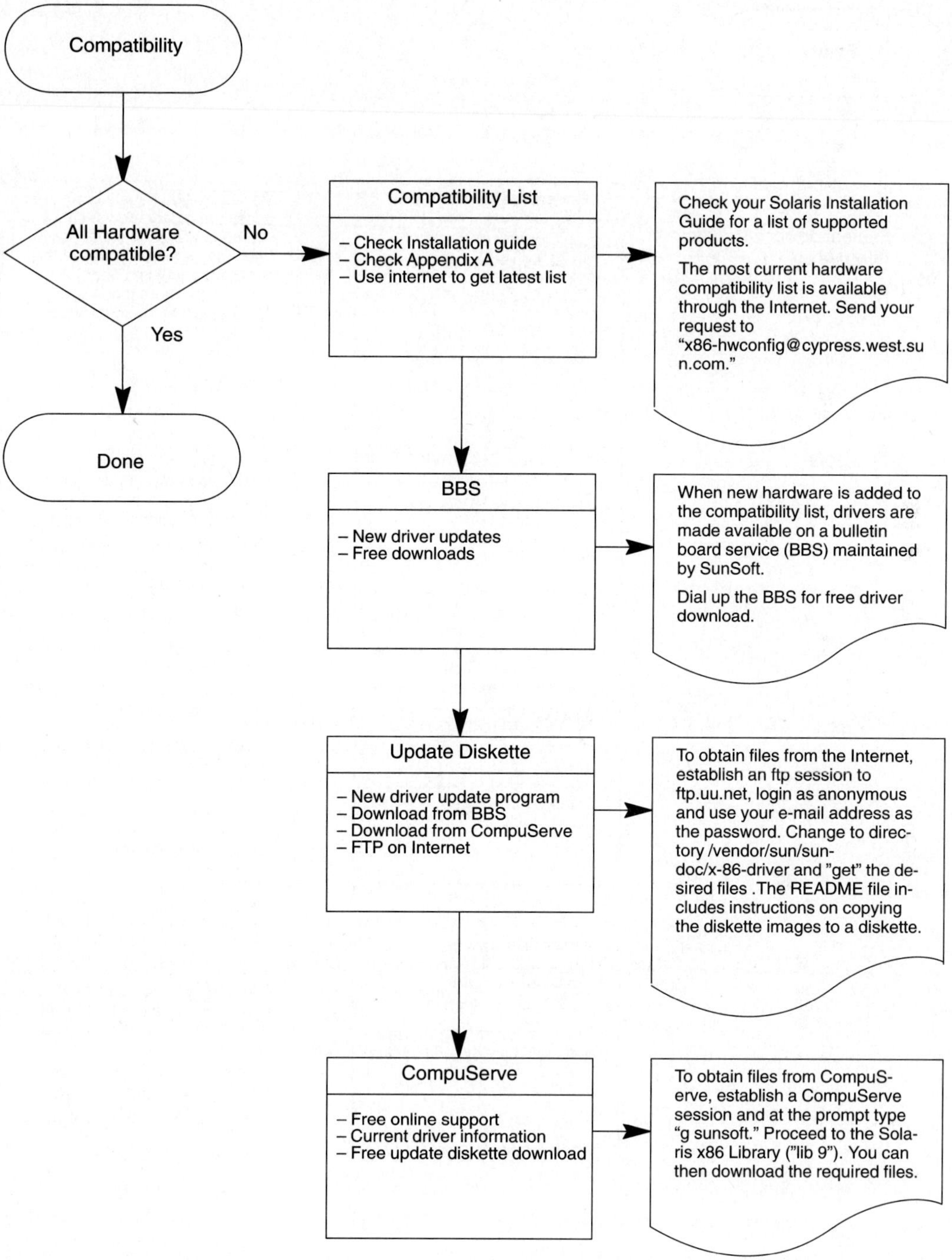
Compatibility
All Hardware compatible?
No
Yes
Done
Compatibility List
– Check Installation guide
– Check Appendix A
– Use internet to get latest list
Check your Solaris Installation Guide for a list of supported products.
The most current hardware compatibility list is available through the Internet. Send your request to "x86-hwconfig@cypress.west.sun.com."
BBS
– New driver updates
– Free downloads
When new hardware is added to the compatibility list, drivers are made available on a bulletin board service (BBS) maintained by SunSoft.
Dial up the BBS for free driver download.
Update Diskette
– New driver update program
– Download from BBS
– Download from CompuServe
– FTP on Internet
To obtain files from the Internet, establish an ftp session to ftp.uu.net, login as anonymous and use your e-mail address as the password. Change to directory /vendor/sun/sun-doc/x-86-driver and "get" the desired files .The README file includes instructions on copying the diskette images to a diskette.
CompuServe
– Free online support
– Current driver information
– Free update diskette download
To obtain files from CompuServe, establish a CompuServe session and at the prompt type "g sunsoft." Proceed to the Solaris x86 Library ("lib 9"). You can then download the required files.

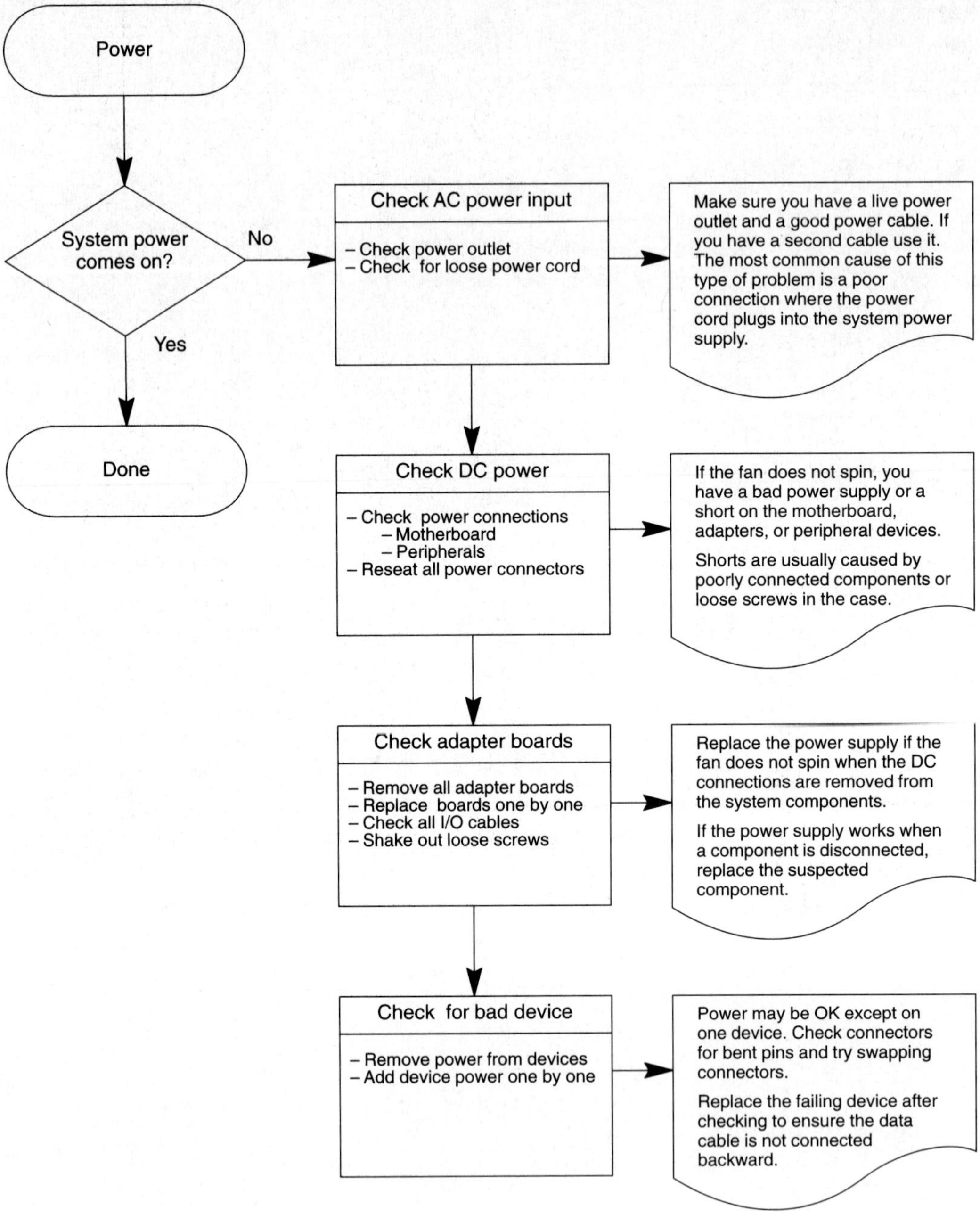
Power
System power comes on?
No
Yes
Done
Check AC power input
– Check power outlet
– Check for loose power cord
Make sure you have a live power outlet and a good power cable. If you have a second cable use it. The most common cause of this type of problem is a poor connection where the power cord plugs into the system power supply.
Check DC power
– Check power connections
– Motherboard
– Peripherals
– Reseat all power connectors
If the fan does not spin, you have a bad power supply or a short on the motherboard, adapters, or peripheral devices.
Shorts are usually caused by poorly connected components or loose screws in the case.
Check adapter boards
– Remove all adapter boards
– Replace boards one by one
– Check all I/O cables
– Shake out loose screws
Replace the power supply if the fan does not spin when the DC connections are removed from the system components.
If the power supply works when a component is disconnected, replace the suspected component.
Check for bad device
– Remove power from devices
– Add device power one by one
Power may be OK except on one device. Check connectors for bent pins and try swapping connectors.
Replace the failing device after checking to ensure the data cable is not connected backward.

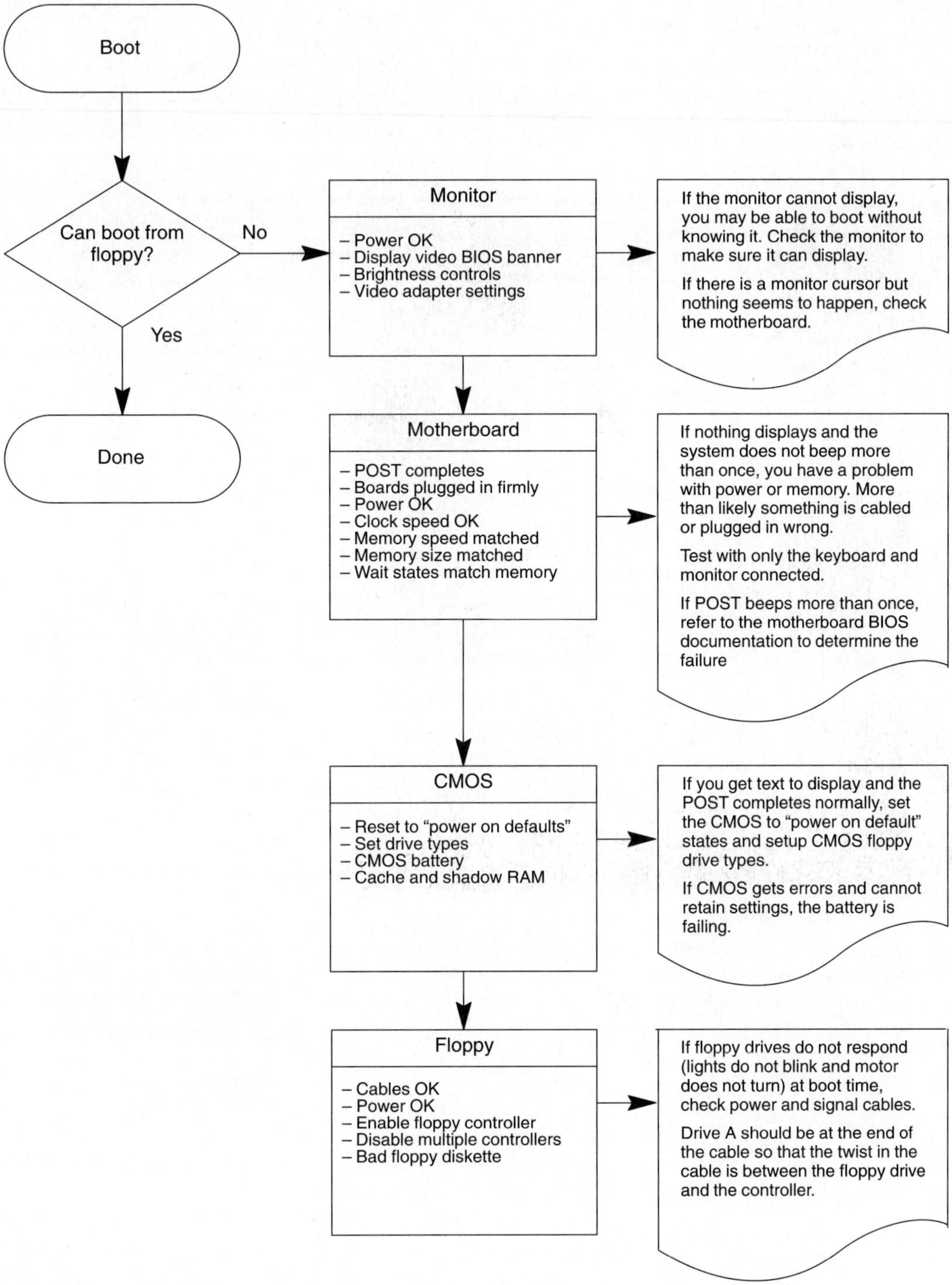
Boot
Can boot from floppy?
No
Yes
Done
Monitor
– Power OK
– Display video BIOS banner
– Brightness controls
– Video adapter settings
If the monitor cannot display, you may be able to boot without knowing it. Check the monitor to make sure it can display.
If there is a monitor cursor but nothing seems to happen, check the motherboard.
Motherboard
– POST completes
– Boards plugged in firmly
– Power OK
– Clock speed OK
– Memory speed matched
– Memory size matched
– Wait states match memory
If nothing displays and the system does not beep more than once, you have a problem with power or memory. More than likely something is cabled or plugged in wrong.
Test with only the keyboard and monitor connected.
If POST beeps more than once, refer to the motherboard BIOS documentation to determine the failure
CMOS
– Reset to "power on defaults"
– Set drive types
– CMOS battery
– Cache and shadow RAM
If you get text to display and the POST completes normally, set the CMOS to "power on default" states and setup CMOS floppy drive types.
If CMOS gets errors and cannot retain settings, the battery is failing.
Floppy
– Cables OK
– Power OK
– Enable floppy controller
– Disable multiple controllers
– Bad floppy diskette
If floppy drives do not respond (lights do not blink and motor does not turn) at boot time, check power and signal cables.
Drive A should be at the end of the cable so that the twist in the cable is between the floppy drive and the controller.

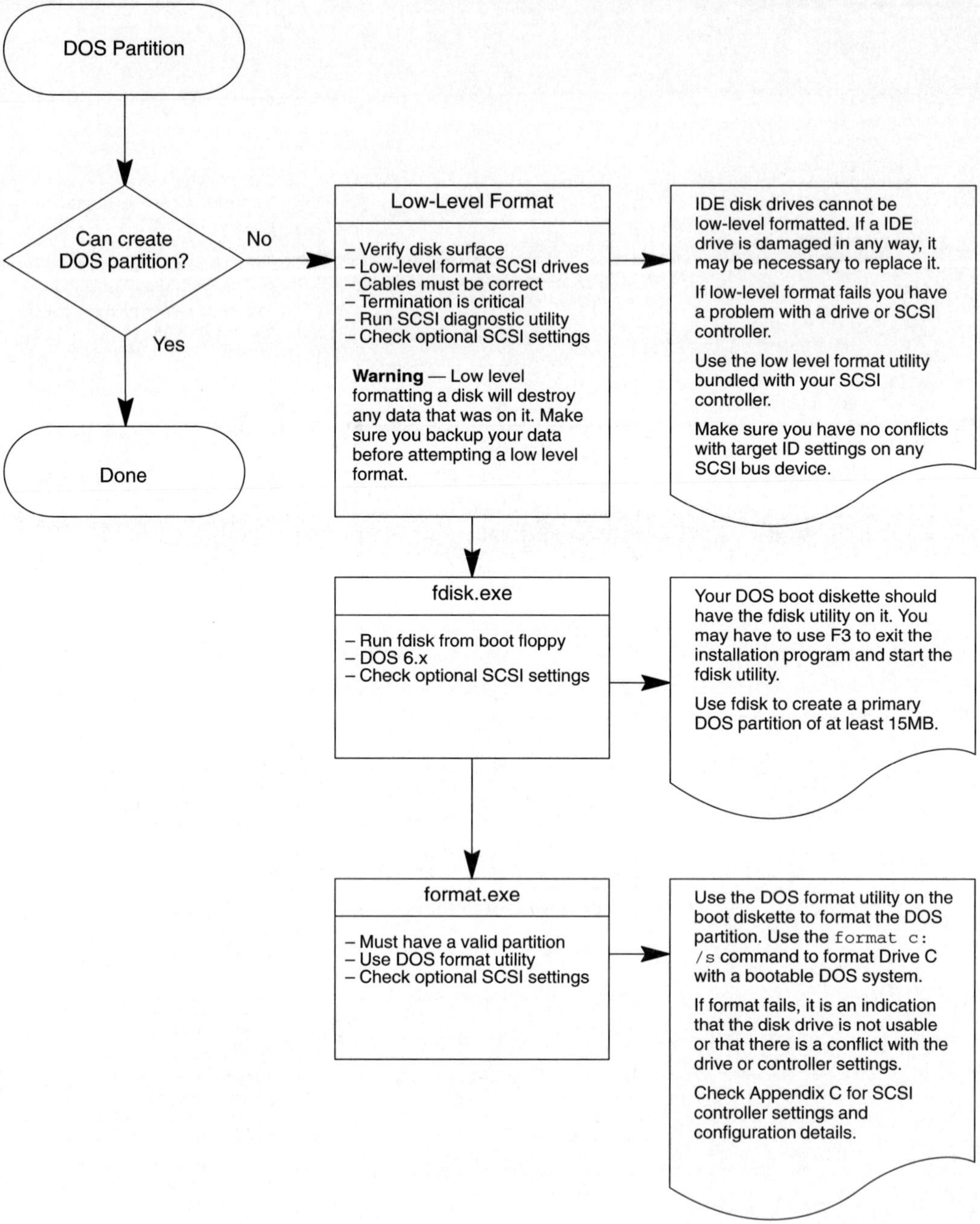
DOS Partition
Can create DOS partition?
No
Yes
Done
Low-Level Format
– Verify disk surface
– Low-level format SCSI drives
– Cables must be correct
– Termination is critical
– Run SCSI diagnostic utility
– Check optional SCSI settings
Warning — Low level formatting a disk will destroy any data that was on it. Make sure you backup your data before attempting a low level format.
IDE disk drives cannot be low-level formatted. If a IDE drive is damaged in any way, it may be necessary to replace it.
If low-level format fails you have a problem with a drive or SCSI controller.
Use the low level format utility bundled with your SCSI controller.
Make sure you have no conflicts with target ID settings on any SCSI bus device.
fdisk.exe
– Run fdisk from boot floppy
– DOS 6.x
– Check optional SCSI settings
Your DOS boot diskette should have the fdisk utility on it. You may have to use F3 to exit the installation program and start the fdisk utility.
Use fdisk to create a primary DOS partition of at least 15MB.
format.exe
– Must have a valid partition
– Use DOS format utility
– Check optional SCSI settings
Use the DOS format utility on the boot diskette to format the DOS partition. Use the `format c: /s` command to format Drive C with a bootable DOS system.
If format fails, it is an indication that the disk drive is not usable or that there is a conflict with the drive or controller settings.
Check Appendix C for SCSI controller settings and configuration details.

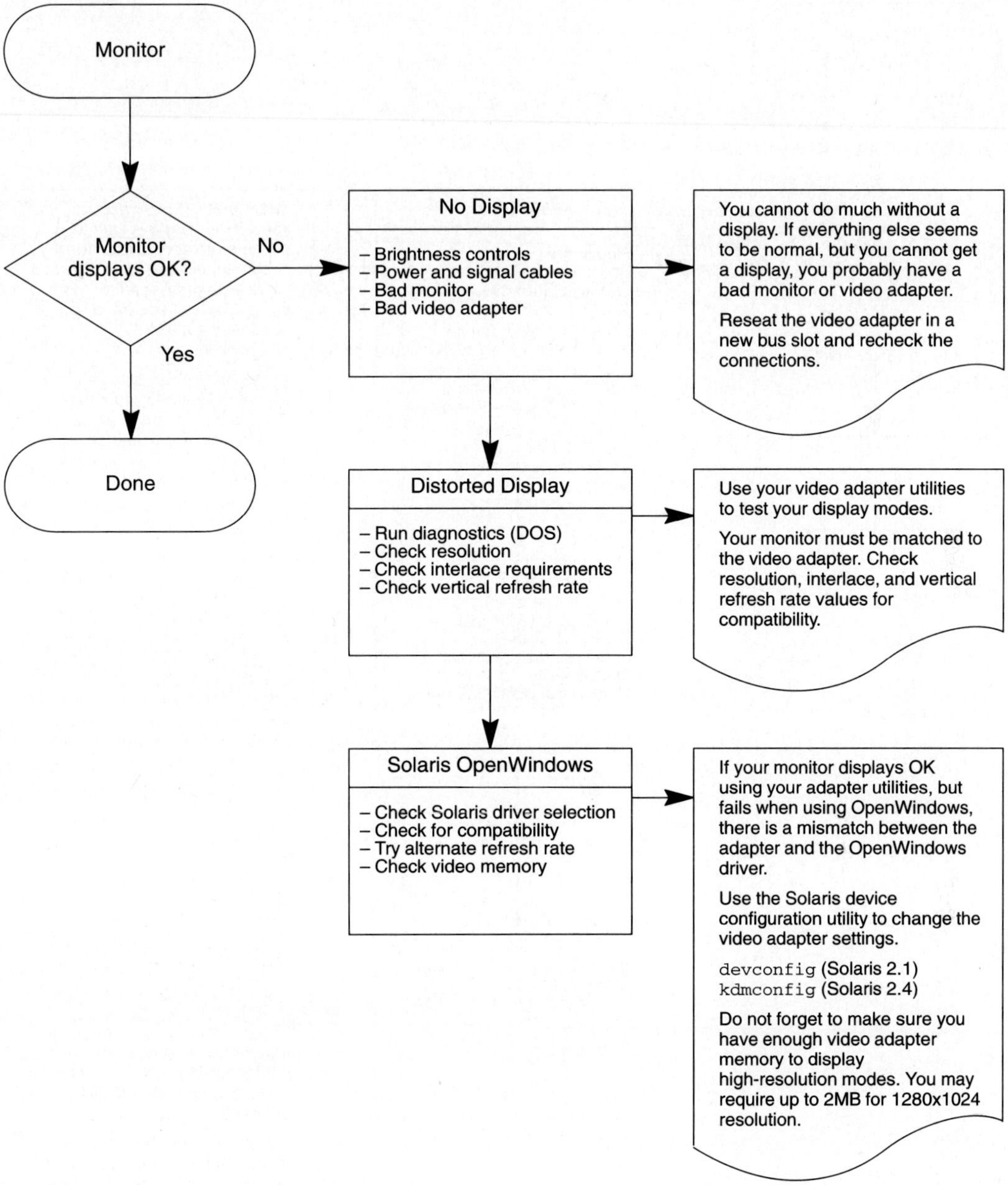
Monitor
Monitor displays OK?
No
Yes
Done
No Display
– Brightness controls
– Power and signal cables
– Bad monitor
– Bad video adapter
You cannot do much without a display. If everything else seems to be normal, but you cannot get a display, you probably have a bad monitor or video adapter.
Reseat the video adapter in a new bus slot and recheck the connections.
Distorted Display
– Run diagnostics (DOS)
– Check resolution
– Check interlace requirements
– Check vertical refresh rate
Use your video adapter utilities to test your display modes.
Your monitor must be matched to the video adapter. Check resolution, interlace, and vertical refresh rate values for compatibility.
Solaris OpenWindows
– Check Solaris driver selection
– Check for compatibility
– Try alternate refresh rate
– Check video memory
If your monitor displays OK using your adapter utilities, but fails when using OpenWindows, there is a mismatch between the adapter and the OpenWindows driver.
Use the Solaris device configuration utility to change the video adapter settings.
devconfig (Solaris 2.1)
kdmconfig (Solaris 2.4)
Do not forget to make sure you have enough video adapter memory to display high-resolution modes. You may require up to 2MB for 1280x1024 resolution.

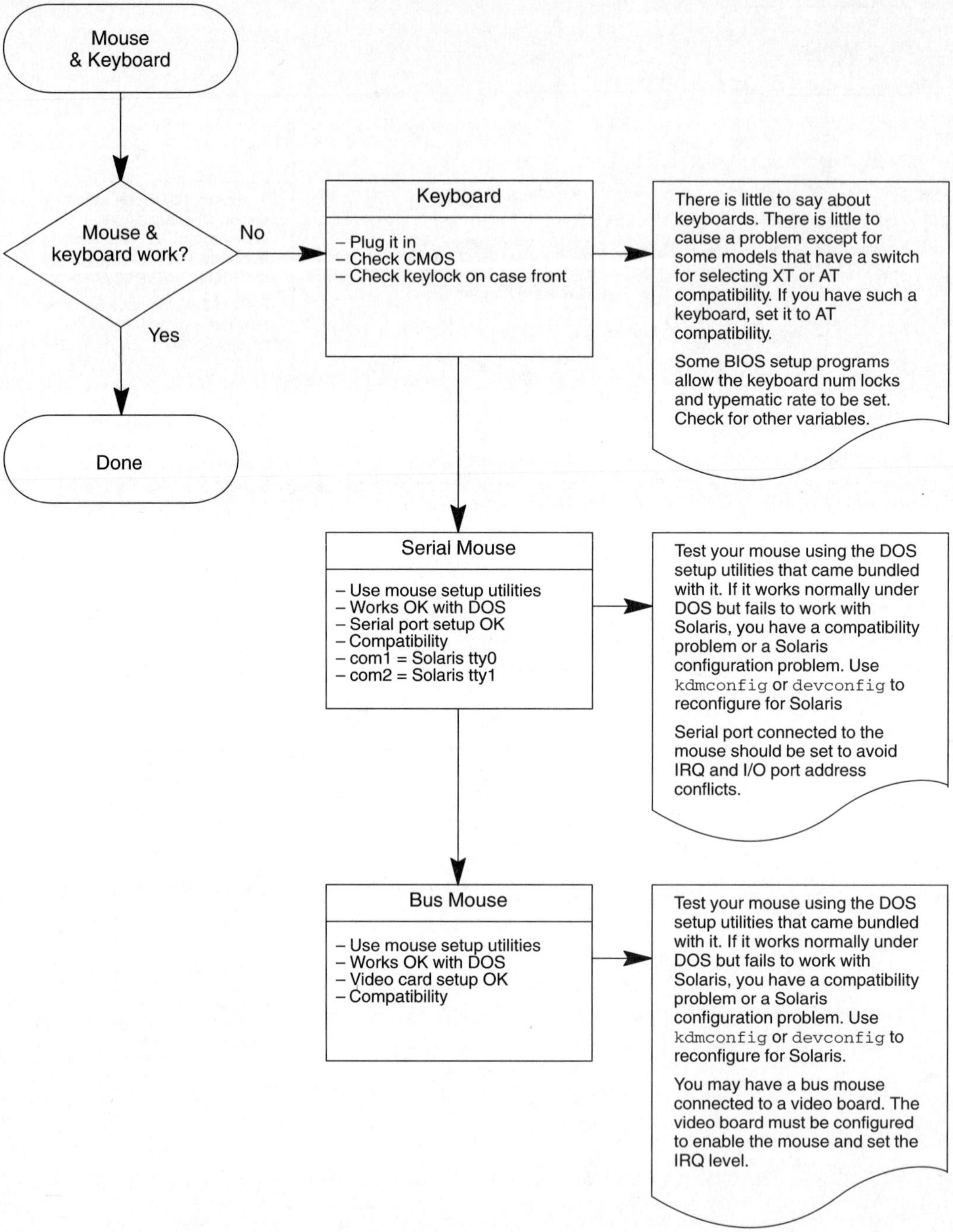
Mouse & Keyboard
Mouse & keyboard work?
No
Yes
Done
Keyboard
– Plug it in
– Check CMOS
– Check keylock on case front
There is little to say about keyboards. There is little to cause a problem except for some models that have a switch for selecting XT or AT compatibility. If you have such a keyboard, set it to AT compatibility.
Some BIOS setup programs allow the keyboard num locks and typematic rate to be set. Check for other variables.
Serial Mouse
– Use mouse setup utilities
– Works OK with DOS
– Serial port setup OK
– Compatibility
– com1 = Solaris tty0
– com2 = Solaris tty1
Test your mouse using the DOS setup utilities that came bundled with it. If it works normally under DOS but fails to work with Solaris, you have a compatibility problem or a Solaris configuration problem. Use kdmconfig or devconfig to reconfigure for Solaris
Serial port connected to the mouse should be set to avoid IRQ and I/O port address conflicts.
Bus Mouse
– Use mouse setup utilities
– Works OK with DOS
– Video card setup OK
– Compatibility
Test your mouse using the DOS setup utilities that came bundled with it. If it works normally under DOS but fails to work with Solaris, you have a compatibility problem or a Solaris configuration problem. Use kdmconfig or devconfig to reconfigure for Solaris.
You may have a bus mouse connected to a video board. The video board must be configured to enable the mouse and set the IRQ level.

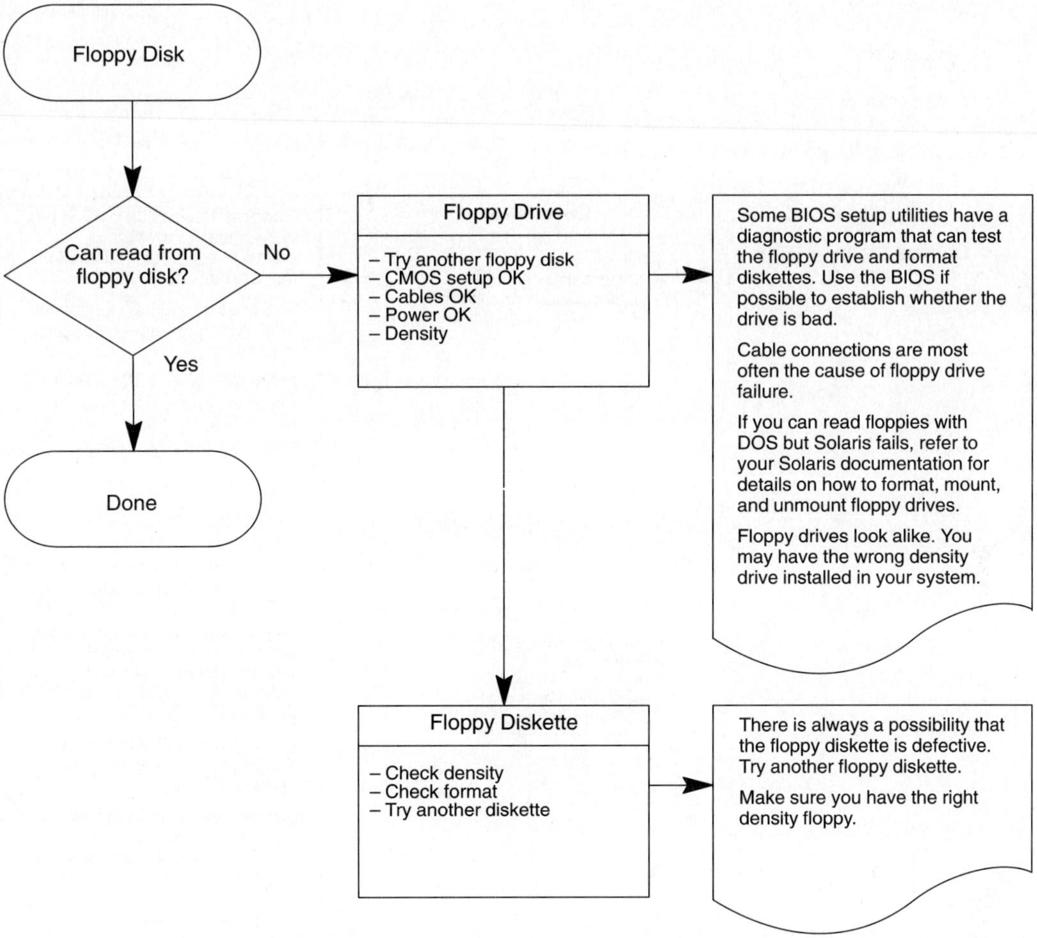
Floppy Disk
Can read from floppy disk?
No
Yes
Done
Floppy Drive
– Try another floppy disk
– CMOS setup OK
– Cables OK
– Power OK
– Density
Some BIOS setup utilities have a diagnostic program that can test the floppy drive and format diskettes. Use the BIOS if possible to establish whether the drive is bad.
Cable connections are most often the cause of floppy drive failure.
If you can read floppies with DOS but Solaris fails, refer to your Solaris documentation for details on how to format, mount, and unmount floppy drives.
Floppy drives look alike. You may have the wrong density drive installed in your system.
Floppy Diskette
– Check density
– Check format
– Try another diskette
There is always a possibility that the floppy diskette is defective. Try another floppy diskette.
Make sure you have the right density floppy.

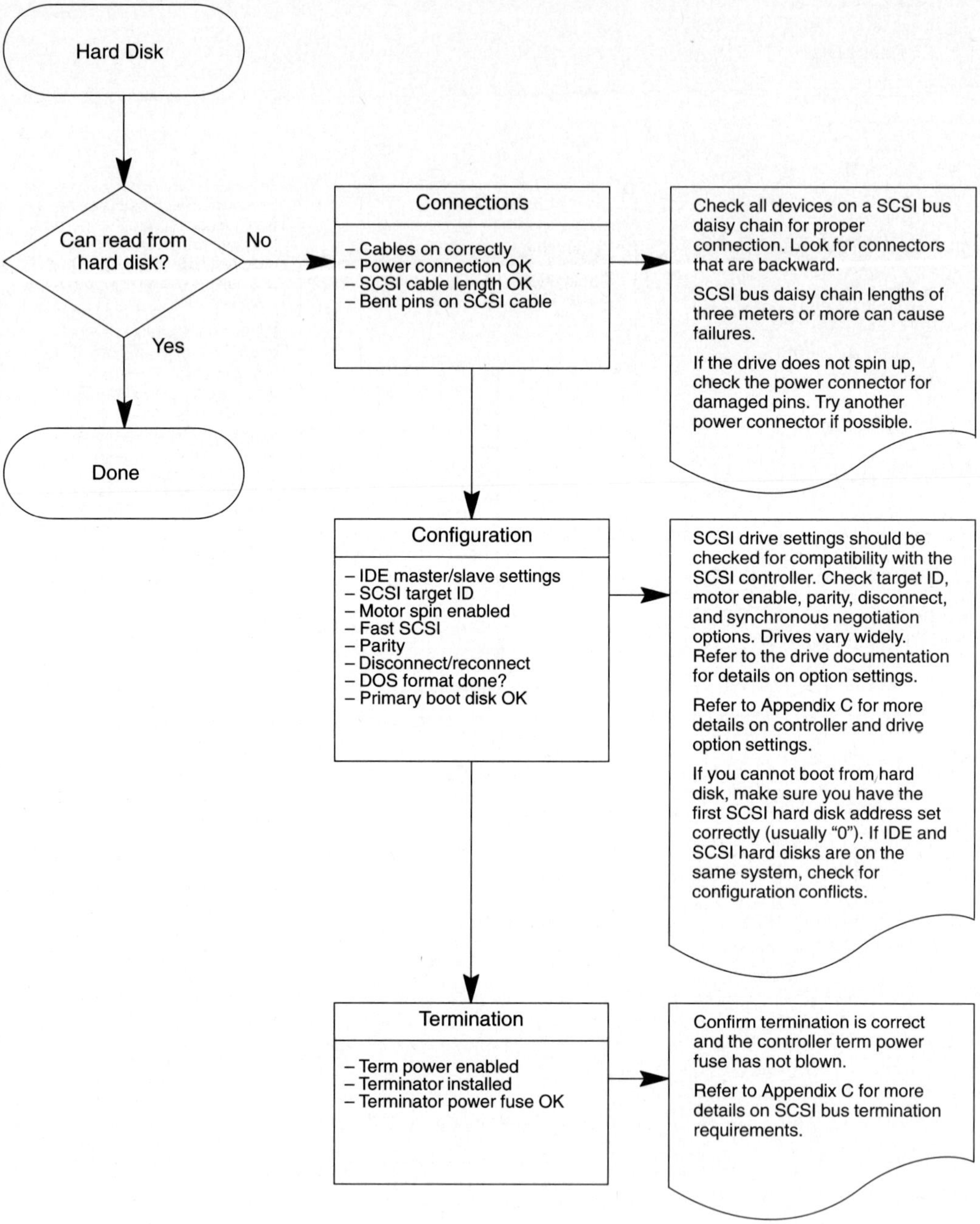
Hard Disk
Can read from hard disk?
No
Yes
Done
Connections
– Cables on correctly
– Power connection OK
– SCSI cable length OK
– Bent pins on SCSI cable
Check all devices on a SCSI bus daisy chain for proper connection. Look for connectors that are backward.
SCSI bus daisy chain lengths of three meters or more can cause failures.
If the drive does not spin up, check the power connector for damaged pins. Try another power connector if possible.
Configuration
– IDE master/slave settings
– SCSI target ID
– Motor spin enabled
– Fast SCSI
– Parity
– Disconnect/reconnect
– DOS format done?
– Primary boot disk OK
SCSI drive settings should be checked for compatibility with the SCSI controller. Check target ID, motor enable, parity, disconnect, and synchronous negotiation options. Drives vary widely. Refer to the drive documentation for details on option settings.
Refer to Appendix C for more details on controller and drive option settings.
If you cannot boot from hard disk, make sure you have the first SCSI hard disk address set correctly (usually "0"). If IDE and SCSI hard disks are on the same system, check for configuration conflicts.
Termination
– Term power enabled
– Terminator installed
– Terminator power fuse OK
Confirm termination is correct and the controller term power fuse has not blown.
Refer to Appendix C for more details on SCSI bus termination requirements.

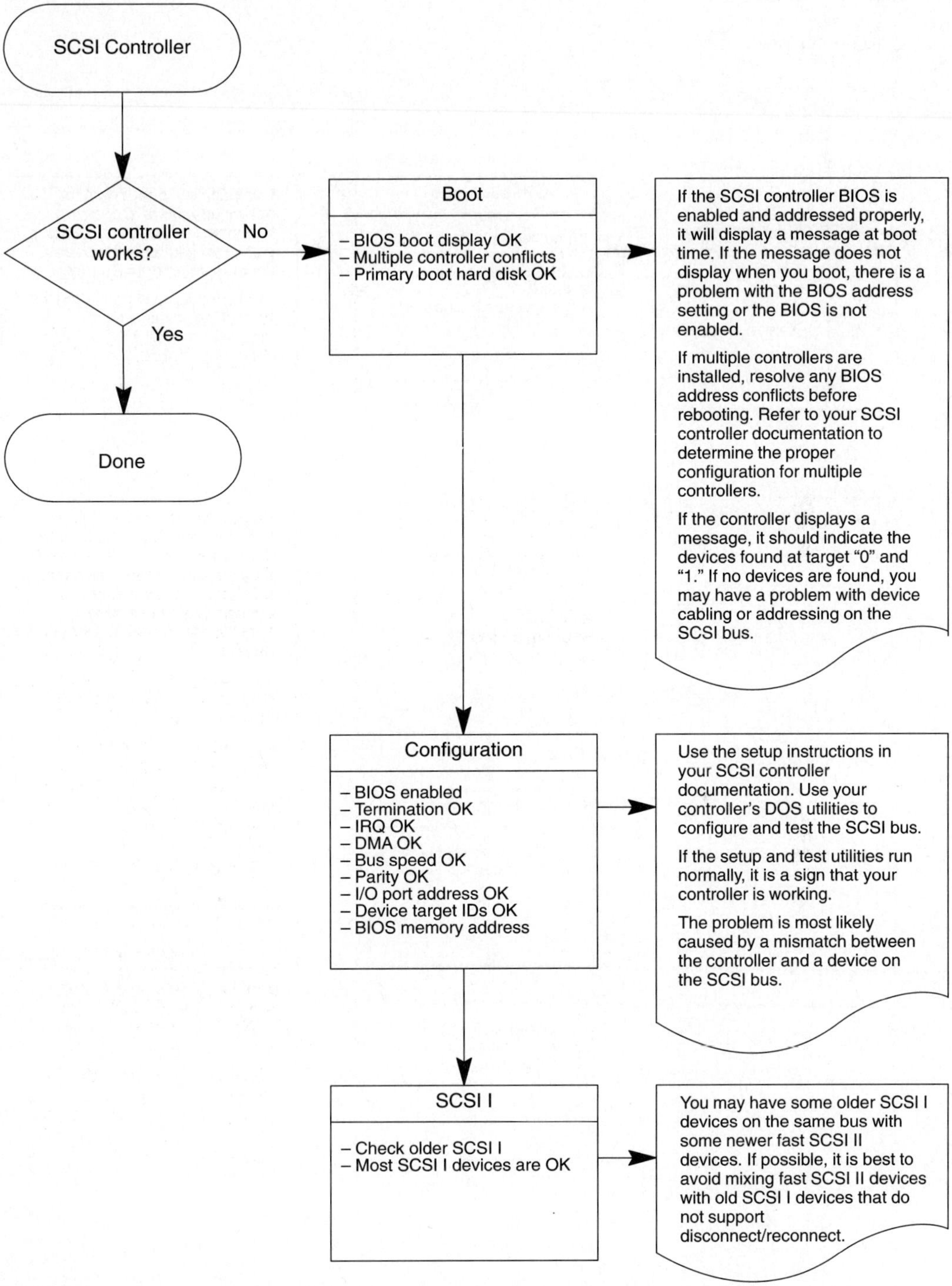
SCSI Controller
SCSI controller works?
No
Yes
Done
Boot
– BIOS boot display OK
– Multiple controller conflicts
– Primary boot hard disk OK
If the SCSI controller BIOS is enabled and addressed properly, it will display a message at boot time. If the message does not display when you boot, there is a problem with the BIOS address setting or the BIOS is not enabled.
If multiple controllers are installed, resolve any BIOS address conflicts before rebooting. Refer to your SCSI controller documentation to determine the proper configuration for multiple controllers.
If the controller displays a message, it should indicate the devices found at target "0" and "1." If no devices are found, you may have a problem with device cabling or addressing on the SCSI bus.
Configuration
– BIOS enabled
– Termination OK
– IRQ OK
– DMA OK
– Bus speed OK
– Parity OK
– I/O port address OK
– Device target IDs OK
– BIOS memory address
Use the setup instructions in your SCSI controller documentation. Use your controller's DOS utilities to configure and test the SCSI bus.
If the setup and test utilities run normally, it is a sign that your controller is working.
The problem is most likely caused by a mismatch between the controller and a device on the SCSI bus.
SCSI I
– Check older SCSI I
– Most SCSI I devices are OK
You may have some older SCSI I devices on the same bus with some newer fast SCSI II devices. If possible, it is best to avoid mixing fast SCSI II devices with old SCSI I devices that do not support disconnect/reconnect.

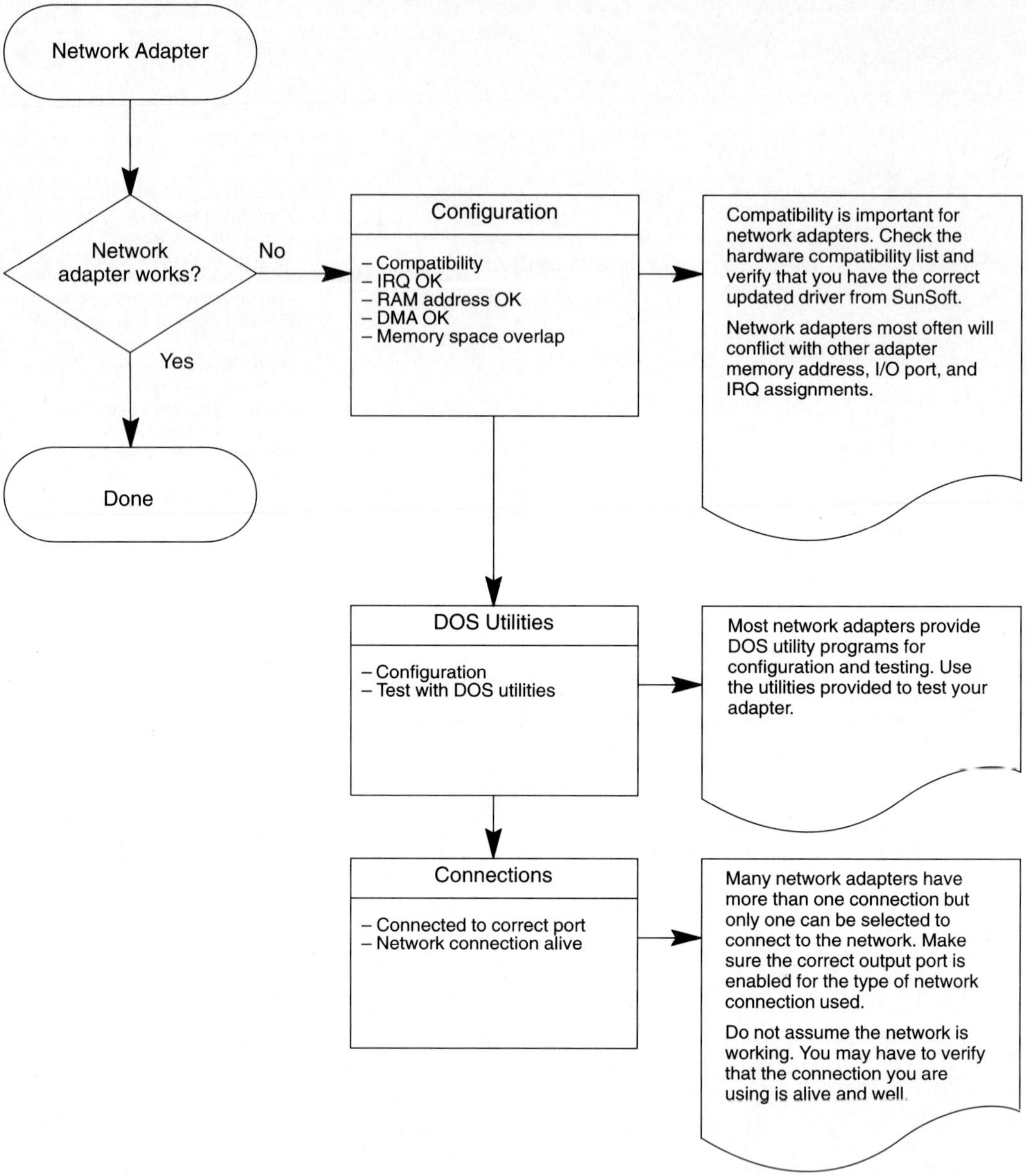
Network Adapter
Network adapter works?
No
Yes
Done
Configuration
– Compatibility
– IRQ OK
– RAM address OK
– DMA OK
– Memory space overlap
Compatibility is important for network adapters. Check the hardware compatibility list and verify that you have the correct updated driver from SunSoft.
Network adapters most often will conflict with other adapter memory address, I/O port, and IRQ assignments.
DOS Utilities
– Configuration
– Test with DOS utilities
Most network adapters provide DOS utility programs for configuration and testing. Use the utilities provided to test your adapter.
Connections
– Connected to correct port
– Network connection alive
Many network adapters have more than one connection but only one can be selected to connect to the network. Make sure the correct output port is enabled for the type of network connection used.
Do not assume the network is working. You may have to verify that the connection you are using is alive and well.

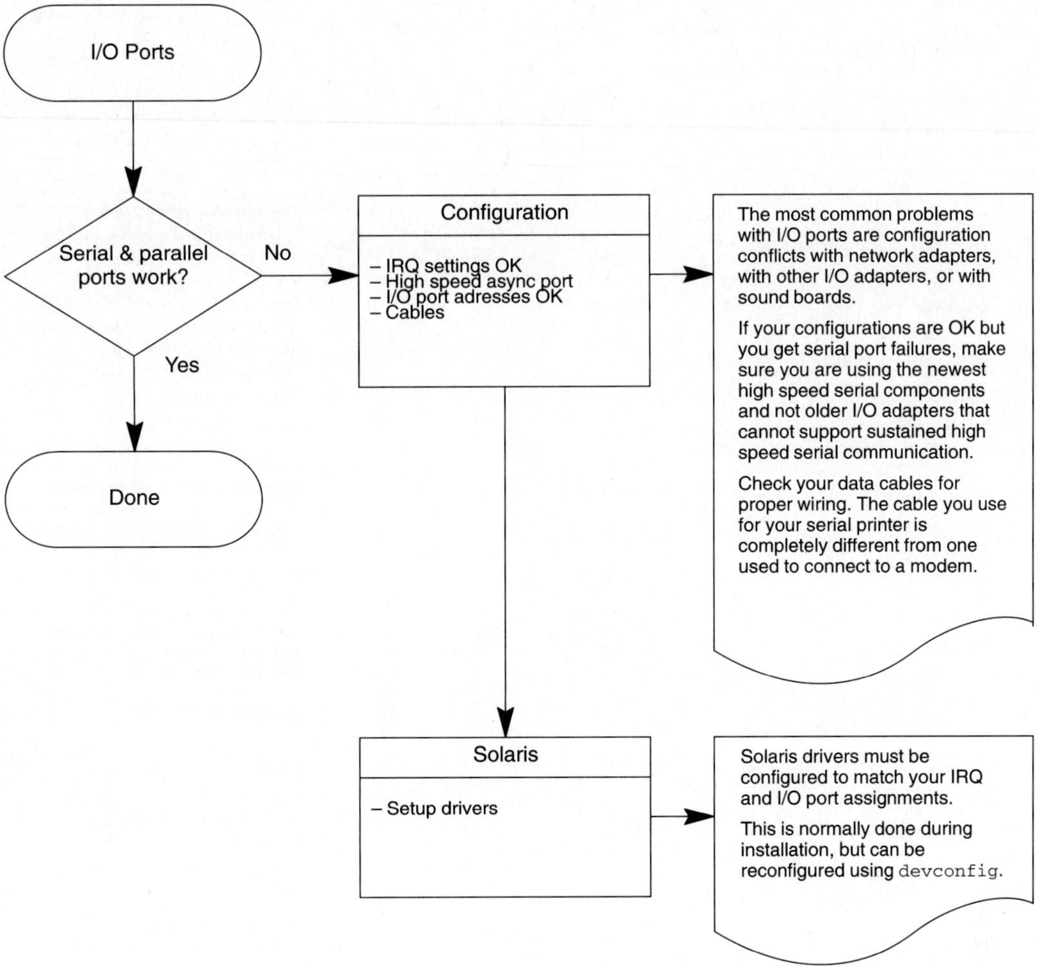
I/O Ports
Serial & parallel ports work?
No
Yes
Done
Configuration
– IRQ settings OK
– High speed async port
– I/O port adresses OK
– Cables
The most common problems with I/O ports are configuration conflicts with network adapters, with other I/O adapters, or with sound boards.
If your configurations are OK but you get serial port failures, make sure you are using the newest high speed serial components and not older I/O adapters that cannot support sustained high speed serial communication.
Check your data cables for proper wiring. The cable you use for your serial printer is completely different from one used to connect to a modem.
Solaris
– Setup drivers
Solaris drivers must be configured to match your IRQ and I/O port assignments.
This is normally done during installation, but can be reconfigured using devconfig.

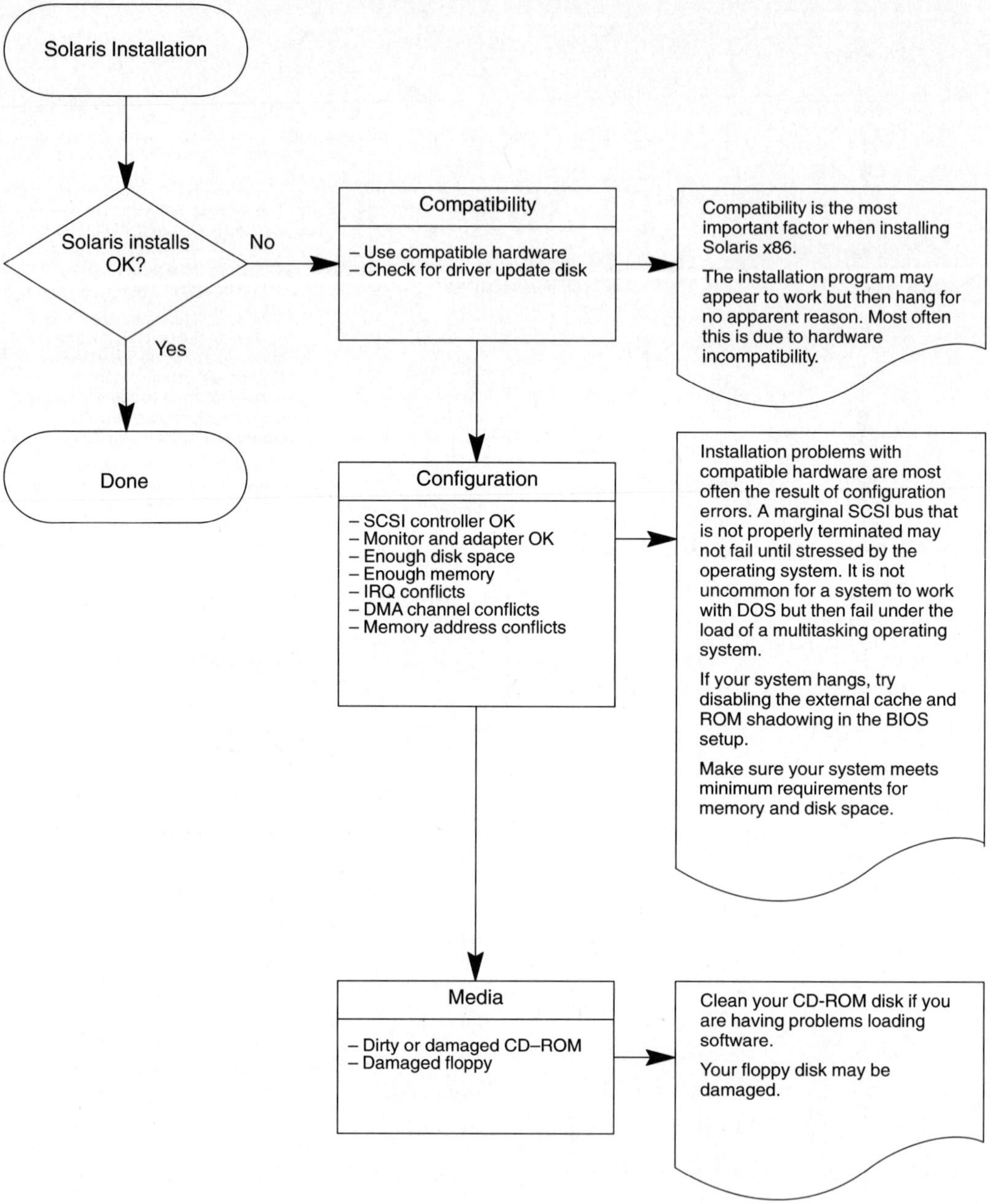
Solaris Installation
Solaris installs OK?
No
Yes
Done
Compatibility
– Use compatible hardware
– Check for driver update disk
Compatibility is the most important factor when installing Solaris x86.
The installation program may appear to work but then hang for no apparent reason. Most often this is due to hardware incompatibility.
Configuration
– SCSI controller OK
– Monitor and adapter OK
– Enough disk space
– Enough memory
– IRQ conflicts
– DMA channel conflicts
– Memory address conflicts
Installation problems with compatible hardware are most often the result of configuration errors. A marginal SCSI bus that is not properly terminated may not fail until stressed by the operating system. It is not uncommon for a system to work with DOS but then fail under the load of a multitasking operating system.
If your system hangs, try disabling the external cache and ROM shadowing in the BIOS setup.
Make sure your system meets minimum requirements for memory and disk space.
Media
– Dirty or damaged CD–ROM
– Damaged floppy
Clean your CD-ROM disk if you are having problems loading software.
Your floppy disk may be damaged.

Appendix A

COMPATIBILITY

This appendix contains a list of hardware that is compatible with Solaris x86 and instructions on how to get:

- Current compatibility information
- New drivers from SunSoft
- New PMI files from SunSoft
- Patches from SunSoft

Accessing Information

The list changes as new hardware is added. More current information is available through:

- CompuServe on–line service
- SunSoft bulletin board service (BBS)
- Internet

SunSoft BBS

The SunSoft BBS contains the latest versions of drivers for compatible products. The drivers are free and available for downloading.

- 8–bit, 1 stop bit, no parity
- VT100 or AT386 terminal emulation
- Login: guest
- Password: guest1
- 9600 baud V.32bis access # (310) 348–8641
- 1200/2400 baud access # (310) 348–8638

The bulletin board also provides free access to a frequently asked question (FAQ) list. There is no technical support provided on this BBS.

Internet

The most current hardware compatibility list is available through the Internet. Send your request to `x86-hwconfig@cypress.west.sun.com`.

If you are a user of UUNET services, you can obtain PMI and driver update files from the Internet. Establish an ftp session to ftp.uu.net, login as anonymous and use your E–mail address as the password. Change to directory `/vendor/sun/sun-doc/x-86-driver` and “get” the desired files. The README file includes instructions for copying the diskette images to a diskette.

For more information about accessing UUNET contact:

UUNET Technologies Inc.
Falls Church, Virginia
(703) 204–8000

SunSoft's Automated Support System

The latest information regarding the availability of new drivers and PMI files can be obtained by calling SunSoft's Automated Support System at (310) 348–6070 or by sending electronic mail to `support@cypress.West.Sun.COM`.

SunSoft Catalyst[SM] Fax-on-Demand

Fax Server (800) 769–4000

CompuServe

To obtain PMI (video adapter) files and driver update files from CompuServe, establish a CompuServe session and at the prompt type “g sunsoft.” Proceed to the Solaris x86 Library (“lib 9”). You can then download the required files.

HARDWARE COMPATIBILITY LIST

Computer Systems

The following systems were tested by SunSoft during the development of Solaris x86 version 2.1.

Manufacturer	Model	Description
Acer America	ACERFrame 1000	Model 1750
Apricot	FTe	Tower
AST	Power Premium 4/33	486/33
AST	Premium SE 4/66D	486DX2/66
Compaq	Deskpro 4/33 i	486/33
Compaq	Prolinea 4/33	486/33
Compaq	LTE Lite 4/25C	Laptop*
Compaq	LTE Lite 4/33C	Laptop*

Manufacturer	Model	Description
CompuAdd	433E	Tower EISA
CompuAdd	450	Desktop
CompuAdd	466EDX2	486DX2/66
CompuAdd	MC 466EDX2	486DX2/66
Dell	450SE	486/50
Dell	450DE	486DX/50
Dell	433DE	486DX/33
Dell	466/T	486DX2/66
Dell	466/ME	486DX2/66
Gateway 2000	486/33E	Tower
Gateway 2000	4DX2–66V	Tower
Grid	MFP/450+	486/50
IBM	PS/2 Model 57	MCA Bus
IBM	PS/2 Model 77	MCA Bus
IBM	PS/2 Model 95	MCA Bus
ICL	DRS 3000	
LEO	486DX2–66	Tower
NEC	Powermate 466	486DX2/66
NEC	Powermate DX2/66Te	486DX2/66
NCR	System 3000	Model 3350
Tatung	TCS9650E	Desktop
Toshiba	T4400C	Laptop*
Toshiba	T4600C	Laptop*
Wyse	Decision	486se
Zenith	Z–Server 433DE	486DX/33
Zenith	Z–Server LT 466XE	486DX/66

* Laptop systems require the following:

- Minimum of 12MB of memory, preferably 20MB
- Minimum of 180MB of disk
- Docking bay must be used for the installation
- Use 4400c PMI file for the Toshiba 4600C

System Configuration Notes

Configurations were tested with an add-on video adapter; the vendor's standard video controller may not be supported. When an add-on adapter is used, the integrated controller must be disabled.

Configurations were tested with an add-on SCSI adapter; the vendor's standard SCSI host adapter may not be supported. When an add-on adapter is used, the integrated controller must be disabled.

Vendor-Tested Hardware

The hardware products listed below were certified at vendor sites using SunSoft certification test suites. All systems were tested using peripheral devices that are certified as Solaris compatible listed above. In all cases, factory configurations had to be changed in order to successfully install and run Solaris.

Listed below are cards and configurations that were used for certification.

Card Type	Manufacturer / Model	Configuration
Video	ATI Wonder	8514 Mode
Video	ATI Graphics	8514 Mode
Ethernet	SMC Ethernet Plus	IRQ: 3 – Mem:d000 – DMA: 2
Multimedia	Sound Blaster Pro	IRQ: 10 – I/O: 220
SCSI	Adaptec 1740	IRQ: 11 – I/O:330 – DMA: 3

List of Vendor-Tested Systems

Manufacturer	Model	Description
Advanced Digital Systems	486 Upgradable EISA/ VESA	486DX2/66
Advanced Digital Systems	486 Upgradable ISA/ VESA	486DX2/66
Advanced Digital Systems	ADS 3486 Upgradable	486DX2/66
Advanced Digital Systems	ADS EISA	486DX2/66
Advanced Digital Systems	LDB 486 VESA Upgradable	486DX2/50
Advanced Digital Systems	LDB 486 VESA Upgradable	486DX2/66
ACER	3000/50	486DX/50 EISA Tower
ACER	3000/33	486DX/33 EISA Tower
ACER	ACROS 486/33	486DX/33 Desktop ISA

Manufacturer	Model	Description
ACER	Power 486E	486DX/33 EISA Tower
ACER	Power 486E	486DX/33 EISA Desktop
ALR	Evolution IVe	486DX2/66 – EISA Bus
ALR	Evolution IV	486 DX/33– ISA Bus
ALR	Evolution IV Pentium	Pentium /60 – ISA
ALR	Evolution V Pentium	Pentium/66, Tower
ALR	Evolution V Desktop	486DX2/66 – EISA
ALR	Evolution Ve	486DX2/66 – EISA
ALR	Flyer 32 DT	486DX/33 – ISA
ALR	Power Business/V EISA	486DX2/66 – EISA
ALR	ProV EISA 486DX2/66	EISA Bus
ALR	ProV EISA w/Pentium	Pentium/60 Upgrade
ALTOS	900	486DX/33 Desktop ISA
ALTOS	15000	486DX/50 EISA Tower
ALTOS	10000	486DX/33 EISA Tower
ALTOS	1700	486DX/33 EISA Desktop
ASI	GigaLine ATI MACH32	486DX2/66Tower ISA w/VLB
ASI	GigaLine Cirrus GDL–5426	486DX2/66Tower ISA w/3xVLB
ASI	GigaLine WDC31	486DX2/66Tower EISA
ASI	GigaLine WDC31	486DX2/66Tower ISA w/3xVLB
AST	Bravo 4/33	Model 213W
AST	Bravo 4/50D	Model 213W
AST	Bravo 4/66D	Model 213W
AST	Power Premium 4/33	Model 213W
AST	Power Premium 4/66D	Model 213W
AST	Premium SE 4/50D	Model 1003
AST	Premium SE 4/50D	Model 503
AST	Premium SE 4/66D	Model 1003
AST	Premium SE 4/66D	Model 503
AST	Premmia 4/33	Model 373W
AST	Premmia 4/66D	Model 373W

Manufacturer	**Model**	**Description**
Austin Computer Green PC	486DX/25	ISA Desktop
Austin Computer Green PC	486DX/33	ISA Desktop
Austin Computer Green PC	486DX2/50	ISA Desktop
Austin Computer Green PC	486DX2/66	ISA Desktop
Austin Computer Patriot	486DX/33	EISA Tower
Austin Computer Patriot	486DX2/50	EISA Tower
Austin Computer Patriot	486DX2/66	EISA Tower
Centrex	CX486 ISA	486DX2/66 ISA Bus Desktop
Centrex	CX486 VESA	486DX2/66 ISA/VL Bus Tower
Compaq	DeskPro 4/66i	486DX2/66
Compaq	DeskPro 5/60	Pentium 60 Mhz
Compaq	DeskPro 50M	486DX2/50
Compaq	DeskPro 66M	486DX2/66
Compaq	Prolinea 4/50	486DX2/50
Compuadd	C433D Desktop	486DX/33 ISA
Compuadd	C450D Desktop	486DX2/50 ISA
Compuadd	C466D Desktop	486DX2/66 ISA
Compuadd	C433D Low Profile	486DX/33 ISA
Compuadd	C450D Low Profile	486DX2/50 ISA
Compuadd	C466D Low Profile	486DX2/66 ISA
Compuadd	C433D Mini Tower	486DX/33 ISA
Compuadd	C450D Mini Tower	486DX2/50 ISA
Compuadd	C466D Mini Tower	486DX2/66 ISA
Compuadd	C433D Tower	486DX/33 ISA
Compuadd	C450D Tower	486DX2/50 ISA
Compuadd	C466D Tower	486DX2/66 ISA
DELL	433/L	486DX Slimline Desktop
DELL	450/L	486DX2/50 Slimline Desktop
DELL	466/L	486DX2/66 Slimline Desktop
DELL	433/M	486DX EISA Desktop

Manufacturer	Model	Description
DELL	450/M	486DX2/50 Desktop
DELL	466/M	486DX2/66 Desktop
DELL	433/ME	486DX EISA Desktop
DELL	450/ME	486DX2/50 EISA Desktop
DELL	466/ME	486DX2/66 EISA DEsktop
DELL	433/SE	486DX/33 EISA Tower
DELL	450/SE	486DX2/50 EISA Tower
DELL	466/SE	486DX2/66 EISA Tower
DELL	433/T	486DX/33 Tower
DELL	433/T	486DX Tower
DELL	450/T	486DX2/50 Tower
DELL	466/T	486DX2/66 Tower
DELL	4033/XE	486DX/33 EISA Desktop
DELL	4050/XE	486DX2/50 EISA Desktop
DELL	4066/XE	486DX2/66 EISA Desktop
DELL	4560/XE	Pentium 60 Mhz EISA Desktop
DELL	Dimension 486/33	486DX/33 ISA Desktop
DELL	Dimension 486/50	486DX2/50 ISA Desktop
DELL	Dimension 486/66	486DX2/66 ISA Desktop
DELL	Netplex 433/P	486DX/33 ISA
DELL	Netplex 450/P	486DX2/50 ISA
DELL	Netplex 466/P	486DX2/66 ISA
DELL	Optiplex 433/L	486DX/33 ISA
DELL	Optiplex 450/L	486DX2/50 ISA
DELL	Optiplex 466/L	486DX2/66 ISA
DELL	Optiplex 433/LV	486DX/33 ISA
DELL	Optiplex 450/LV	486DX2/50 ISA
DELL	Optiplex 466/LV	486DX2/66 ISA
DELL	Optiplex 433/MX	486DX/33 ISA
DELL	Optiplex 450/MX	486DX2/50 ISA
DELL	Optiplex 466/MX	486DX2/66 ISA
DELL	Optiplex 433/MXV	486DX/33 ISA
DELL	Optiplex 450/MXV	486DX2/50 ISA

Manufacturer	Model	Description
DELL	Optiplex 466/MXV	486DX2/66 ISA
DTK	BDE4D33V	486DX/33 Destkop ISA
DTK	BDE4D33V	486DX/33 Mini Tower ISA
DTK	BDE4T66V	486DX/33 Desktop ISA
DTK	BDE4T66V	486DX33 Mini Tower ISA
DTK	FEAT03–D33	486DX/33 Desktop ISA VL
DTK	FEAT33–D33	486DX/33 Tower ISA VL
DTK	FEAT33–D34	486DX/33 Mini Tower ISA
DTK	FEAT03–D50	486DX/50 Desktop ISA VL
DTK	FEAT33–D50	486Dx/50 Mini Tower ISA VL
DTK	FEAT34–D50	486DX/50 Tower ISA VL
DTK	FEAT03–T66	486DX2/66 Desktop ISA VL
DTK	FEAT33–T66	486DX2/66 Mini Tower ISA VL
DTK	FEAT34–T66	486DX2/66 Tower ISA VL
DTK	FEAT 5030D33	486DX/33 Desktop ISA
DTK	FEAT 5031D33	486DX/33 Tower ISA
DTK	FEAT5030T66	486DX2/66 Desktop ISA
DTK	FEAT5031T66	486DX2/66 Tower ISA
DTK	GEMMA4L–33	486DX/33 Desktop ISA VL
DTK	GEMMA4L–50	486DX/50 Desktop ISA VL
DTK	GEMMA 4L–66	486DX2/66 Desktop ISA VL
DTK	Grafika 4A	486DX/33 Tower ISA
DTK	Grafika 4E	486DX/50 Tower EISA
DTK	Grafika 4C	486DX/33 Desktop ISA
DTK	Grafika 4G	486DX/50 Tower EISA
DTK	Grafika 4I	486Dx2/66 Tower ISA
DTK	Grafika 4J	486DX2/66 Desktop ISA
DTK	Grafika 4V1D–D3	486DX/33 Destkop ISA
DTK	Grafika 4V2D–D3	486DX/33 Desktop ISA VL
DTK	Grafika 4V2D–D5	486DX/50 Desktop ISA VL
DTK	Grafika 4V2D–D6	486DX2/66 Desktop ISA VL
DTK	Grafika 4V2T–D3	486DX/33 Tower ISA VL
DTK	Grafika 4V2T–D5	486DX/50 Tower ISA VL

Manufacturer	Model	Description
DTK	Grafika 4V2T–D6	486DX2/66 Tower ISA VL
DTK	SPAN0030	486DX2/66 Tower EISA
DTK	SPAN3330	486DX/33 Tower EISA
DTK	SPAN5030	486Dx/50 Tower EISA
DTK	SPAN01–D33	486Dx/33 Desktop EISA
DTK	SPAN01–D50	486DX/50 Desktop EISA
DTK	SPAN01–D66	486DX2/66 Desktop EISA
Epson	Power Span DX/66	496DX2/66 EISA
Everex	Step 486DX/33	EISA (12 Slot) Cube Chassis
Everex	Step 486DX2/50	EISA (12 Slot) Cube Chassis
Everex	Step 486DX2/66	EISA (12 Slot) Cube Chassis
Everex	Step 486DX/33	EISA (8 Slot) Tower Chassis
Everex	Step 486DX2/50	EISA (8 Slot) Tower Chassis
Everex	Step 486DX2/66	EISA (8 Slot) Tower Chassis
Everex	Step 486DX/33	EISA (8 Slot) Large Chassis
Everex	Step 486DX2/50	EISA (8 Slot) Large Chassis
Everex	Step 486DX2/66	EISA (8 Slot) Large Chassis
Everex	Step 486DX/33	ISA Tower Chassis
Everex	Step 486DX/33	ISA Large Chassis
Everex	Step 486DX/33	ISA Small Chassis
Everex	Step 486DX2/50	ISA Tower Chassis
Everex	Step 486DX2/50	ISA Large Chassis
Everex	Step 486DX2/50	ISA Small Chassis
Everex	Step 486DX2/66	ISA Tower Chassis
Everex	Step 486DX2/66	ISA Large Chassis
Everex	Step 486DX2/66	ISA Small Chassis
Everex	Step VL EISA 486DX/33	Baby Chassis
Everex	Step VL EISA 486DX2/50	Baby Chassis
Everex	Step VL EISA 486DX2/66	Baby Chassis
Everex	Step VL EISA 486DX/33	Tower Chassis
Everex	Step VL EISA 486DX2/50	Tower Chassis
Everex	Step VL EISA 486DX2/66	Tower Chassis
Everex	Step VL ISA 486DX/33	Baby Chassis

Manufacturer	**Model**	**Description**
Everex	Step VL ISA 486DX2/50	Baby Chassis
Everex	Step VL ISA 486DX2/66	Baby Chassis
Everex	Step VL ISA 486DX/33	Slimline Chassis
Everex	Step VL ISA 486DX2/50	Slimline Chassis
Everex	Step VL ISA 486DX2/66	Slimline Chassis
Everex	Step VL ISA 486DX/33	Tower Chassis
Everex	Step VL ISA 486DX2/50	Tower Chassis
Everex	Step VL ISA 486DX2/66	Tower Chassis
First International	LEO 6646 486DX2/66	EISA Computer
Future Tech	System 425eV–i	486DX/25 EISA ISA Tower
Future Tech	System 433eV–i	486DX/33 EISA ISA Tower
Future Tech	System 452eV–i	486DX2/50 EISA ISA Tower
Future Tech	System 462eV–i	486DX2/60 EISA ISA Tower
Future Tech	System 425eV–s	486DX/25 EISA ISA Tower
Future Tech	System 433eV–s	486DX/33 EISA ISA Tower
Future Tech	System 452eV–s	486DX2/50 EISA ISA Tower
Future Tech	System 462eV–s	486DX2/60 EISA ISA Tower
Gateway 2000	4DX–33	486DX/33 Slimline
Gateway 2000	4DX2/66E	486DX2/66 Desktop EISA
Gateway 2000	4DX2/66E	486DX2/66 Tower EISA
Gateway 2000	4DX–33V	486DX/33 Desktop ISA VL
Gateway 2000	4DX–33V	486DX/33 Tower ISA VL
Gateway 2000	4DX2–50V	486DX2/50 Desktop ISA VL
Gateway 2000	4DX2–50V	486DX2/50 Tower ISA VL
Gateway 2000	4DX2/66V	486DX2/66 Desktop ISA VL
Gateway 2000	4DX2/66V	486DX2/66 Tower ISA VL
Intel	Professional GX	486DX2/66 Standard Resolution
Intel	Professional GX	486DX2/66 High Resolution
Intel	L486 Series	486DX2/66 High Resolution
Intel	L486 Series	486DX2/66 Standard Resolution
Intel	Xpress Deskside Server	486DX2/66
Intel	Xpress Deskside Server	486DX2/50
Intel	Xpress Deskside Server	Pentium 60Mhz

Manufacturer	**Model**	**Description**
Intel	Classic R–series	486/33
IPI	Predator I	486DX/33 ISA
IPI	Predator I	486DX2/66 ISA
IPI	Super Voyager VLB	486DX/33 ISA
IPI	Super Voyager VLB	486DX2/66 ISA
Leading Edge	D4/MTDX–33	486DX/33 ISA Mini Tower
Leading Edge	D4/DX–33	486DX/33 ISA Desktop
Leading Edge	D4/Dx33 Plus	486DX/33 ISA
Leading Edge	Winpro 486e/DX33	486DX/33 ISA
Metrologie	Professional GX	EISA DX2/66 Desktop w/ATI8514
Metrologie	OEM Intel Classic "R"	i486DX33 ISA
Metrologie	GmbH PGX PGX station	i486DXD2/66 EISA
Metrologie PGX	OEM Intel PGX	i486DX2/66 EISA
Micro Access	New Orleans	486DX/33 EISA
Micro Access	New Orleans	486DX/66 EISA
Micro Access	Omaha	486DX/33 ISA
Micro Access	Omaha	486DX/66 ISA
Micro Access	San Francisco	486DX/33 EISA
Micro Access	San Francisco	486DX/66 EISA
Micro Access	Savannah	486DX/33 ISA
Micro Access	Savannah	486DX/66 ISA
Mobius Comp.	Protege P466ECS	486DX2/66 Workstation
Mobius Comp.	Protege P560Is/560M	Pentium 80586/60 Multi–User
NCR	System 3230	486DX/25 ISA Desktop
NCR	System 3230	486DX/33 ISA Desktop
NCR	System 3230	486DX/50 ISA Desktop
NCR	System 3333	486DX/25 ISA Desktop
NCR	System 3333	486DX/33 ISA Desktop
NCR	System 3333	486DX/50 ISA Desktop
NCR	System 3333	486DX2/66 ISA Desktop
NEC	Express/II p601 LT	Pentium 60
NEC	PowerMate 466	486DX2/66 ISA
NEC	PowerMate 486/50Te	486DX2/50 EISA

Manufacturer	**Model**	**Description**
NEC	PowerMate 486/66Te	486DX2/66 EISA
NEXCOM International Co. Ltd.	Nextation 4	486DX2/66 Workstation
NEXCOM International Co. Ltd.	Nextation 4	486DX3/100 Workstation
NorthGate	Elegance ZXP	486DX2/66 Desktop ISA
NorthGate	Elegance ZXP	486DX/33 Desktop ISA
NorthGate	ZXP Eisa Vesa Server	486DX/25 EISA
NorthGate	ZXP Eisa Vesa Server	486DX/33 EISA
NorthGate	ZXP Eisa Vesa Server	486DX2/50 EISA
NorthGate	ZXP Eisa Vesa Server	486DX2/66 EISA
Olivetti	LSX 5010	486DX/25 Tower
Olivetti	LSX 5020	486DX/33 Tower
Peacock AG	Peacock UNIX Tower	486DX50 EISA + VLB
Peacock AG	Peacock UNIX Tower	486DX2/50 ISA
Research Machines	Centra	Desktop 486DX2–66 ISA/VL
Research Machines	SystemBase	Tower 486DX33 EISA
Research Machines	Centra V560	Pentium/60 ISA
Samsung	Deskmaster	486DX/66 ISA VLB
Siemens ANL	SiiX Server 1 Tower	EISA DX50 w/WDC31 video
Siemens ANL	SiiX Station 1 Desktop	EISA DX2/66 w/Mach32 video
Siemens Nixdorf	PCD–4C	PGX EISA 486DX2/66
Siemens Nixdorf	PCD–4H Desktop	ISA DX2/66 w/Cirrus GLD–5426 VLB
Siemens Nixdorf	PCD–4H/VL Desktop	ISA/VLB 486DX2/66 w/S3 ISA/VLB
Siemens Nixdorf	PCE–4T Tower	EISA DUAL DX50 w/WDC31 ISA video
Siemens Nixdorf	PCD–5H	Pentium 60Mhz ISA + PCI
Siemens Nixdorf	PCE–5S Tower	EISA Pentium/60 w/WDC31 ISA
Siemens Nixdorf	PCE–5S Tower	EISA Pentium/60 w/WDC31 ISA
Tatung	900T	Desk Top
Tatung	9800T	Tower System
Viglen	Contender Exec	Small desktop ISA 486DX33
Viglen	Genie Exec	Desktop 486DX2–66 ISA

Manufacturer	Model	Description
Viglen	EX Desktop/Tower	Pentium EISA
Wyse	Decision 486se/66	486DX2/66 Desktop
Wyse	Decision 486se/33	486DX/33 Desktop
Wyse	Decision 486se/66	486DX2/66 Tower
Wyse	Decision 486se/33	486DX/33 Tower
Wyse	Decision 486si/33	486DX/33 Tower
Wyse	Decision 486si/66	486DX2/66 Tower
Wyse	7000i, Model 760mp	486DX2/66 Tower (single processor only)
Zenith Data	Z–Server EX433DE	486DX/33 EISA Tower
Zenith Data	Z–Server EX450DE	486DX2/50 EISA Tower
Zenith Data	Z–Server LT433DX	486DX/33 EISA Tower
Zenith Data	Z–Server LT466XE	486DX2/66 EISA Tower
Zenith Data	Z–Server LTP60E	Pentium EISA Tower

x86 Multiprocessor Computer Systems

Manufacturer	Model	Description
Acer	AcerFrame 3000MP	Multiprocessor System
AST	Manhattan SMP	Multiprocessor System
Wyse	Series 7000i	486DX Processors

Laptops

Manufacturer	Model	Description
AST	Power Exec 4/33	640x480 16 Color
Compaq	LTE 4/33	
NEC	Ultralite Versa	
Texas Instruments	4000E	
Toshiba	1950CT	640x480 16 Color
Toshiba	T4400C	
Toshiba	T4600	640x480 16 Color
Toshiba	T4700C	640x480 16 Color
Twinhead	Slimnote II 486E	640x480 16 Color

x86 Motherboards Tested

Manufacturer or Type	Model	Description
386 Motherboard	UMC 82C491F Chipset	AMD386 DX–40 CPU
AMI	Enterprise III	486DX2/60
AMI	Super Voyager VLB II	486DX/33
AMI	Super Voyager VLB II	486DX/50
AMI	Voyager	486DX2/66
CMS	EISA Mirage	486DX/50 EISA
CMS	ISA Mirage	486DX/33 ISA
EliteGroup	SL486VE	486DX2/66 EISA + VLB
EliteGroup	UC4917G	486DX2/66 ISA + VLB
EliteGroup	UM486V	486DX2/66 ISA + VLB
EliteGroup	UM4910	AMD486DX40 ISA VLB
EliteGroup	UM4910	486DX/33 ISA + VLB
Escom	ISA/PCI Pentium	Pentium/60
Escom	ISA/VLB	486DX2/66
Micronics	EISA–3	486DX/33
Micronics	EISA–3	486DX2/66
Micronics	EISA–VL	486DX/33
Micronics	EISA–VL	486DX2/66
Micronics	ISA VBL	486DX/33
Micronics	ISA VBL	486DX2/66
Micronics	JX30/66	486DX/33
Micronics	JX30/66	486DX2/66
VEGA	486F–3VL	Symphony SL82C461, SL82C362, SL1287 chipset, and 486DX2/66 CPU

Appendix B

MOTHERBOARD CONFIGURATION (GENERAL)

Memory

Memory must be of the correct speed and type. You should have already verified the correct memory type and speed for your system. Although most retail stores will put the proper memory in their systems, make sure to verify memory speed yourself. Problems with mismatched memory are usually intermittent and hard to identify.

POST

The power on self test (POST) can indicate test failures by a pattern of audible beeps on the system speaker. Make sure your speaker is connected to the motherboard if you do not hear a beep after POST completes.

Most BIOS implementations use a pattern of beeps to indicate failures. Check your motherboard documentation for information on decoding the pattern in your system. If your BIOS manufacturer is AMI, your BIOS will emit the following pattern:

POST Beep Codes

Review your motherboard documentation for information regarding BIOS messages. Most BIOS programs communicate POST status by beeps on the speaker or by messages displayed on the monitor. AMI is a common BIOS used on PC motherboards. My particular test system uses the pattern of beeps listed below:

Fatal errors

1	DRAM refresh failure
2	Parity failure
4	System timer failure
5	Processor failure
6	Keyboard controller gate A20 error
7	Virtual mode exception error

Nonfatal errors

3	Base 64K RAM failure
8	Display memory R/W test failure
9	ROM–BIOS checksum failure

NICE/HINT Motherboard

I was not able to get the NICE (EISA, ISA, VESA) motherboard with the HINT chip set to work. I tried several boards and had compatibility problems with all of them. I cannot recommend this motherboard. The system hangs intermittently and usually will not work at all when connected to a network.

I did not have the time to resolve the problems with this type of motherboard. If you have problems similar to mine, I suggest you contact the manufacturer for assistance.

Power Supply and Signal Connections

The power supply seldom requires any special configuration. You may have to add additional power connectors or lengthen existing power supply cables to reach some devices. This is usually only required in extreme cases. Cable extensions and splitters are available at most computer retail stores.

Motherboard Power

The power connectors on AT compatible motherboards are connected to two power supply cables. The cable connectors are unique and easy to match.

Make sure that when the connectors are installed, the red and orange wires are at the two ends of the motherboard pin row.

The connectors are keyed. It is impossible to get the connectors on backward unless you use a substantial amount of force — ouch!

Name	Color	Pin #	
+5 volts	Red	6	P9
+5 volts	Red	5	P9
+5	Red	4	P9
–5	White	3	P9
Ground	Black	2	P9
Ground	Black	1	P9
Ground	Black	6	P8
Ground	Black	5	P8
–12 volts	Blue	4	P8
+12 volts	Yellow	3	P8
Not used	N/A	2	P8
+5 pwr good	Orange	1	P8

Peripheral Power

The disk drives and other peripheral devices are connected to the power supply via 4-pin connectors that supply +5 volts and +12 volts DC. A typical power supply will have four peripheral device power connections. If you need more power connectors, you can add Y cables that split a single power connector into two separate connectors.

Name	Color	Pin #
+5 volts	Red	4
Ground	Black	3
Ground	Black	2
+12 volts	Yellow	1

Battery Power

Motherboard Pin #	Signal Name
1	Ground
2	Not Used
3	Not Used
4	+6 Volts

Speaker Connection

Motherboard Pin #	Signal Name
1	Audio
2	Not Used
3	Ground
4	+5 Volts

Keyboard Connection

Motherboard Pin #	Signal Name
1	Clock
2	Data
3	Not Used
4	Ground
5	+5 Volts

Appendix C

This appendix contains information on SCSI controllers, floppy drives, and IDE drives.

SCSI HBA (CONTROLLERS)

The SCSI controller is usually the most complicated adapter to install and configure. This section of the appendix contains general SCSI information and specific installation and configuration details for some popular SCSI controllers.

Compatibility and Features

The following SCSI adapters and SCSI controller chips are compatible with Solaris x86.

Manufacturer	Model	Solaris Driver
Aculogic	PCIport Adapter (NCR 810 Chip)	ncrs
Adaptec	AHA 1520/1522	aic
Adaptec	AHA 1540B/1542B	aha
Adaptec	AHA 1540C/1542C	aha
Adaptec	AHA 1540CF/1542CF	aha
Adaptec	AHA 1640	aha
Adaptec	AHA 1740A/1742	eha
Adaptec	AHA 2740/2742	esa
Adaptec	AIC 6260/6360 – Intel Prof GX w/6360	aic
Adaptec	AIC 7770 Chip	esa
BusLogic	BT–445S, VL Bus	blogic
BusLogic	BT–542B	blogic
BusLogic	BT–545S	blogic
BusLogic	BT–646S	blogic
BusLogic	BT–742A	blogic
BusLogic	BT–747S	blogic
BusLogic	BT–757S	blogic
BusLogic	BT–946C	blogic
Corollary	MP System (NCR 810 Chip)	ncrs

Manufacturer	Model	Solaris Driver
Creative Labs	Sound Blaster Pro 16 SCSI-II	aic
DPT	PM2011	dpt
DPT	PM2012B	dpt
DPT	PM2021	dpt
DPT	PM2022	dpt
DPT	PM2122	dpt
Future Domain	MCS–600 (MCA Bus)	tmf
Future Domain	MCS–700 (MCA Bus)	tmf
Future Domain	TMC–1650/1670	tmf
Future Domain	TMC–1660/1680	tmf
IBM	LACUNA SCSI	tmf
IBM	PS/2 SCSI, MCA Bus	mcis
Intel	IntelExpress	esa
Intel	PCI Motherboard (NCR 810 Chip)	ncrs
NCR	8250 PCI Adapter (NCR 810 Chip)	ncrs
NCR	NCR C710 Chip – Compaq Fast SCSI-II – Compaq Prosignia	ncrs
NCR	NCR C810 Chip – Dell Omniplex 560 – Digital DEC PC 560	ncrs
Specter	NEC 466ST Express II	dpt
Trantor	T348 Mini SCSI Plus	trantor
Unisys	DT1	esa
Unisys	DT2	esa
Unisys	6000/100	esa
Unisys	6000/300	esa

Disk Arrays

The following SCSI disk array products are compatible with Solaris x86.

Manufacturer	Model	Solaris Driver
Dell	Dell SCSI Array	dsa
IBM	DMC–960 (Passplay) SCSI Array	dac
Mylex	DAC–960 SCSI Array	mlx

Boot Disk

The Solaris operating system bootable partition can only be installed on the boot disk. Only one of the hard disks on a system is designated as the boot disk. The PC BIOS expects the boot disk to be the first available hard-disk drive on the primary disk controller. The primary disk controller BIOS is usually found at memory location C8000. When there is no valid BIOS at C8000, the system will use the first valid disk controller BIOS found.

If your primary disk controller is a SCSI controller, you can avoid problems by setting the target address of your boot disk to 0. Most SCSI controllers use the disk drive with the lowest target address as the boot disk. Some controllers do not work properly if a device other than a disk drive is set to target address 0. As usual, there is an exception to the rule. On PS/2 SCSI controllers, the primary hard disk has to be set to SCSI target address six. If you own a PS/2 type system, you already know this. If you don't have a PS/2 type system, forget I mentioned this!

Multiple Controllers

The need may arise to add additional IDE or SCSI controllers to a system. This can be done, but requires good planning to make sure there are no conflicts between the controllers. There should only be one IDE adapter installed, and it is by default the primary boot disk interface.

Primary Disk Controller

If you intend to have multiple disk controllers in your configuration, install the primary disk controller with memory BIOS address set to C8000. Set any secondary controllers to one of the optional addresses (DC000, D8000, D4000, D0000, or CC000). If there is only one controller in the configuration, select C8000 as the BIOS address. Some controllers do not have a C8000 BIOS address option. Choose a primary controller value such as CC000 or D0000, and make sure you do not conflict with the network adapter RAM address.

Termination

Term Power

The termination circuit requires power to function. The term (termination) power is supplied to the SCSI bus by one or more of the devices connected to the bus. The SCSI adapter usually provides term power (must be enabled), but most SCSI peripherals also have the ability to supply term power. It is standard practice for term power sources to be fused to protect a SCSI bus short from causing serious damage.

You must always ensure that at least one device on the SCSI bus is supplying term power, or the bus will not work correctly. Term power is usually enabled by setting a jumper on the SCSI host bus adapter or SCSI device.

Terminators

All single-ended SCSI bus configurations require proper electrical termination at both ends of the bus. Proper termination assures that the bus will operate reliably at high speed. The placement of termination resistors varies depending on the bus configuration you choose. The three valid termination configurations are:

- Internal bus only
- External bus only
- Both internal and external busses

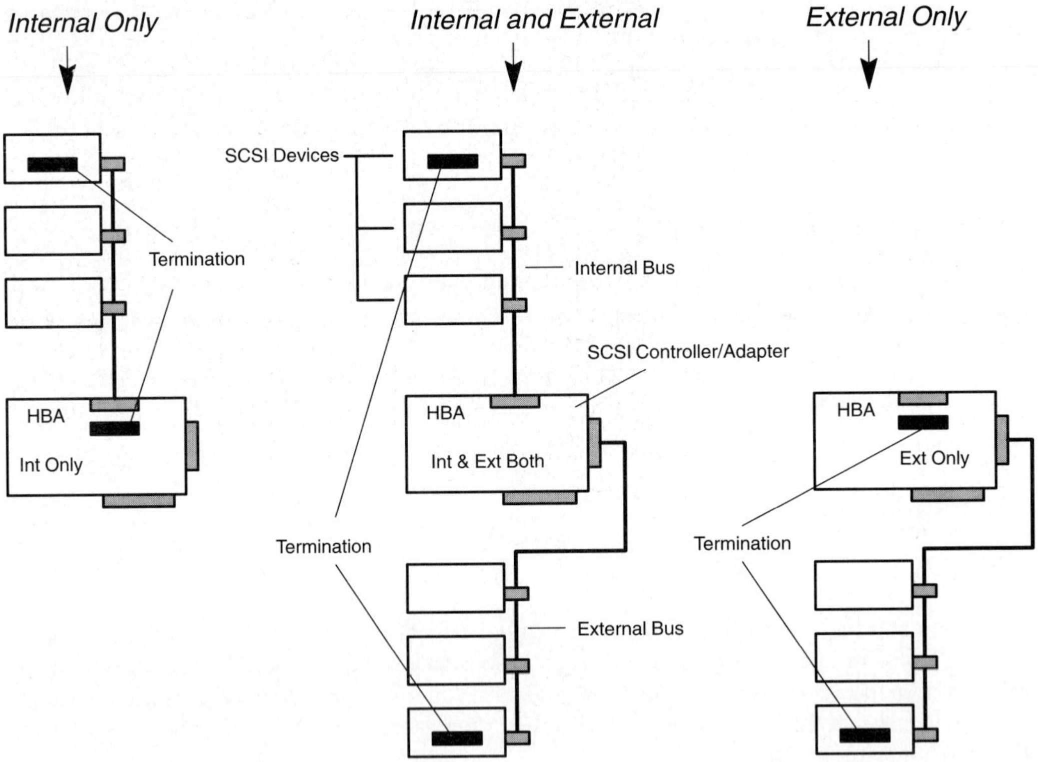

Proper termination is accomplished by removing termination resistors or disabling termination on all devices (including the adaptor), except the two at each end of the bus. It is important to check each device you install on a SCSI bus to ensure proper termination. Improperly terminated busses may appear to work, but you will get unpredictable results.

Cables

Controllers may or may not come with cables for both SCSI devices and floppy-disk drives. Even if the controller includes cables, they often are too short and usually include connectors for at most two SCSI devices. Check this out before you purchase any controller that requires cables. There is a good chance you will have to modify or replace the cables supplied with your SCSI adapter.

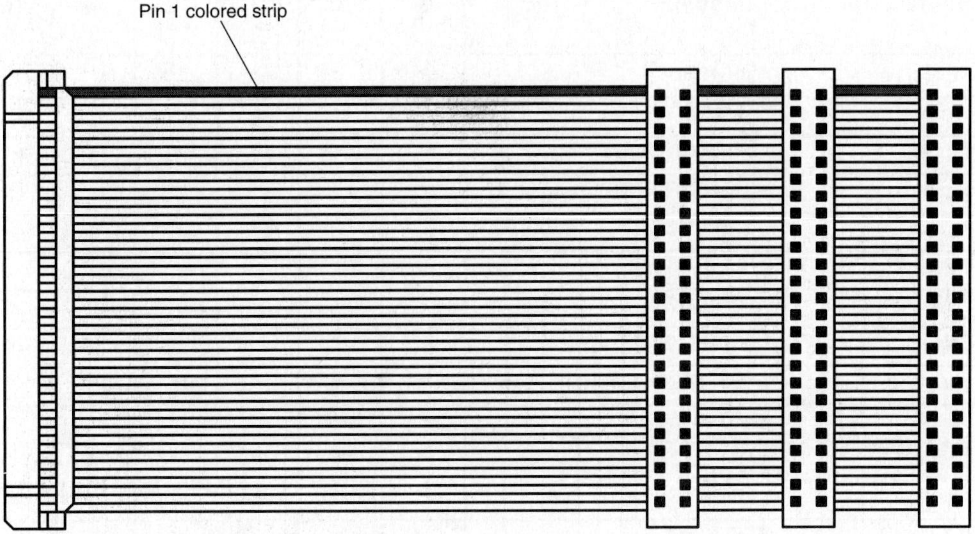

The colored strip along the cable ribbon indicates the location of pin 1. It is important to match the pin-1 side of the cable with the corresponding pin-1 side of the connectors on the SCSI devices and the SCSI controller.

Note: *Pin 1 is usually designated on cable connectors, devices, and adapters by a triangle, arrow, dot, square, numeral 1, or other such mark. Look closely at your cables, devices, and adaptors to locate pin 1.*

The cable can be connected to devices in any order as long as the device connected to the end of the cable is properly terminated. If you only have one internal SCSI device, it should be terminated and connected to the end of the internal SCSI ribbon cable.

Disable Unused Floppy Controllers

Only one floppy controller can be active on a system. It is important to disable all floppy controllers except for the one attached to the floppy drives. Most SCSI adapters that provide a floppy drive controller also provide a configuration option to disable and enable the floppy controller. If you cannot disable an extra floppy controller, consider replacing the offending adapter or motherboard.

Interrupt Selection (IRQ)

Each controller must be set to use one of the available system interrupt request lines. The following table lists some common SCSI host bus adapters. You can use the blank lines in the table as a worksheet to add new host bus adapters.

SCSI Controller Interrupt Table

Manufacturer	Model	9	10	11 *	12 ***	14	15 **
Adaptec	1540B	✓	✓	✓	✓	✓	
Adaptec	1542B	✓	✓	✓	✓	✓	✓
Adaptec	1540C/1542C	✓	✓	✓	✓	✓	✓
Adaptec	1540CF/1542CF	✓	✓	✓	✓	✓	✓
Adaptec	1640/1642			✓			
Adaptec	1740A/1742						
Adaptec	2740/2742	✓	✓	✓	✓	✓	✓
Adaptec	2740T/2742T	✓	✓	✓	✓	✓	✓
Buslogic	BT–542D	✓	✓	✓	✓	✓	✓
Buslogic	BT–545S	✓	✓	✓	✓	✓	✓
Buslogic	BT–742A	✓	✓	✓	✓	✓	✓
Buslogic	BT–747S	✓	✓	✓	✓	✓	✓
DPT	PM2011				✓	✓	✓
DPT	PM2012B Rev. J or higher			✓			✓

✓ Indicates which interrupts can be selected on the SCSI controller. Most controllers can be set to any available interrupt between 9–15. Controllers that do not provide a wide range of interrupt choices can be more difficult to install in "loaded" systems.

Interrupt 13 is reserved for the math coprocessor and is not available on any of the controllers.

11* Recommended setting for first (primary) controller
15** Recommended setting for second controller
12*** Recommended setting for third controller

SCSI Target ID

I recommend you maintain a consistent pattern to addressing your SCSI devices. You should always start with the disk drives at address "0" and add devices in sequence and in the following order: disk, tape, and CD–ROM.

Note: *The SCSI controller is always set to address "7" and has highest priority when arbitration is required on the SCSI bus. SCSI target ID "7" has the highest SCSI-bus priority and target ID "0" has the lowest SCSI-bus priority. Higher target ID numbers have greater priority than lower target ID numbers.*

Hard-Disk Preparation

SCSI disk drives should come from the factory with a valid low-level format. In cases where the drive is not new or is not properly formatted, you can use the utilities provided with your SCSI adapter to low-level format the drives or verify surface integrity.

Disk-surface verification is always a good idea when setting up a new system. It helps to establish that the drives are functioning properly before you begin partitioning. Establishing that the SCSI controller can communicate properly with the disk drives is an important troubleshooting technique. Most SCSI controllers come with a BIOS program that provides low-level formatting, surface verification, and diagnostics.

COMMON SCSI CONTROLLER OPTIONS

Each SCSI controller provides some range of optional features that can be configured to improve performance and compatibility. The following list represents a sampling of the most common options:

- Initiate synchronous negotiation
- Fast SCSI transfer rate
- Maximum DMA transfer rate
- Start unit command
- Disconnection feature
- Error if device not found
- Include in BIOS scan
- Support removable disks as fixed disks

Note: *You may hear the term "wide SCSI" used in reference to the SCSI data lines. This term is not related to either SCSI-I or SCSI-II. Wide 16-bit SCSI data lines are defined by the new SCSI-III standard. SCSI-III host bus adapters and devices are not currently available for testing and are not discussed here. Because there is a new wider SCSI bus, you may hear the 8-bit SCSI-I and SCSI-II bus called "narrow SCSI."*

Initiate Synchronous Negotiation

SCSI controllers will respond to requests for synchronous negotiation from SCSI devices on the bus. The controller can initiate the negotiation if synchronous negotiation is enabled. Older SCSI devices may not work correctly if the SCSI controller initiates a request for synchronous data transfer. This is why SCSI controllers can be set with initiate synchronous negotiation enabled or disabled.

If you have older SCSI devices, you may want to disable the initiate synchronous negotiation feature on your controller. Older controllers most likely will default to disable initiate synchronous negotiation, but newer controllers are more likely to default to enable synchronous negotiation.

If you have a combination of devices that both *support* and *not support* synchronous negotiation, you can leave the controller set to *disabled.* When synchronous negotiation is disabled on most controllers, the controller will still respond correctly when a SCSI device negotiates for synchronous transfer. Some controllers can be configured for synchronous negotiation enabled on a per-device basis.

It is safe to disable this feature in all cases. If you have newer SCSI devices that support synchronous negotiation, you can set the device to enable synchronous negotiation.

Fast SCSI Transfer Rate

Fast SCSI refers to the data transfer rate between the SCSI device and the SCSI controller. Fast SCSI will transfer data at up to 10MB/s. Fast SCSI controllers may give the option of setting the maximum transfer rate on the SCSI bus if synchronous negotiation is not initiated by the controller or the device. This option may be useful if you have an older SCSI device that cannot handle fast SCSI transfer rates.

If you have not figured it out yet, there is a message here. It is best to avoid mixing slow SCSI devices with fast SCSI devices.

Maximum DMA Transfer Rate

It is easy to confuse memory transfer rates with SCSI bus transfer rates. The SCSI controller is usually rated for transfer speed between the controller and the target device (SCSI bus rate), and also for data transfer speed between the controller and system memory (DMA transfer speed).

Note: *As a rule of thumb, you can assume that ISA bus transfer rates are the slowest. EISA and MCA bus rates are faster, and VESA local bus and PCI bus transfers are fastest.*

Start Unit Command

SCSI controllers may have the ability to issue start unit commands to each SCSI target. This is unnecessary in most cases, but occasionally it is necessary if a device on the SCSI bus requires the start unit command to start the motor.

Some SCSI devices such as hard disks can be set to wait for a command from the SCSI controller before initiating motor spin. If you install a SCSI device set to start on command from the controller, make sure you set the controller to issue the start unit command to the appropriate SCSI target device.

Note: *The start unit command is used most often to stagger the motor startup cycle of SCSI devices. This avoids power supply surges that may result from many devices drawing startup current simultaneously.*

Disconnection Feature

The disconnect/reconnect feature is usually enabled except in the case of older SCSI devices that do not support it. This feature enables the controller to be more efficient by disconnecting from a device after issuing a command, and reconnecting when the device needs service. This enables the controller to work efficiently with multiple devices on the SCSI bus.

Error if Device Not Found

This option is available on some controllers, and when enabled, will display an error message if a predetermined device is not found on the SCSI bus. This option is usually set individually for each target ID on the SCSI bus. The default setting is disabled.

Include in BIOS Scan

This feature determines if a device on the SCSI bus is controlled by the SCSI controller BIOS program or ignored. If you choose to ignore a target ID on the SCSI bus, the ignored device can only be addressed by a driver. The normal default is to include all devices on the SCSI bus in the BIOS scan.

Support Removable Disks as Fixed Disks

This option provides for the configuration of devices supported by the SCSI controller BIOS. The normal default setting is that only the boot device is supported as a removeable device.

ADAPTEC AHA-1640

Features

- Micro Channel bus
- 8MB/second DMA
- 50–pin SCSI-II External Connector
- Automatic Configuration (no jumpers and switches)

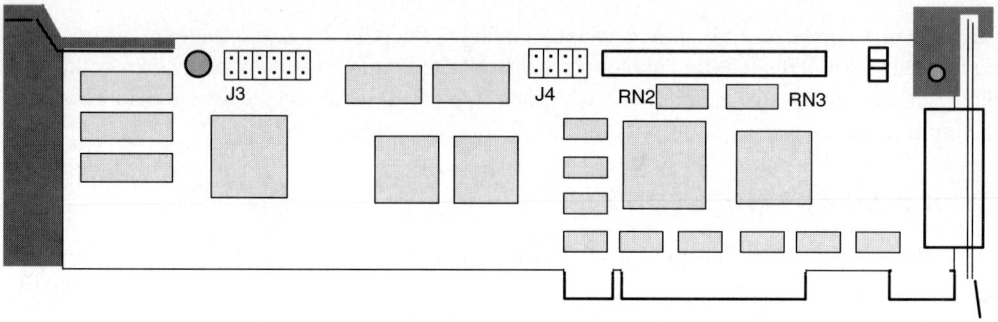

Configuration

Primary SCSI Controller Settings

	IRQ Level	DMA Channel	I/O Port Address	BIOS Address	RAM Address
Factory Defaults	11	5	330	DC000	N/A
Recommended	11	6	330	C8000	N/A

Termination

Termination is enabled when the dual in–line (DIP) resistor chips RN2 and RN3 are installed on the controller. These two resistor chips must be manually removed or inserted to set the termination on the controller.

Hard Disk Preparation

The controller BIOS provides utilities for testing the DMA channel and for low-level format of the hard disks. You can access the utility through the use of the DOS debug utility program.

- Use debug command `g=C800:6` to access the format utility

Configuration Notes

SunSoft recommends leaving the IRQ setting at the default of IRQ 11 to avoid the difficulty of manual configuration.

The adapter descriptor file (`@0F1F.ADF`) is provided on a diskette and must be transfered to the system reference diskette. Install the descripter file on the refernce diskette if it is not already installed.

Factory Default Settings

The adapter is automatically configure using the system reference diskette. The following options are available:

• Port I/O Address	330
• Arbitration Level	5
• Interrupt Level	non–conflicting
• Adapter BIOS Address	Only one BIOS should be enabled
• SCSI Address	7
• SCSI Parity	On
• Sync Xfer Started by AHA-1640	Yes
• Fairness	On
• Synchronous Transfer Negotiation	On

Known Problems

The AHA-1640 will only function with Solaris x86 if set to DMA 6. The aha driver assumes DMA 6 and cannot accurately locate the AHA-1640 if it is not set to DMA 6.

ADAPTEC AHA-1540B/1542B

Features

- SCSI-II compatible
- 1542B includes floppy controller
- Centronics® -type external connector

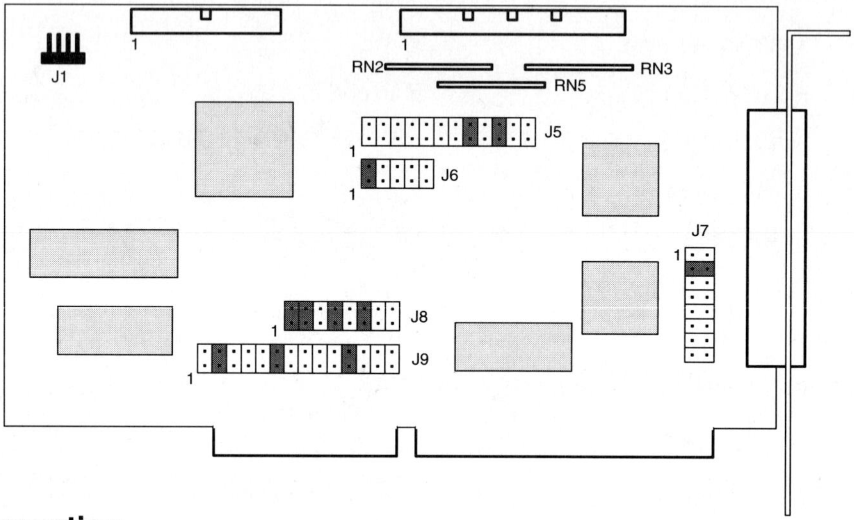

Configuration

Primary SCSI Controller Settings

	IRQ Level	DMA Channel	I/O Port Address	BIOS Address	RAM Address
Factory Defaults	11	5	330	DC000	N/A
Recommended	11	5	330	C8000	N/A

Termination

Termination is enabled and resistor packs RN2, RN3, and RN5 are installed on the adapter by default. These three resistor packs must be manually removed or inserted to set the termination on the controller.

Hard-Disk Preparation

The controller BIOS provides utilities for testing the DMA channel and for low-level format of the hard disks. You can access the utility through the use of the DOS debug utility program.

- Use debug command `g=C800:6` to access the format utility
- Use debug command `g=C800:9` to access the DMA test utility

Diagnostics

At powerup or after a hard reset, the red LED on the controller will flash. If the LED continuously emits a repeating sequence of flashes, it is an indication of controller diagnostic failure. Check your controller documentation for more details.

Jumpers and Switches

This adapter is more difficult than most to configure. It is configured manually by the use of jumpers. You can leave the IRQ setting at the default of IRQ 11 to avoid the difficulty of manual configuration.

I/O Port	**J7** 2	3	4
334	0	0	0
330 *	1	0	0
234	0	1	0
230	1	1	0
134	0	0	1
130	1	0	1
not used	0	1	1
not used	1	1	1

IRQ Level	**J5** 9	10	11	**J9** 9	10	11	12	13	14
9	0	0	0	1	0	0	0	0	0
10	1	0	0	0	1	0	0	0	0
11 *	0	1	0	0	0	1	0	0	0
12	1	1	0	0	0	0	1	0	0
14	0	0	1	0	0	0	0	1	0
15	1	0	1	0	0	0	0	0	1

BIOS Addr	**J7** 7	8
DC000 *	0	0
CC000	1	0
D8000	0	1
C8000	1	1

BIOS Enabled	**J6** 1
Enabled *	1
Disabled	0

I/O Chrdy Delay	**J7** 5	6
0 ns *	0	0
100 ns	1	0
200 ns	0	1
300 ns	1	1

Floppy I/O Addr	**J7** 1
Primary port *	0
Secondary port	1

Floppy Enable	**J8** 1	2	3	4	5	6	7	8
Enabled *	1	1	0	1	0	1	0	0
Disabled	0	0	0	0	0	0	0	0

Not present on 1540B

Not Used	**J6** 2	3	4
Not used *	0	0	0

Diag Factory Only	**J5** 2
Enabled	1
Disabled*	0

Auto Sense	**J6** 5
Enabled *	0
Disabled	1

Synchronous Negotiation	**J5** 1
Enabled	1
Disabled *	0

SCSI Bus Parity	**J5** 3
Disable Parity	1
Enable Parity *	0

DMA Req/Ack	**J9** 2	3	4	5	6	7	8
DREQ5 *	1	0	0				
DREQ 6	0	1	0				
DREQ 7	0	0	1				
DACK 0				1	0	0	0
DACK 5 *				0	1	0	0
DACK 6				0	0	1	0
DACK 7				0	0	0	1

DMA Speed	**J5** 12	13
5.0 MB/s	0	0
5.7 MB/s	1	0
6.7 MB/s	0	1
8.0 MB/s	1	1

DMA Level	**J5** 7	8
7	0	0
6	1	0
5 *	0	1
0	1	1

SCSI Target	**J5** 4	5	6
7 *	0	0	0
6	1	0	0
5	0	1	0
4	1	1	0
3	0	0	1
2	1	0	1
1	0	1	1
0	1	1	1

Switches: 0=off
1=on
Jumpers: 0=not installed
1=installed
*=Default Settings

ADAPTEC AHA-1540C/1542C AND AHA-1540CF/1542CF

Features

- SCSI-II compatible
- 10 MB/sec DMA bus mastering
- Fast SCSI support on model CF
- 5 MB/sec maximum SCSI bus synchronous rate
- Software controlled configuration resident in BIOS

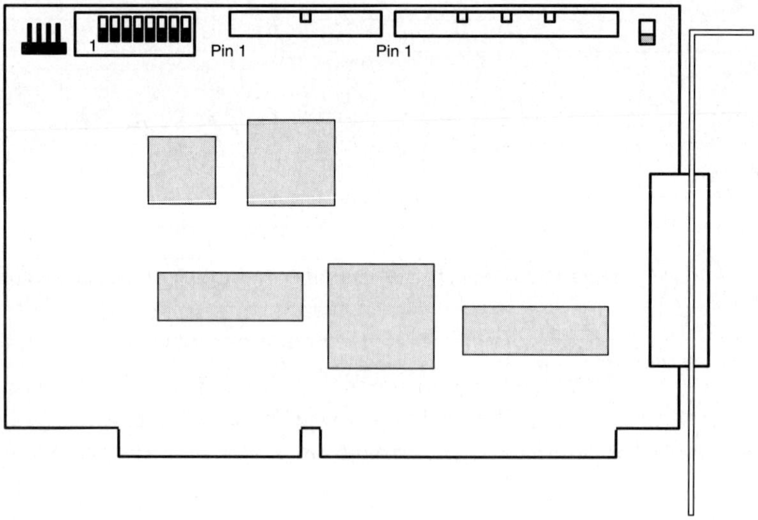

Configuration

Primary SCSI Controller Settings

	IRQ Level	DMA Channel	I/O Port Address	BIOS Address	RAM Address
Factory Defaults	11	5	330	DC000	N/A
Recommended	11	6	330	C8000	N/A

Termination

Termination on the controller is enabled by default. This will work on configurations that do not have devices on both the external and internal SCSI bus cable. If you have SCSI devices on both internal and external cables, you can disable the controller termination with the software configuration program.

Hard-Disk Preparation

The software configuration program is menu driven and provides for low-level formatting and drive-surface verification.

Configuration Program Notes

The aha driver was updated after Solaris 2.1 was released. The driver update incorporated support for the AHA-1540CF/1542CF fast SCSI HBA. See Appendix A for driver update information.

The AHA-154xC/154xCF boards all have an option that should be disabled using the manufacturer-supplied setup utility. The option to support greater than 1 Gbyte (1024 cylinders) on the disk (Extended BIOS Translation for DOS Drives > 1 GByte) should be disabled.

Disable Synchronous Negotiation for CD–ROM drives, and do not change the default DMA transfer rate unless your motherboard specifically supports it.

Note: *The DMA transfer rate for the 1540CF should be left at the default unless your motherboard supports higher rates. Use of the built-in configuration program and DIP switch assignments are documented in the installation guide that comes with the Adaptec 154x board.*

BIOS Setup (Control–A hot key)

The configuration on this model of SCSI adapter is partly software controlled by the BIOS code resident on the adapter. The I/O port and BIOS address must be set on the configuration switch SW1, but other settings are accessed through the BIOS routines.

You can access the configuration software by pressing Ctrl–A while the system is booting (watch the screen at boot time for a message prompting you to press Ctrl–A). You can also access the configuration software by using a debug program to run the adapter configuration program.

Use the command: `g=c800:6`

Copy any optional DOS software to your DOS partition for use with DOS applications.

Jumpers and Switches

I/O port and BIOS address must be set using switch SW1 on the board.

BIOS Address	SW1			I/O Port Address	SW1			Floppy Disk Controller	SW1	Termination	SW1
	8	7	8		2	3	4		5		1
*DC000	0	0	0	*330–333	0	0	0	*Enabled	0	Installed	1
D8000	1	0	0	334–337	1	0	0	Disabled	1	*Software controlled	0
D4000	0	1	0	230–233	0	1	0				
D0000	1	1	0	234–237	1	1	0				
CC000	0	0	1	130–133	0	0	1				
C8000	1	0	1	134–137	1	0	1				
Reserved	0	1	1	Reserved	0	1	1				
Disabled	1	1	1	Reserved	1	1	1				

Switches: 0=off
1=on
Jumpers: 0=not installed
1=installed

*=Default Settings

ADAPTEC AHA-1740/1742A

Features

- SCSI-II compatible
- EISA to 10MB/sec fast SCSI-II devices
- Host memory 32-bit wide burst transfer rates of 33MB/sec
- Programmable active SCSI termination

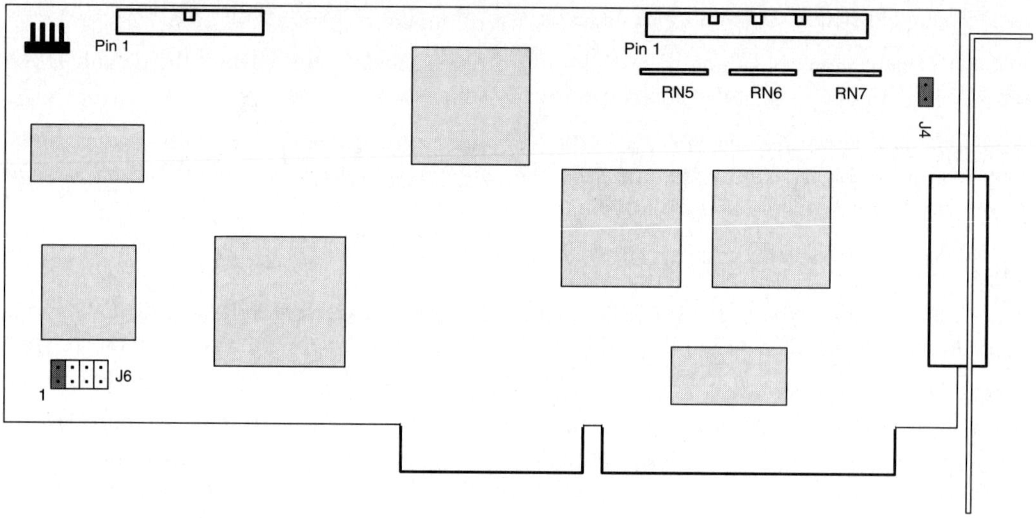

Configuration

Primary SCSI Controller Settings

	IRQ Level	DMA Channel	I/O Port Address	BIOS Address	RAM Address
Factory Defaults	11	N/A	N/A	D8000	N/A
Recommended	N/A	N/A	N/A	C8000	N/A

Termination

Termination is enabled, and resistor packs RN5, RN6, and RN7 are installed on the controller by default. These three resistor packs must be manually removed or inserted to set termination on the controller.

Hard-Disk Preparation

The diskettes shipped with the controller contain low-level format and diagnostic utility programs.

EISA Configuration Files

The EISA configuration files are provided on floppy diskette. You cannot configure your controller without the files contained on the diskette. Do not lose your utility diskette! The EISA configuration program is accessed by booting from the DOS partition or from a DOS diskette.

Floppy Controller

The floppy controller on the 1742 is enabled with Jumper J4. Remove J4 to disable the floppy controller.

Floppy Controller	Jumper J4
Disabled	0
*Enabled	1

Switches: 0=off
1=on
Jumpers: 0=not installed
1=installed

*=Default Settings

Configuration Notes

The adapter must be in slots 1 to 8 of the motherboard. Solaris x86 will not boot if the HBA is not found in one of these slots.

Enable synchronous negotiation for all targets except the NEC Intersect CD–ROM 74/84.

Operating this SCSI adapter in 154x emulation mode may cause data corruption. Use enhanced mode. Use the Adaptec EISA NVRAM DOS download utility to change the following three fields:

1. Host Adapter Interface Mode
2. Standard Mode Resource Selection I/O Port Definition
3. Standard Mode Resource Selection DMA Channel Definition

ADAPTEC AHA-2740/2742 AHA-2740T/2742T

Features

- SCSI-II compatible
- Twin Channel (T models support up to 14 devices)
- EISA to 10MB/sec fast SCSI-II devices
- Host memory 32-bit wide burst transfer rates of 33MB/sec
- Programmable active SCSI termination

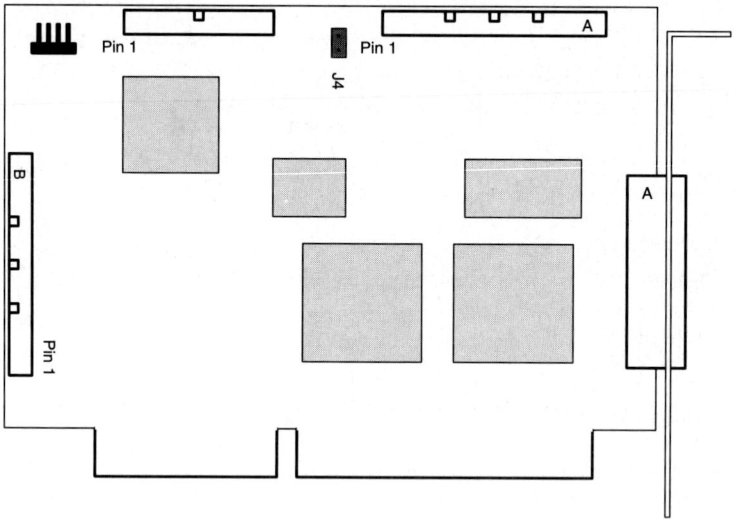

Configuration

Primary SCSI Controller Settings

	IRQ Level	DMA Channel	I/O Port Address	BIOS Address	RAM Address
Factory Defaults	11	N/A	N/A	D8000	N/A
Recommended	11	5	N/A	D8000	N/A

Termination

Termination is controlled through the EISA configuration program. On twin channel controllers, termination for each channel (SCSI bus) is independently controlled. Only the A channel allows for external SCSI bus connection, and only the A channel can contain the bootable disk.

Hard-Disk Preparation

The diskettes shipped with the adapter contain EISA configuration files, a low-level format utility, and a diagnostic utility.

Jumpers and Switches

There are no jumpers and switches to set, except for J4 (floppy enable jumper) on models with floppy controllers. The default IRQ and BIOS address settings are used by the controller until the EISA configuration program is used to change them. BIOS address C8000 is not a valid choice on this controller. You can use the default BIOS address D8000.

The esa driver supports the Adaptec AHA-2740 and AHA-2742 host bus adapters, and motherboards that integrate the Adaptec AIC-7770 chip such as the Intel Express.

For systems with two channels, whether on the motherboard or on the EISA 274x controller, make sure the boot device is on the first channel (A), and is target 0. The hard-disk drive that will be used to boot Solaris should be connected to channel A.

Run the BIOS configuration and make sure that the BIOS support for drives greater than 1 GByte is disabled and that BIOS support for more than two drives is disabled.

Note: *If you have a motherboard with an AMI BIOS, the Adaptec 2740 EISA configuration file requires version 2.01 or later of the AMI EISA configuration utility.*

EISA Configuration

This controller is configured using configuration files provided on floppy diskette.

The EISA configuration program is accessed by booting from the DOS partition or from a DOS diskette.

The 2740T and 2742T have a twin SCSI interface. The two SCSI busses are designated A and B. The A bus has both internal and external connections, while the B bus has only internal bus connection.

Floppy Controller

The floppy controller on the 2742 and 2742T is enabled with Jumper J4. Remove J4 to disable the floppy controller.

Floppy Controller 2742/2742T only	**Jumper J4**
Disabled	0
*Enabled	1

Switches: 0=off
1=on
Jumpers: 0=not installed
1=installed

*=Default Settings

BUSLOGIC BT445S

Features

- SCSI-II compatible
- VL bus 32-bit master DMA
- 10MB/sec Synchronous fast SCSI-II
- Floppy controller

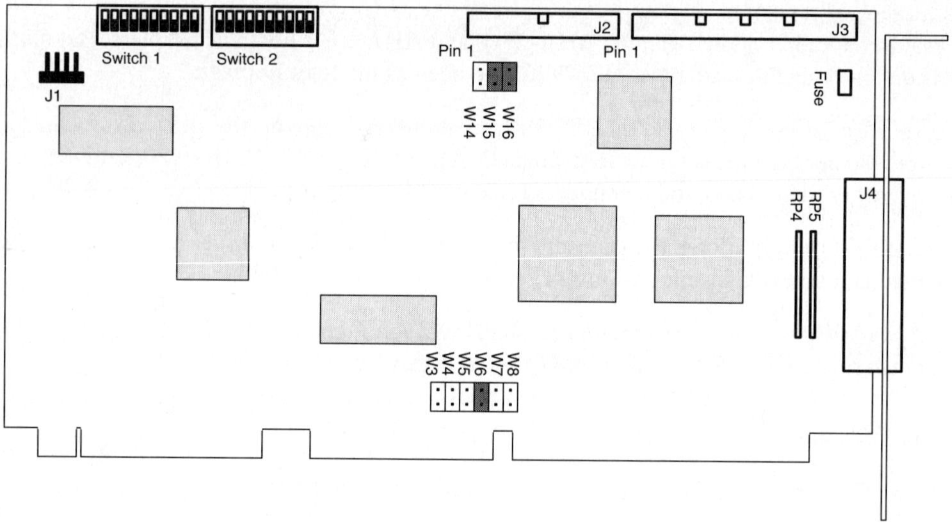

Configuration

Primary SCSI Controller Settings

	IRQ Level	DMA Channel	I/O Port Address	BIOS Address	RAM Address
Factory Defaults	11	n/a	330	DC000	N/A
Recommended	11	n/a	334	C8000	N/A

Termination

Resistor packs RP4 and RP5 are manually inserted or removed to set termination on the controller. The controller is shipped with terminators installed.

Hard-Disk Preparation

Low-level format and diagnostic utilities are provided on floppy diskettes.

Jumpers and Switches

Configuration is done manually by a combination of jumpers and switches.

Solaris 2.1 supported the BusLogic SCSI HBA with the `aha` driver. A new `blogic` driver is now available on the driver update diskette. See Appendix A for information on driver update diskettes. With the `blogic` driver, the BusLogic SCSI HBAs can be used in native mode.

Note: *ISA Bus models of BusLogic boards must have their IRQ set in two places–with switches and jumpers. The Host Interrupt Request switch and the Host Interrupt Channel jumper must have settings that match or the board will not work.*

Set the I/O Address on the board to 334. The board will automatically use the `aha` driver if the address is 330 and the `blogic` driver if the address is 334. No other I/O Addresses are valid.

SCSI Target ID	Switch 1		
	1	2	3
0	0	0	0
1	1	0	0
2	0	1	0
3	1	1	0
4	0	0	1
5	1	0	1
6	0	1	1
*7	1	1	1

CPU Clock Mhz	Switch 1		
	8	9	10
20	1	1	0
25	0	1	0
33,40	1	1	1
50	1	0	1
DX2/50	0	1	0
*DX2/66	1	1	1

BIOS Address	Switch 2	
	4	5
C8000	0	0
Disable	1	0
D8000	0	1
*DC000	1	1

I/O Port Address	Switch 2		
	1	2	3
Reserved	0	0	0
134–137	1	0	0
234–237	0	1	0
334–337	1	1	0
Reserved	0	0	1
130–133	1	0	1
230–233	0	1	1
*330–333	1	1	1

Synchronous Negotiation	Switch 1
	6
Enabled	0
*Disabled	1

DOS Disk >1GB	Switch 1
	5
Enabled	0
*Disabled	1

Synchronous Max Rate	Switch 1
	7
10MB/s	0
*5MB/s	1

SCSI Bus Parity	Switch 1
	4
Disable Parity	0
*Enable Parity	1

IRQ Level	Jumper
15	W3
14	W4
12	W5
*11	W6
10	W7
9	W8

IRQ Level	Switch 2		
	6	7	8
Res	0	0	0
Res	1	0	0
15	0	1	0
14	1	1	0
12	0	0	1
9	1	0	1
10	0	1	1
*11	1	1	1

Floppy Controller	Jumper		
	W14	W15	W16
Disabled	0	0	0
*Enable Primary	0	1	1
Enable Secondary	1	1	1

Switches: 0=off
1=on
Jumpers: 0=not installed
1=installed

*=Default Settings

BUSLOGIC BT545S

Features

- SCSI-II compatible
- Fast SCSI-II
- Floppy controller
- ISA bus

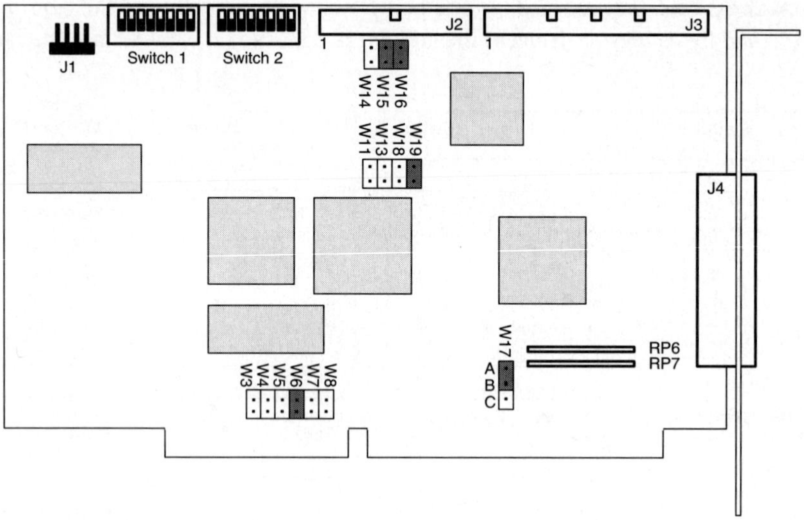

Configuration

Primary SCSI Controller Settings

	IRQ Level	DMA Channel	I/O Port Address	BIOS Address	RAM Address
Factory Defaults	11	5	330	DC000	N/A
Recommended	11	5	334	C8000	N/A

Termination

Resistor packs RP6 and RP7 are manually inserted or removed to set termination on the controller. The controller is shipped with terminators installed.

Hard-Disk Preparation

Low-level format and diagnostic utilities are provided on floppy diskettes.

Jumpers and Switches

Configuration is done manually by a combination of jumpers and switches.

Solaris 2.1 supported the BusLogic SCSI HBA with the `aha` driver. A new `blogic` driver is now available on the driver update diskette. See Appendix A for information on driver update diskettes. With the `blogic` driver, the BusLogic SCSI HBAs can be used in native mode.

Host DMA Channel	Switch 1 (7 8)	BIOS Address	Switch 2 (4 5)	SCSI Target ID	Switch 1 (1 2 3)	I/O Port Address	Switch 2 (1 2 3)
Disabled	0 0	C8000	0 0	0	0 0 0	Reserved	0 0 0
7	1 0	Disable	1 0	1	1 0 0	134–137	1 0 0
6	0 1	D8000	0 1	2	0 1 0	234–237	0 1 0
*5	1 1	*DC000	1 1	3	1 1 0	334–337	1 1 0
				4	0 0 1	Reserved	0 0 1
				5	1 0 1	130–133	1 0 1
				6	0 1 1	230–233	0 1 1
				*7	1 1 1	*330–333	1 1 1

Synchronous Max Rate	Jumper W19	Synchronous Negotiation	Switch 1 (6)	DOS Disk >1GB	Switch 1 (5)	SCSI Bus Parity	Switch 1 (4)
10MB/s	0	Enabled	0	Enabled	0	Disable Parity	0
*5MB/s	1	*Disabled	1	*Disabled	1	*Enable Parity	1

IRQ Level	Jumper	IRQ Level	Switch 2 (6 7 8)	Host Bus Speed	Jumper (W11 W13)	Floppy Controller	Jumper (W14 W15 W16)
15	W3	Res	0 0 0	*5.0 MB/s	0 0	Disabled	0 0 0
14	W4	Res	1 0 0	5.7 MB/s	0 1	*Enable Primary	0 1 1
12	W5	15	0 1 0	6.7 MB/s	1 0	Enable Secondary	1 1 1
*11	W6	14	1 1 0	8.0 MB/s	1 1		
10	W7	12	0 0 1				
9	W8	9	1 0 1				
		10	0 1 1				
		*11	1 1 1				

Host I/O Read	Jumper W17	Reserved	Jumper W18
*Enable	A–B	*not used	0
Disable	B–C		

Switches: 0=off
1=on
Jumpers: 0=not installed
1=installed
*=Default Settings

Note: *ISA Bus models of BusLogic boards must have their IRQ set in two places–with switches and jumpers. The Host Interrupt Request switch and the Host Interrupt Channel jumper must have settings that match or the board will not work.*

Set the I/O Address on the board to 334. The board will automatically use the `aha` driver if the address is 330 and the `blogic` driver if the address is 334. No other I/O Addresses are valid. Adapter settings not listed above may be used in their default settings.

BUSLOGIC BT542B

Features

- SCSI-II compatible
- Fast SCSI-II
- Floppy-disk controller

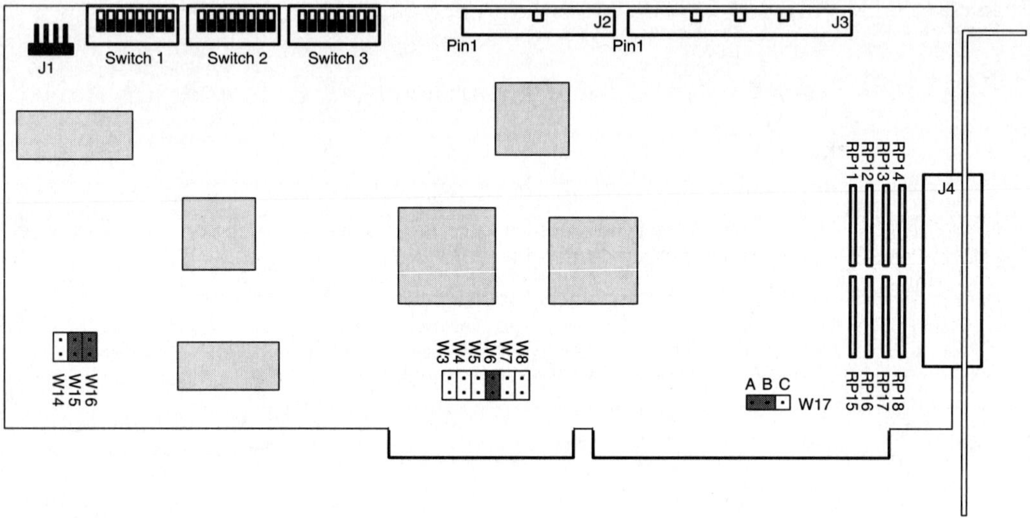

Configuration

Primary SCSI Controller Settings

	IRQ Level	DMA Channel	I/O Port Address	BIOS Address	RAM Address
Factory Defaults	11	5	330	DC000	N/A
Recommended	11	5	334	C8000	N/A

Termination

Resistor packs RP11 through RP18 are manually inserted or removed to set termination on the controller. The controller is shipped with terminators installed.

Hard-Disk Preparation

Low-level format and diagnostic utilities are provided on floppy diskettes.

Jumpers and Switches

Configuration is done manually by a combination of jumpers and switches.

I/O Port Address	Switch 2	Host DMA Channel	Switch 1	SCSI Target ID	Switch 1	BIOS Address	Switch 3
	1 2 3		7 8		1 2 3		3 4 5
Reserved	0 0 0	Disabled	0 0	0	0 0 0	Disabled	0 0 0
134–137	1 0 0	7	1 0	1	1 0 0	Reserved	1 0 0
234–237	0 1 0	6	0 1	2	0 1 0	C8000	0 1 0
334–337	1 1 0	*5	1 1	3	1 1 0	CC000	1 1 0
Reserved	0 0 1			4	0 0 1	D0000	0 0 1
130–133	1 0 1			5	1 0 1	D4000	1 0 1
230–233	0 1 1			6	0 1 1	D8000	0 1 1
*330–333	1 1 1			*7	1 1 1	*DC000	1 1 1

Synchronous Negotiation	Switch 1	DOS Disk >1GB	Switch 1	Synchronous Max Rate	Switch 3	SCSI Bus Parity	Switch 1
	6		5		6		4
Enabled	0	Enabled	0	10MB/s	0	Disable Parity	0
*Disabled	1	*Disabled	1	*5MB/s	1	*Enable Parity	1

IRQ Level	Jumper	IRQ Level	Switch 2	Host I/O Read	Jumper	Floppy Controller	Jumper
			6 7 8		W17		W14 W15 W16
15	W3	Res	0 0 0	*Enable	A–B	Disabled	0 0 0
14	W4	Res	1 0 0	Disable	B–C	*Enable Primary	0 1 1
12	W5	15	0 1 0			Enable Secondary	1 1 1
*11	W6	14	1 1 0				
10	W7	12	0 0 1				
9	W8	9	1 0 1				
		10	0 1 1				
		*11	1 1 1				

Host Bus Speed	Switch 3	Reserved	Switch 3
	1 2		7 8
*5.0 MB/s	1 1	*not used	0 0
5.7 MB/s	0 1		
6.7 MB/s	1 0		
8.0 MB/s	0 0		

Switches: 0=off
1=on
Jumpers: 0=not installed
1=installed

*=Default Settings

Solaris 2.1 supported the BusLogic SCSI HBA with the `aha` driver. A new `blogic` driver is now available on the driver update diskette. See Appendix A for information on driver update diskettes. With the `blogic` driver, the BusLogic SCSI HBAs can be used in native mode.

Note: *ISA Bus models of BusLogic boards must have their IRQ set in two places–with switches and jumpers. The Host Interrupt Request switch and the Host Interrupt Channel jumper must have settings that match or the board will not work.*

Set the I/O Address on the board to 334. The board will automatically use the `aha` driver if the address is 330 and the `blogic` driver if the address is 334. No other I/O Addresses are valid. Adapter settings not listed above may be used in their default settings.

BUSLOGIC BT742A

Features

- SCSI-II compatible
- Floppy controller
- EISA bus transfer up to 33MB/second

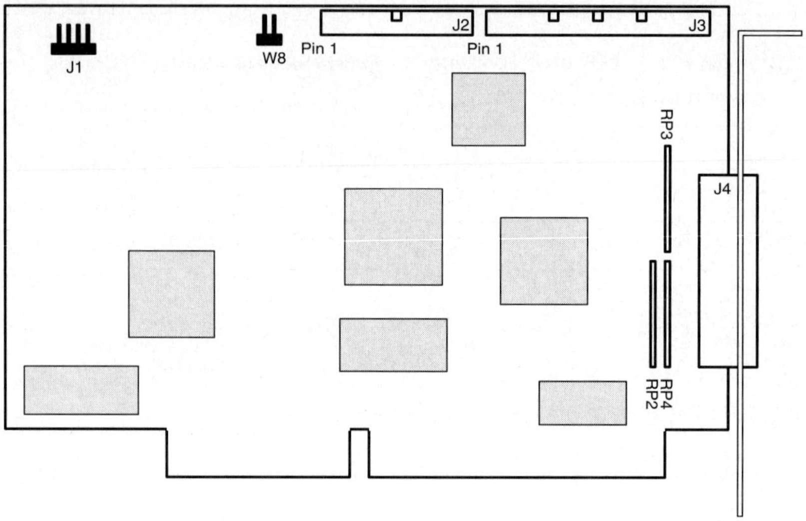

Configuration

Primary SCSI Controller Settings

	IRQ Level	DMA Channel	I/O Port Address	BIOS Address	RAM Address
Factory Defaults	11	5	330	DC000	N/A
Recommended	11	5	334	C8000	N/A

Termination

Resistor packs RP2, RP3, and RP4 are manually inserted or removed to set termination on the controller. The controller is shipped with terminators installed.

Hard-Disk Preparation

Low-level format and diagnostic utilities are provided on floppy diskettes.

Jumpers and Switches

There are no jumpers or switches to set.

EISA Configuration

The EISA configuration files are provided on floppy diskette. You cannot configure your controller without the files contained on the diskette. The EISA configuration program is accessed by booting from the DOS partition or from a DOS diskette. Do not lose your utility diskette!

The default IRQ and BIOS address settings are used by the controller until the EISA configuration program is used to change them.

Solaris 2.1

Solaris 2.1 supports the BusLogic SCSI HBA with the `aha` driver. A newer `blogic` driver is available on the driver update diskette. See Appendix A for information on driver update diskettes. With the `blogic` driver, the BusLogic SCSI HBAs can be used in native mode.

Set the I/O Address to 334. The board will automatically use the `aha` driver if the address is 330 and the `blogic` driver if the address is 334. No other I/O Addresses are valid.

Adapter settings not listed above may be used in their default settings.

BUSLOGIC BT747S

Features

- SCSI-II compatible
- 32-bit Fast SCSI-II
- Floppy-disk controller (2.88MB support)

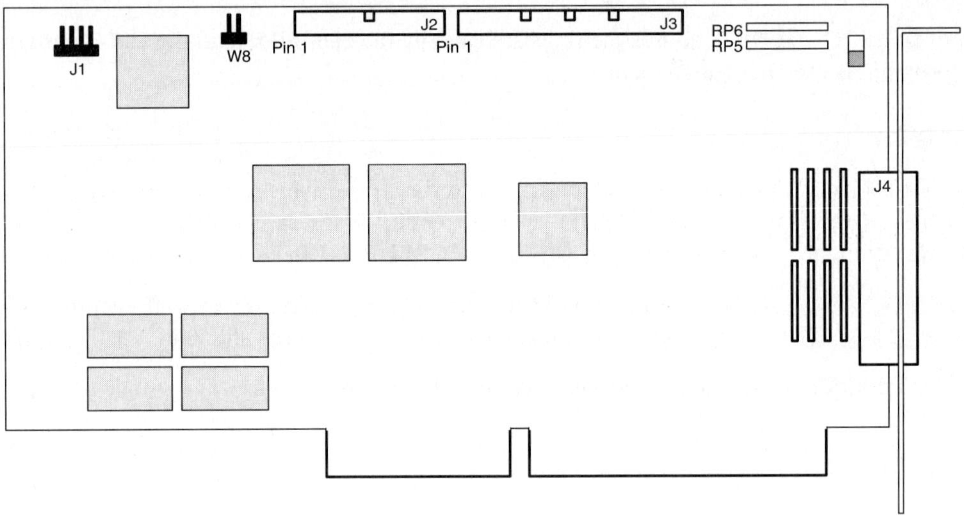

Configuration

Primary SCSI Controller Settings

	IRQ Level	DMA Channel	I/O Port Address	BIOS Address	RAM Address
Factory Defaults	11	5	330	DC000	N/A
Recommended	11	5	334	C8000	N/A

Termination

Resistor packs RP5 and RP6 are manually inserted or removed to set termination on the controller. The controller is shipped with terminators installed.

Hard-Disk Preparation

Low-level format and diagnostic utilities are provided on floppy diskettes.

Jumpers and Switches

There are no jumpers or switches to set.

EISA Configuration

The EISA configuration files are provided on floppy diskette. You cannot configure your controller without the files contained on the diskette. The EISA configuration program is accessed by booting from the DOS partition or from a DOS diskette. Do not lose your utility diskette!

The default IRQ and BIOS address settings are used by the controller until the EISA configuration program is used to change them.

Solaris 2.1

Solaris 2.1 supports the BusLogic SCSI HBA with the `aha` driver. A newer `blogic` driver is available on the driver update diskette. See Appendix A for information on driver update diskettes. With the `blogic` driver, the BusLogic SCSI HBAs can be used in native mode.

Set the I/O Address on the board to 334. The board will automatically use the `aha` driver if the address is 330 and the `blogic` driver if the address is 334. No other I/O Addresses are valid.

Adapter settings not listed above may be used in their default settings.

DPT 2011/2021

Features

- SCSI-II compatible
- ISA
- Optional cache memory
- Optional floppy controller

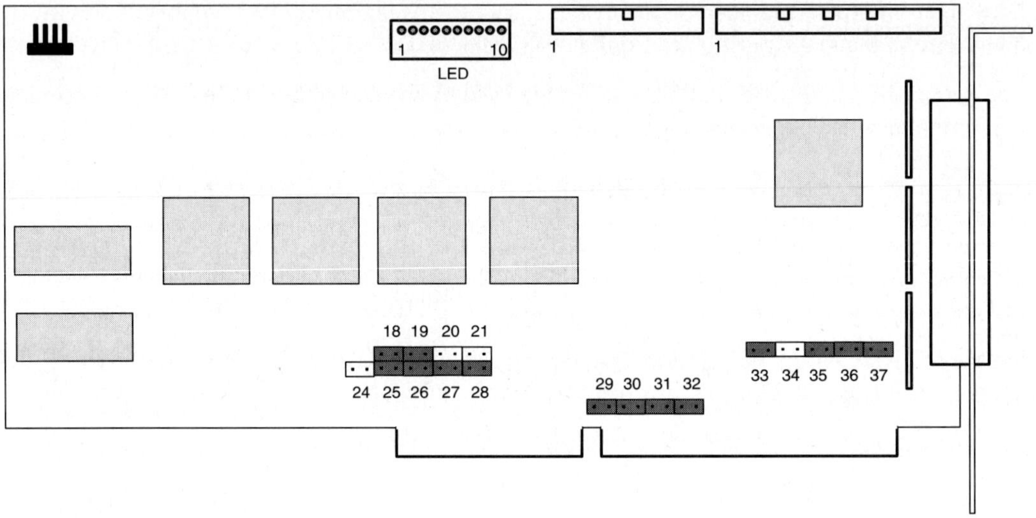

Configuration

Primary SCSI Controller Settings

	IRQ Level	DMA Channel	I/O Port Address	BIOS Address	RAM Address
Factory Defaults	14	5	1F0	C8000	N/A
Recommended	15	5	1F0	C8000	N/A

Termination

Resistor packs are manually inserted or removed to set termination on the controller. The controller is shipped with terminators installed.

Configuration Notes

The `dpt` driver, which supports the DPT 2011 ISA host bus adapter, also supports the DPT 2021. To install the DPT 2021 you must run the DPT SCSI Storage Manager Utility, DPTMGR, under DOS and select Solaris as the operating system. This must be done prior to installing Solaris.

Note: *When using the Solaris driver update diskette an error message similar to the following may be displayed while DPTMGR is running:*

```
Unable to find any drivers in the DRIVERS Directory
```

This message can be ignored. The driver will be installed when the Solaris 2.1 Driver Update software is installed.

A system with a DPT 2021 or 2022 HBA installed may hang when the command "`uadmin` 2 x" is run. `uadmin` is called by both the `reboot` and `halt` commands.

Jumpers and Switches

The DPT 2021 ISA jumper settings should be set as follows:

- IRQ 12 or 15, (first controller should be at IRQ 15)
- I/O Address 1F0 or 170

Ensure that the controller board is properly installed in any slot between 1 and 7. Slots 8 and above are not supported.

SCSI Target ID	Jumper Y 25	18	26	I/O Port Address	Jumper Y 35	33	BIOS Address	Jumper Y 36	37	LED Legend	LED #
0	0	0	0	*1F0–1F8	1	1	*C8000	1	1	Busy	1
1	1	0	0	170–178	1	0	D8000	1	0	CPU bus xfer to controller	2
2	0	1	0	330–338	0	1	DC000	0	1	CPU bus xfer from controller	3
3	1	1	0	230–238	0	0	Disabled	0	0	Cache hit	4
4	0	0	1							Disk read-ahead active	5
5	1	0	1							Disk read	6
6	0	1	1							Disk write	7
*7	1	1	1							Controller reset	8
										Controller IRQ pending	9
										DRQ asserted to CPU	10

Host DMA Channel	Jumper Y 31	32	IRQ Level	Jumper Y 29	30	LA and SA Line Driver	Jumper Y 19	Floppy Controller	Jumper Y 20
*5	1	1	*14	1	1	LA17–19	0	Disabled	1
6	1	0	15	1	0	*SA/LA 17–19	1	*Enable	0
7	0	1	12	0	1				
0	0	0	Disable	0	0				

EPROM Size	Jumper Y 23	Speed	Jumper Y 27	Memory	Jumper Y 21	28	Floppy Address	Jumper Y 34
*256K	Bottom	*4MB/sec	1	*16 bit	0	1	370	1
512K	Top	5MB/sec	0	8 or 16 bit	1	0	*3F0	0

*=Default Settings

Switches: 0=off
1=on
Jumpers: 0=not installed
1=installed

DPT 2012/2022

Features

- SCSI-II compatible
- EISA
- Optional cache memory
- Optional floppy controller

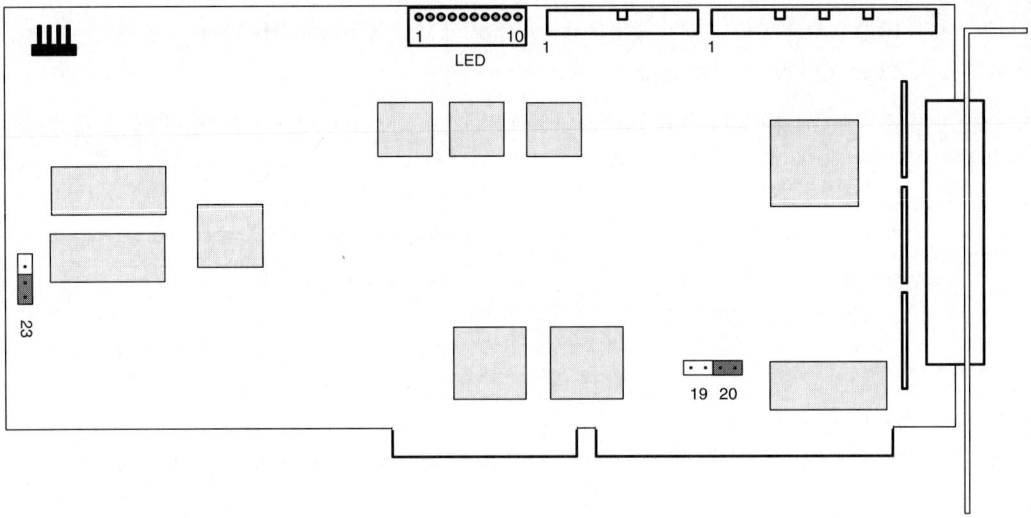

Configuration

Primary SCSI Controller Settings

	IRQ Level	DMA Channel	I/O Port Address	BIOS Address	RAM Address
Factory Defaults	14	5			N/A
Recommended	15	5		C8000	N/A

Termination

Resistor packs are manually inserted or removed to enable and disable termination on the controller. The controller is shipped with terminators installed.

Configuration Notes

The dpt driver, which supports the DPT 2012 EISA host bus adapter, also supports the DPT 2022. To install the DPT 2022 you must run the DPT SCSI Storage Manager Utility, DPTMGR, under DOS and select Solaris as the operating system. This must be done prior to installing Solaris.

Note: *The PROM revisions on the board should be the latest. The BIOS Prom must be at revision level 5C and the SmartROM Prom must be at revision level 2C. Earlier revisions (A or B Proms) will cause problems with Solaris. The Storage Manager Program revision should be rev 1C. If your board has an earlier release of firmware, contact your DPT representative for a BIOS/SmartROM upgrade.*

Jumpers and Switches

Ensure that the controller board is properly installed in any slot between 1 and 7. Slots 8 and above are not supported in this release.

When using the EISA configuration program make sure the following parameters are set as shown:

- WD1003 Boot Address — Enabled at Primary
- IRQ — 12 or 15 (first controller should be at IRQ 15)
- Interrupts — Edge-triggered interrupts
- SCSI BIOS ROM Address — Default
- HBA SCSI ID — Default 7

EISA Configuration

This controller is configured using configuration files provided on floppy diskette.

The EISA configuration program is accessed by booting from the DOS partition oEr from a DOS diskette.

EPROM Size	Jumper Y	8K/16K Select	Jumper Y	Floppy Controller	Jumper Y	LED Legend	LED #
	23		19		20		
*256K	Bottom	*8K	0	Disabled	1	Busy	1
512K	Top	16K	1	*Enable	0	CPU bus xfer to controller	2
						CPU bus xfer from controller	3
						Cache hit	4
						Disk read-ahead active	5
						Disk read	6
						Disk write	7
						Controller reset	8
						Controller IRQ pending	9
						DRQ asserted to CPU	10

*=Default Settings

Switches: 0=off
1=on
Jumpers: 0=not installed
1=installed

TRANTOR T348 MINI-SCSI PARALLEL HBA

Features

- SCSI-II compatible
- Uses parallel port
- No jumpers and switches

Configuration

The Trantor T348 is supported on the Solaris *driver update diskettes*. If your version of Solaris does not support this adapter, get the latest driver update diskette before installing Solaris. See Appendix A for more information on driver update diskettes.

The Trantor T348 Parallel SCSI HBA is easy to install. It has no switches, no software-settable options, and does not require any manual configuration. However, the adapter may require special cabling to obtain electrical power and to connect to certain devices.

The Trantor MiniSCSI Plus host adapter obtains its electrical power from the TERMPWR signal on the SCSI cable. The adapter will not receive power and will not work unless the first (or only) device connected to it supplies TERMPWR. The T348 and attached devices must also be plugged in and powered on at boot time in order to be available during that session.

The Trantor MiniSCSI Plus HBA ends in a male SCSI-I connector, suitable for plugging into a SCSI-I device. If you want to connect it to a SCSI-II device, you will need a SCSI-I to SCSI-II cable (which has a male SCSI-I connector on one end and a male SCSI-II connector on the other end) and a SCSI-I female–to–female adapter (to connect the male end of the T348 to the male end of the SCSI-I to SCSI-II cable).

The Solaris T348 `trantor` driver does not support the Trantor T338 or T358.

Solaris does not support concurrent use of other parallel devices on the same port as the Trantor T348 or on the T348 pass-through port. If you want to switch between the T348 and some other parallel port device, such as a printer or Ethernet adapter, shut down Solaris and power off the computer and any SCSI devices attached to the T348. With the power turned off, disconnect the old device and connect the new one. If switching to the T348, power up any SCSI devices you intend to use. Turn on the power to the computer and do a reconfigure reboot.

If the SCSI devices attached to the T348 fail to respond after a reconfigure reboot, and the parallel port had previously been used for a different device, it might be necessary to do a second reconfigure reboot. This situation occurs when the driver from the previous device interferes with the T348 driver's attempt to detect the presence of the T348 device.

Note: *If you need to reconfigure the system later to add other devices, make sure the T348 and all its devices are plugged in and powered up; otherwise they will be removed from the configuration. If you accidentally reconfigure without the T348 plugged in, plug the T348 in and repeat the reconfiguration process.*

AT/IDE CONTROLLERS

The AT bus IDE (Intelligent Drive Electronics) controllers and disk drives are lower performance alternatives to the more expensive, high-performance SCSI disk drives and controllers. IDE drives are easy to configure and install, but only one IDE controller and two IDE disk drives are allowed on a system.

Configuration of IDE hard disks is done using the standard system BIOS setup program. This is an easy process that involves setting the Drive C and Drive D parameters in the standard CMOS setup. Some BIOS setups have auto disk configuration options that will detect your IDE drives and correctly set the CMOS.

Performance and low capacity are usually drawbacks when using the IDE interface. There are, however, some faster IDE adapters that use the VESA local bus and disk caching to achieve higher performance. The IDE interface is a good choice for a low cost desktop system that will not suffer from limited disk capacity and slower disk performance.

Primary Controller

It is important to note that if you install the IDE adapter and hard disk in your system, the IDE interface will always be the primary disk controller, and the system BIOS will try to boot from the IDE master disk. If you add a SCSI controller to your system, the SCSI controller will be your secondary disk controller.

This is important when you consider the operating system will have to boot off of a partition on the IDE drive. If you are planning to use additional SCSI controllers or drives, you will still be required to use the IDE drive for the boot partition unless you disable the IDE interface and remove it from the CMOS drive-type table.

When you are installing the Solaris operating system, the IDE drives will not be listed as boot devices during the initial boot sequence. Only devices on the SCSI controller or network adapter will be listed as possible boot devices. This is normal. The IDE drives will not appear as options until the Solaris installation disk partitioning menu appears.

Master or Slave

The first IDE drive installed is designated as the master and the second drive is designated a slave. IDE drives provide jumper or switch settings to enable the master/slave configuration. There is no other addressing required when using IDE adapters.

Interrupt Request

The AT bus IDE adapter will default to IRQ 14 for the hard-disk controller and IRQ 6 for the floppy disk controller. The IDE adapter does not require a BIOS memory address, RAM address, or any other settings that may conflict with other boards.

Solaris 2.1 Technical Notes

IDE Drive Geometry

Regardless of your CMOS IDE drive-type geometry setting, Solaris x86 installation will succeed, since x86 does not rely on the "TYPE" definition under CMOS to define the geometry of IDE drives.

If the "TYPE" definition of your IDE drive is incorrect (does not match the physical geometry written on the drive) under CMOS configuration, you may not be able to reboot the system after Solaris x86 installation is completed on the IDE drive. If this is a problem on your system, you will get an error message such as:

```
Missing partition boot record
```

Make sure you set the CMOS drive type to reflect the actual geometry of the drive. Refer to your drive documentation or contact the manufacturer for the information.

If you have this problem on your system, you may be able to correct it by using the Solaris x86 installation program to create both the DOS partition and the Solaris partition. Using the DOS `fdisk` utility to create the DOS partition is not recommended in this situation.

Appendix D

VIDEO ADAPTER CONFIGURATION

Video Adapter Specifications

When you match a monitor to your video adapter, you need to know the following key monitor specifications:

- Resolution in pixels (horizontal x vertical)
- Interlaced or noninterlaced (scans twice or once to complete a display)
- Vertical refresh rate (how many times per second the screen is scanned)

You must know the three characteristics listed above to match your monitor to your video adapter card. I have included a sample video adapter specification to give you an idea of how to make a simple chart for your own video adapter. You will need such a chart when you are trying to find the best monitor match for your adapter.

For more details on resolution, interlacing, and vertical refresh rate, refer to Appendix L.

Sample Video Adapter Specification

ATI Ultra/Vantage	Resolution	I	NI	VF (Hz)
	VGA 640x480		x	60
	800x600		x	56
	800x600		x	60
	800x600		x	70
	800x600		x	72
	1024x768		x	60
	1024x768		x	66
	1024x768		x	70
	1024x768		x	72
	1024x768	x		87
I=interlaced NI=noninterlaced VF=vertical frequency				

My Own Video Adapter

Use the template provided below to list the specifications for your video adapter board. This will be helpful during installation and configuration. You will need to match your monitor to your adapter by choosing the best combination of resolution and refresh rate.

	Resolution	I	NI	VF (Hz)

COMPATIBLE VIDEO ADAPTER CARDS

The following adapters and video chips have been tested by SunSoft.

Manufacturer	Model	Description
ATI	Mach32	(1280x1024, 256 colors)
ATI	Graphics Ultra	ATI Mach 8
ATI	8514 Ultra	ATI Mach 8
ATI	VGA Wonder XL	ATI Mach 8
ATI	Ultra Pro	ATI Mach 32
ATI	Ultra Plus	ATI Mach 32
Compaq	QVision 1024/I	Compaq QVision
Compaq	LTE	(640x480, 256 colors)
CompuAdd	Hi–Res	Tseng Labs ET–4000
Dell	SE/DE Series	Tseng Labs ET–4000
Dell	L/M/ME/T	S386C805
Dell	L Series/OptiPlex	ET4000/W32
Dell	L Series/OptiPlex	ET4000/W32i

Manufacturer	Model	Description
Diamond	Speedstar Pro	
Genoa	Super VGA 7000	Tseng Labs ET–4000
IBM	XGA, XGA–2	IBM XGA
IBM	Model VC550	Easy Option
Miro	MiroMagic	
Orchid	ProDesigner IIs	Tseng Labs ET–4000
Orchid	Fahrenheit 1280	S386C911
Orchid	Fahrenheit VA	S386C801
Paradise	Accelerator for Windows	WD90C31
SPEA	V7–Mercury	PMI file
STB	PowerGraph Ergo	Tseng Labs ET–4000
Trident	8900C	PMI File

PMI FILES

The PMI file is at the heart of the video adapter interaction with the operating system. Each video adapter supported by the operating system has an associated PMI file within the OpenWindows directory structure. The PMI file defines the commands necessary for the operating system to communicate with the video adapter. These PMI files must not be modified.

All you need to know about PMI files is that there must be a PMI file on your file system corresponding to the video adapter on your computer, and that support for new adapters can be added by placing additional new PMI files in the correct PMI file directory. When the `devconfig` or `kdmconfig` (configuration program) is executed, it uses the PMI files to create a list of supported adapters. The list is displayed so that you can select the entry matching your adapter. New PMI files copied to the PMI directory are automatically detected when `devconfig` is executed.

There are at least three PMI directories, and new PMI files must be added to the directory that matches the class of adapter you are adding. "`devconfig`" makes configuration assumptions based on which directory it finds the PMI file. Be sure to put the PMI file in the correct directory or as the saying goes — "You'll be sorry." When you run `devconfig` and select a PMI file that is out of place, you will get unpredictable system hangs!

SOLARIS 2.1 REQUIREMENTS

The Solaris 2.1 environment requires a minimum resolution of 1024x768 to display OpenWindows graphics. Like most rules however, this requirement has an exception. To accommodate the 640x480 VGA resolution of compatible laptop computers, the Solaris x86 operating system can simulate VGA 640x480 resolution. The key word here is "simulate." Solaris 2.1 does not support standard 640x480 VGA graphics. If you do not have a compatible laptop, you cannot run standard VGA resolution.

Installation Choices

The following graphic card options are displayed by the Solaris x86 version 2.1 installation program. The order of the list is as displayed by the installation program. Review the list carefully to find a match for your video adapter.

ATI 8514/A
Dell 486/M & 486ME S3 805 (43Hz vertical refresh)
Orchid Fahrenheit 1280 (43Hz vertical refresh)
Orchid Fahrenheit 1280 (60Hz vertical refresh)
Orchid Fahrenheit 1280 (70Hz vertical refresh)
Orchid Fahrenheit VA (43Hz vertical refresh)
Orchid Fahrenheit VA (60Hz vertical refresh)
Orchid Fahrenheit VA (70Hz vertical refresh)
IBM 8514/A
IBM PS/Valuepoint Display Adapter (43Hz vertical refresh)
ATI VGA Wonder + (43Hz interlaced vertical refresh)
ATI VGA Wonder + (60Hz vertical refresh)
ATI VGA Wonder –6 (43Hz vertical refresh)
ATI VGA Wonder –6 (60Hz vertical refresh)
ATI VGA Wonder –6 (70Hz vertical refresh)
ATI VGA Wonder XL (43Hz interlaced vertical refresh)
ATI VGA Wonder XL (60Hz vertical refresh)
ATI VGA Wonder XL (70Hz vertical refresh)
Cirrus Logic CL–GD542x VGA (1024x768x256x60Hz mode 60h)
Compaq 486C
Compuadd Hi–Rez/Plus VGA (43Hz vertical refresh)
Compuadd Hi–Rez/Plus VGA (60Hz vertical refresh)
Compuadd Hi–Rez/Plus VGA (70Hz vertical refresh)
Dell 433DE & 450DE ET4000 VGA
Genoa 7000 VGA (43Hz interlaced vertical refresh)
Genoa 7000 VGA (60Hz vertical refresh)
Genoa 7000 VGA (72Hz vertical refresh)
Orchid Prodesigner II VGA (43Hz interlaced vertical refresh)
Orchid Prodesigner II VGA (60Hz vertical refresh)
Orchid Prodesigner II VGA (72Hz vertical refresh)
Compaq Prolinea ET4000 VGA
Qvision /1024 Triton VGA 60Hz
Qvision /1024 Triton VGA 66Hz
Qvision /1024 Triton VGA 72Hz
Diamond SpeedStar Plus VGA (43Hz vertical refresh)
Diamond SpeedStar Plus VGA (60Hz vertical refresh)

Diamond SpeedStar Plus VGA (70Hz vertical refresh)
STB Ergo VGA 60Hz
Western Digital WD90C30 and WD90C31 VGA (43Hz interlaced)
Western Digital WD90C30 and WD90C31 VGA (60Hz vertical refresh)
Western Digital WD90C30 and WD90C31 VGA (70Hz vertical refresh)
IBM XGA
ATI VGA Wonder + (70Hz vertical refresh)
Toshiba 4400C portable active matrix TFT 256 colors

SOLARIS 2.4 REQUIREMENTS

Solaris 2.4 supports a greater range of video adapters, including standard VGA 640x480 resolution. 640x480 support may be popular with laptop users, but it is impractical for desktop users. For day-to-day desktop use, you should consider only compatible 1024x768, 256 color video adapters or to a high-end 1280x1024 256 color monitor and video adapter.

Installation Choices

The following graphics card options are displayed by the Solaris x86 version 2.4 installation program. The order of the list is as displayed by the installation program. Review the list carefully to find a match for your video adapter.

16 color 640x480 VGA
16 color 640x480 VGA w/ 800x600 vertical screen
ATI 68800 Mach–32, 60Hz noninterlaced
ATI 68800 Mach–32, 70Hz noninterlaced
ATI 68800 Mach–32, 76Hz noninterlaced
ATI 68800 Mach–32, 87Hz interlaced
ATI 68800 Mach–32, 95Hz interlaced
ATI 8514/A
ATI VGA Wonder XL (43Hz interlaced vertical refresh)
ATI VGA Wonder XL (60Hz vertical refresh)
ATI VGA Wonder XL (70Hz vertical refresh)
ATI VGA Wonder XL–6 (43Hz vertical refresh)
ATI VGA Wonder XL–6 (60Hz vertical refresh)
ATI VGA Wonder XL–6 (70Hz vertical refresh)
ATI VGA Wonder + (43Hz interlaced vertical refresh)
ATI VGA Wonder + (60Hz vertical refresh)
ATI VGA Wonder + (70Hz vertical refresh)
Compaq LTE Lite 4/25C
Cirrus Logic CL–GD542x VGA (1024x768x256x60Hz mode 60h)
Compaq Prolinea ET4000 VGA
Compuadd Hi–Rez/Plus VGA (43Hz vertical refresh)
Compuadd Hi–Rez/Plus VGA (60Hz vertical refresh)
Compuadd Hi–Rez/Plus VGA (70Hz vertical refresh)

Dell 433DE & 450DE ET4000 VGA
Dell 486/M & 486ME S3 805 (43Hz vertical refresh)
Dell L Series, ET4000/w32 (60Hz vertical refresh noninterlaced)
Dell L Series, ET4000/w32 (70Hz vertical refresh noninterlaced)
Dell L Series, ET4000/w32 (87Hz vertical refresh interlaced)
Dell L Series, ET4000/w32i (60Hz vertical refresh noninterlaced)
Dell L Series, ET4000/w32i (70Hz vertical refresh noninterlaced)
Diamond SpeedStar Plus VGA (43Hz vertical refresh)
Diamond SpeedStar Plus VGA (60Hz vertical refresh)
Diamond SpeedStar Plus VGA (70Hz vertical refresh)
Genoa 7000 VGA (43Hz interlaced vertical refresh)
Genoa 7000 VGA (60Hz vertical refresh)
Genoa 7000 VGA (72Hz vertical refresh)
IBM 8514/A
IBM PS/Valuepoint Display Adapter (43Hz vertical refresh)
IBM XGA
IBM XGA II 75Hz
NEC Ultralite Versa 256 color active matrix display
Orchid Fahrenheit VA and 1280 Plus (43Hz vertical refresh)
Orchid Fahrenheit VA and 1280 Plus (60Hz vertical refresh)
Orchid Fahrenheit VA and 1280 Plus (70Hz vertical refresh)
Orchid Prodesigner II VGA (43Hz interlaced vertical refresh)
Orchid Prodesigner II VGA (60Hz vertical refresh)
Orchid Prodesigner II VGA (72Hz vertical refresh)
Orchid Technology Fahrenheit 1280 (43Hz vertical refresh)
Orchid Technology Fahrenheit 1280 (60Hz vertical refresh)
Orchid Technology Fahrenheit 1280 (70Hz vertical refresh)
Pixelworks 8514/A
Qvision /1024 Triton VGA 60Hz
Qvision /1024 Triton VGA 66Hz
Qvision /1024 Triton VGA 72Hz
STB Ergo VGA 60Hz
Toshiba 4400C portable active matrix TFT 256 colors
Toshiba 4600C or AST Powerexec 4/33 SL: WD90C26 256 color TFT
Toshiba 4700 CT or Twinhead Slimnote 486E: WD90C24 256 color TFT
Trident 8900 VGA (60Hz vertical refresh)
V7–Mercury (multiscan 81KHz)
Western Digital WD90C30 and WD90C31 VGA (43Hz interlaced)
Western Digital WD90C30 and WD90C31 VGA (60Hz vertical refresh)
Western Digital WD90C30 and WD90C31 VGA (70Hz vertical refresh)
micro Magic 8514A

Support for additional video adapters may be available on SunSoft supplemental driver diskettes. Please refer to Appendix A for more information concerning the availability of supplemental driver diskettes and PMI files.

ORCHID

Orchid makes several adapters that are compatible with Solaris x86. I have two Orchid boards that I use regularly. The VESA local bus version is my favorite.

- ProDesigner II
- Fahrenheit 1280/1280+
- Fahrenheit VA/VLB

Configuration Notes

- Match the adapter to the monitor
- Add memory if necessary
- Leave other defaults alone

Supported Configurations on Solaris x86 Installation Program

Orchid Fahrenheit VA and 1280 Plus (43Hz vertical refresh)
Orchid Fahrenheit VA and 1280 Plus (60Hz vertical refresh)
Orchid Fahrenheit VA and 1280 Plus (70Hz vertical refresh)
Orchid ProDesigner II VGA (43Hz interlaced vertical refresh)
Orchid ProDesigner II VGA (60Hz vertical refresh)
Orchid ProDesigner II VGA (72Hz vertical refresh)
Orchid Technology Fahrenheit 1280 (43Hz vertical refresh)
Orchid Technology Fahrenheit 1280 (60Hz vertical refresh)
Orchid Technology Fahrenheit 1280 (70Hz vertical refresh)

Orchid Fahrenheit 1280

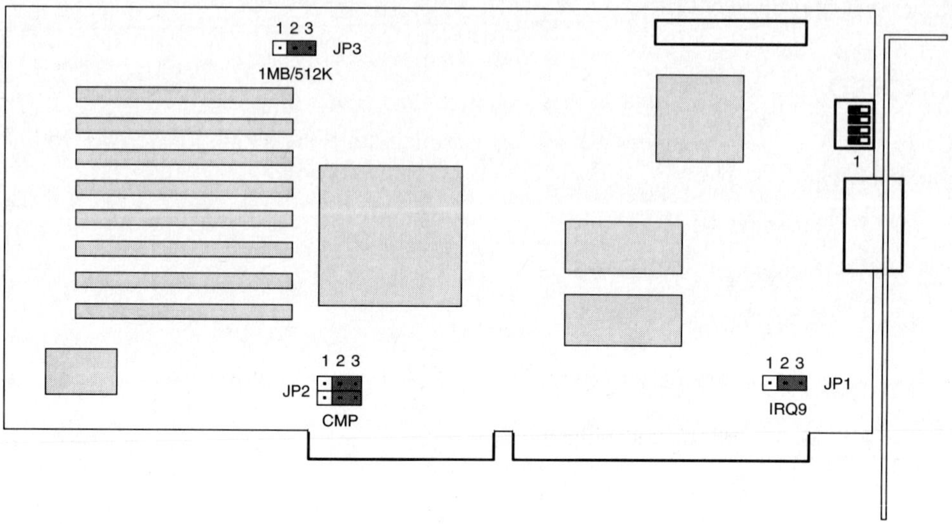

Memory Configuration	JP3	IRQ9 Interrupt	JP1	Motherboard Compatibility	JP2	Reserved	Switch
							3
512K installed	2–3	Enabled	1–2	Enabled	1–2	*not used	0
1MB installed	1–2	*Disabled	2–3	*Disabled	2–3		

Speed Booster	Switch	Monitor 1024x768	Switch
	4		1 2
*Disabled	0	*60Hz	0 0
Enabled	1	70Hz	1 0
		45Hz	0 1
		60Hz	1 1

Switches: 0=off
1=on
Jumpers: 0=installed
1=not installed

*=Default Settings

ATI

ATI makes several adapters that are compatible with Solaris x86.

- ATI Graphics Ultra
- ATI Graphics Vantage
- ATI VLB Mach 32
- ATI 8514A

Configuration Notes

- Match the adapter to the monitor (use ATI DOS utilities)
- Add memory if necessary (2MB required for 1280x1024)
- Leave other defaults alone
- Configure mouse port (if provided)

Supported configurations on Solaris x86 Installation Program

ATI 68800 Mach–32, 60Hz noninterlaced
ATI 68800 Mach–32, 70Hz noninterlaced
ATI 68800 Mach–32, 76Hz noninterlaced
ATI 68800 Mach–32, 87Hz interlaced
ATI 68800 Mach–32, 95Hz interlaced
ATI 8514/A
ATI VGA Wonder XL (43Hz interlaced vertical refresh)
ATI VGA Wonder XL (60Hz vertical refresh)
ATI VGA Wonder XL (70Hz vertical refresh)
ATI VGA Wonder XL–6 (43Hz vertical refresh)
ATI VGA Wonder XL–6 (60Hz vertical refresh)
ATI VGA Wonder XL–6 (70Hz vertical refresh)
ATI VGA Wonder + (43Hz interlaced vertical refresh)
ATI VGA Wonder + (60Hz vertical refresh)
ATI VGA Wonder + (70Hz vertical refresh)

Installing ATI 8514 Mouse

The ATI 8514/A has a bus mouse port that can be used or disabled. If you enable the mouse port, you must use the ATI DOS utility program to setup the mouse I/O port and IRQ settings. When you install Solaris x86, choose the Microsoft bus mouse as your mouse and set the I/O port address and IRQ settings to match the setup on your ATI card mouse port.

ATI Graphics Ultra

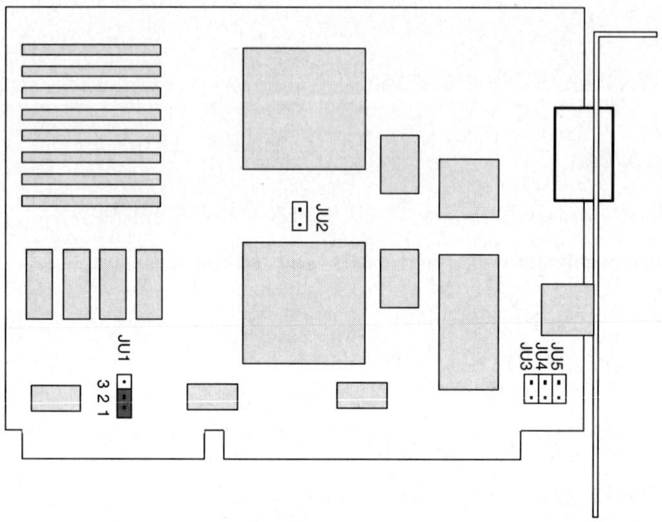

Reserved IRQ5	JU3	Memory Configuration	JU2	Reserved IRQ3	JU4	Coprocessor Bus	JU1
*not used	0	512K installed	1	*not used	0	*16–bit	1–2
		1MB installed	0			8–bit	2–3

Reserved IRQ2	JU5
*not used	0

Switches: 0=off
1=on
Jumpers: 0=installed
1=not installed

*=Default Settings

ATI Graphics Vantage

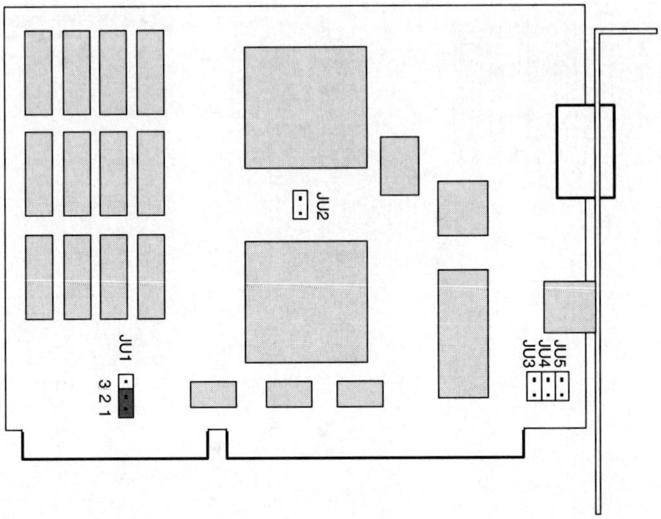

Reserved IRQ5	JU3	Memory Configuration	JU2	Reserved IRQ3	JU4	Coprocessor Bus	JU1
*not used	0	512K installed	1	*not used	0	*16–bit	1–2
		1MB installed	0			8–bit	2–3

Reserved IRQ2	JU5
*not used	0

Switches: 0=off
1=on
Jumpers: 0=installed
1=not installed

*=Default Settings

ATI VLB Mach 32 VRAM

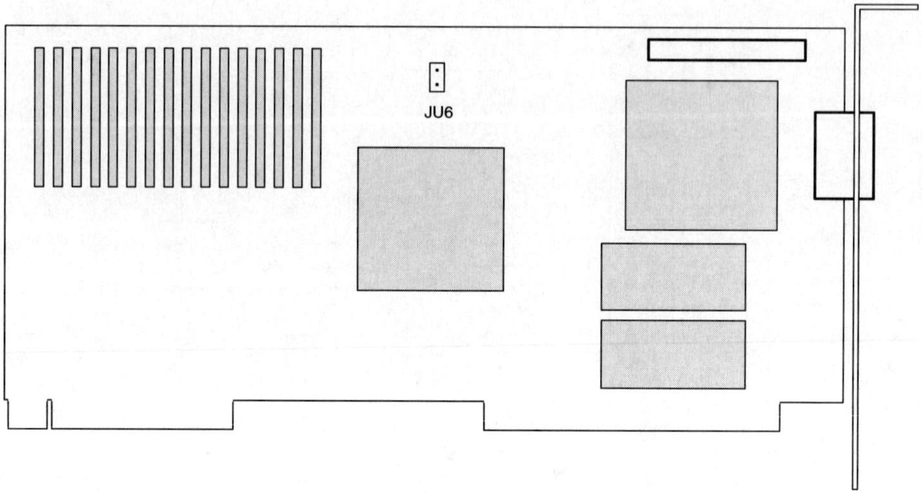

Memory Configuration	JU6
1MB installed	1
2MB installed	0

Switches: 0=off
1=on
Jumpers: 0=installed
1=not installed

*=Default Settings

ATI VLB Mach 32 DRAM

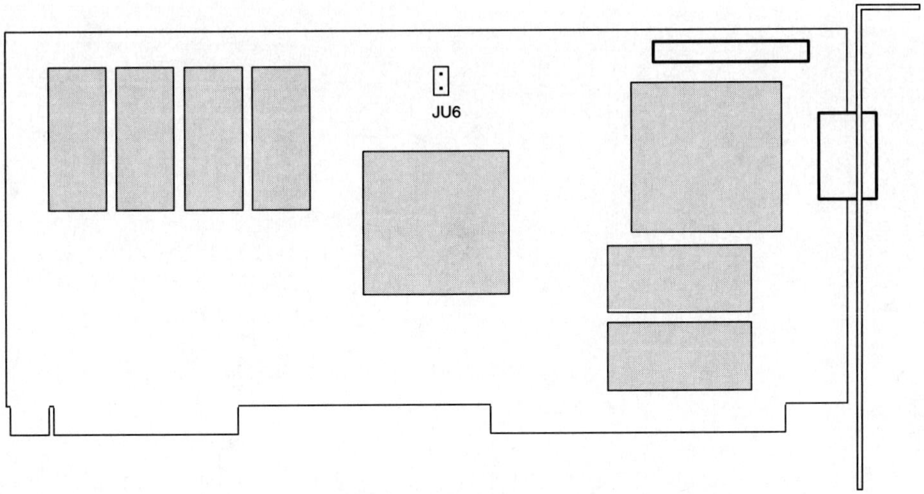

Memory Configuration	JU6
1MB installed	1
2MB installed	0

Switches: 0=off
1=on
Jumpers: 0=installed
1=not installed

*=Default Settings

Appendix E

AUDIO CARDS

The following audio cards are supported by Solaris x86. Refer to Appendix A for information about free *driver update diskettes*.

Manufacturer	Model	Solaris Driver
Creative Sound Labs	SoundBlaster	sbpro
Creative Sound Labs	SoundBlaster PRO	sbpro
Creative Sound Labs	SoundBlaster PRO 16 SCSI II	sbpro

Sound Blaster Pro

Features

- Microphone input jack
- Speaker output jack
- Volume control
- Proprietary CD–ROM interface (not used by Solaris x86)

Jumper Settings

	IRQ Level	DMA Channel	I/O Port Address	BIOS Address	RAM Address
Factory Defaults	5	1	220	N/A	N/A
Recommended	5	1	220	N/A	N/A

Configuration

The Sound Blaster Pro is compatible with Solaris x86. New sound card drivers may be available by the time you read this. Check Appendix A for details on current hardware compatibility.

The FM Synthesizer uses I/O port 338–339 and the game port uses I/O port 200–207. Make a note of this, and do not use those I/O addresses for any other devices.

I/O port 220 may conflict with some token ring cards.

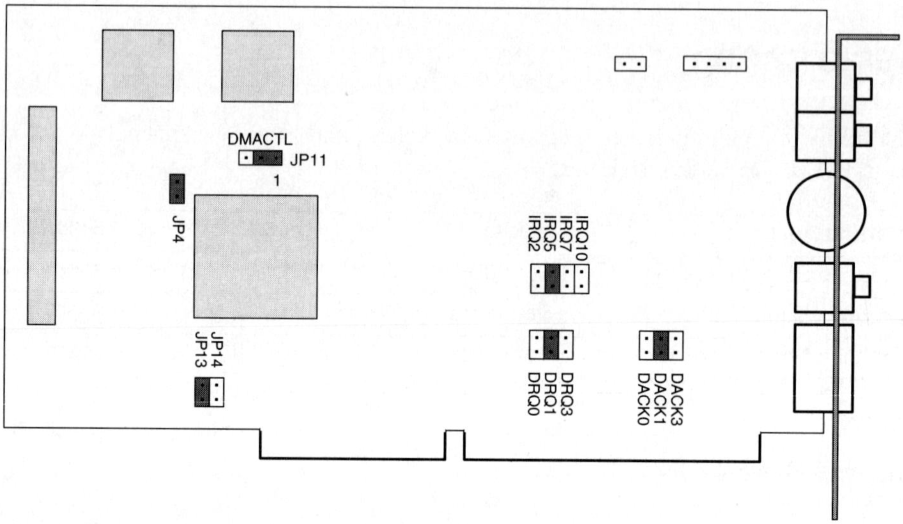

DMA Control	JP	I/O Port Address	JP
	11		13 14
*Not shared	1–2	*220	1 0
Shared	2–3	240	0 1

Switches: 0=off
1=on
Jumpers: 0=installed
1=not installed

*=Default Settings

Configure the sound board as indicated on the drawing. Change the IRQ by moving the IRQ jumper to the desired IRQ #. Change the DMA by moving both the DRQ and DACK jumpers to corresponding #s. You should not change the default I/O port address or DMA control settings. The defaults work fine.

Appendix F

NETWORK ADAPTER CONFIGURATION

Network Cards

The following network cards are supported are Solaris x86:

Manufacturer	Model	Solaris Driver
3COM	EtherLink II (3C503)	el
3COM	EtherLink II/16 (3C503)	el
3COM	EtherLink II/16TP (3C503TP)	el
3COM	EtherLink 16 (3C507)	elink
3COM	EtherLink 16TP (3C507TP)	elink
3COM	EtherLink III (3C509)	elx
3COM	EtherLink III (3C529)	elx
3COM	EtherLink III (3C579)	elx
3COM	TokenLink III 16/4 (3C619) ISA	tr
3COM	TokenLink III 16/4 (3C629) MCA	tr
3COM	TokenLink III 16/4 (3C679) EISA	tr
IBM	Token Ring 4/16	
Intel	EtherExpress 16	iee
Intel	EtherExpress 16C	iee
Intel	EtherExpress 16TP	iee
Intel	EtherExpress 32 (EILA8215)	nee
Intel	EtherExpress Flash32	ieef
Intel	EtherExpress FlashC	iee
Madge	Smart 16/4 MC Ringnode	mtok
Madge	Smart 16/4 MC32 Ringnode	mtok
Madge	Smart 16/4 AT Ringnode	mtok
Madge	Smart 16/4 EISA Ringnode	mtok
Novell	NE2000	nei

Manufacturer	Model	Solaris Driver
Novell	NE3200	nee
SMC	EtherCard Plus Elite32 (8033W)	smce
SMC	EtherCard Plus Elite32T (8033EP)	smce
SMC	EtherCard Elite 16 Ultra (8216)	smc
SMC	EtherCard Elite 16T Ultra (8216T)	smc
SMC	ETherCard Elite 16C Ultra (8216C)	smc
Xircom	PE3 (Pocket Ethernet)	pe

3COM ETHERLINK II (3C503)

The 3COM EtherLink II 3C503 network adapter is not a good choice unless you already have one and want to use it. Since this adapter is very slow by current standards, I strongly recommend that you avoid using this board.

Features

- Thick and thin Ethernet
- Manual configuration

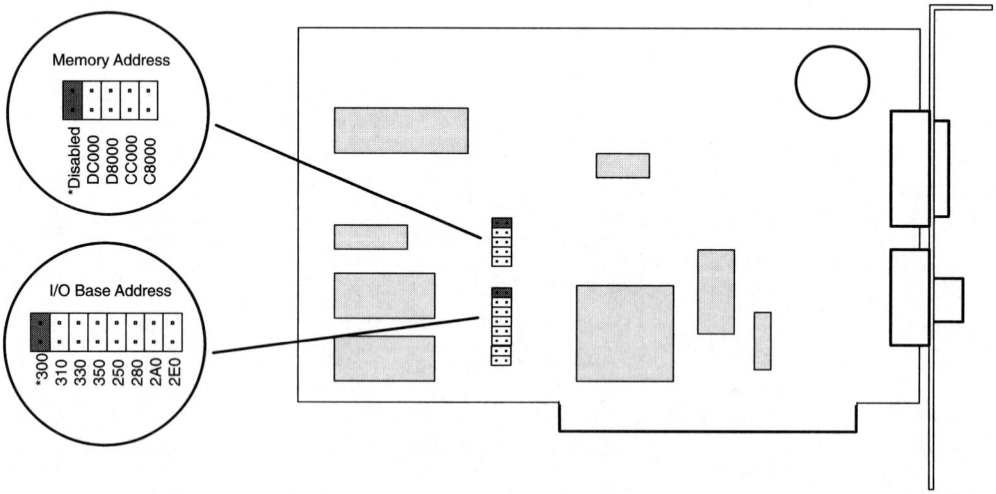

Configuration

Network Adapter Settings

	IRQ Level	DMA Channel	I/O Port Address	BIOS Address	RAM Address
Factory Defaults	3	1	300	N/A	Disabled
Recommended	3	1	300	N/A	Disabled

Configuration Notes

Configuration options are extremely limited on this board. You will not have to change the configuration because Solaris will only use the default settings.

Configuration and Test Utility

This adapter is configured using both jumpers and a diagnostic program called `3C503.exe`. The diagnostic program is provided on a diskette.

Use the xcopy command to copy the 3COM utility diskette and its subdirectories to a directory on your hard disk.

Example:

```
c:\>mkdir c:\3com
c:\>xcopy a:\ c:\3com /s
c:\>cd \3com
c:\3com>3c503
```

3COM ETHERLINK III (3C509)

The 3COM EtherLink III series of network adapters are excellent. They are easy to install and configure. They are my personal choice for easy installation.

Features

- Thick, thin, and UTP Ethernet
- Software configuration
- Optional boot ROM
- No memory required

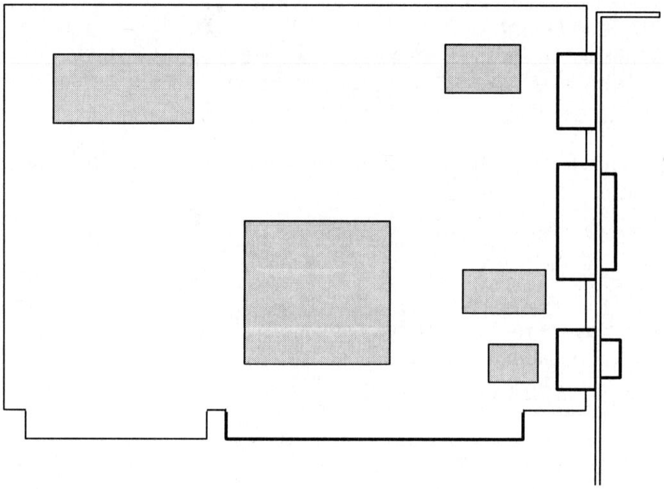

Configuration

Network Adapter Settings

	IRQ Level	DMA Channel	I/O Port Address	BIOS Address	RAM Address
Factory Defaults	10	N/A	300	N/A	N/A
Recommended	10	N/A	300	N/A	N/A

Configuration notes

The configuration of the 3C509 is done with a DOS utility program supplied by 3COM. There are no jumpers on the board. The utility program provides an easy-to-use menu interface for both diagnostic and configuration functions.

The configuration program will automatically select IRQ and I/O port addresses that do not conflict with other boards. The default configuration settings made by the configuration program will probably work fine. Check them to make sure you do not have a conflict with other IRQs and I/O port assignments.

This adapter is an excellent choice for systems that require maximum memory space for DOS environments. The adapter uses programmed I/O that does not require a block of memory. There is no RAM address or DMA setting to configure on this board. Simple!

There is a configuration setting for maximum modem speed. If you plan to run a modem at speeds above 9600 baud, you should set the maximum modem speed accordingly.

Configuration Utility

This adapter is configured using a program called `menu.exe`. The menu program is provided on a diskette.

Use the xcopy command to copy the utility diskette and its subdirectories to a directory on your hard disk.

Example:

```
c:\>mkdir c:\3com
c:\>xcopy a:\ c:\3com /s
c:\>cd \3com
c:\3com>menu
```

3COM ETHERLINK III (3C579)

The 3COM EtherLink III series of network adapters is excellent. They are easy to install and configure. They are my personal choice for easy installation.

Features

- Thick, thin, and UTP Ethernet
- Software configuration
- Optional boot ROM
- 32-bit EISA adapter

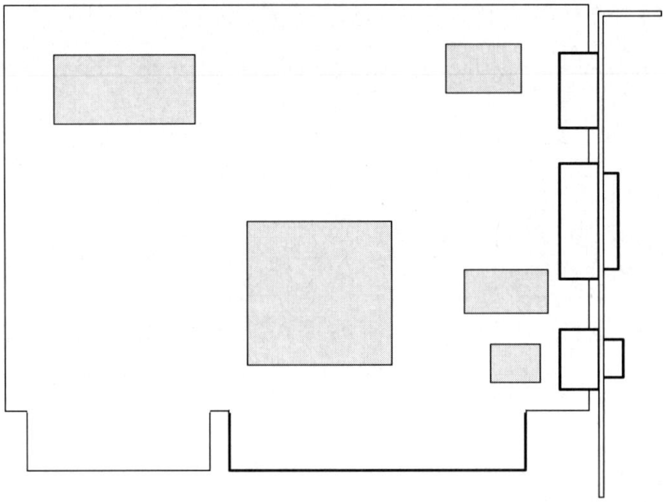

Configuration

Network Adapter Settings

	IRQ Level	DMA Channel	I/O Port Address	BIOS Address	RAM Address
Factory Defaults	10	N/A	300	N/A	N/A
Recommended	10	N/A	300	N/A	N/A

Configuration Notes

The configuration of the 3C579 is done with the EISA configuration program supplied by the motherboard or system manufacturer. There are no jumpers on the board. The EISA configuration program provides automatic configuration of the slot number, IRQ level, boot PROM enable, and transceiver type options. The settings can be changed as required.

The EISA configuration program is accessed by booting from the DOS partition or from a DOS diskette.

The EISA configuration program requires 3COM configuration files that are provided on a floppy diskette. The configuration files are copied to the EISA configuration diskette or to the EISA configuration directory on the hard disk. The EISA configuration program is a DOS utility. The required 3C579 configuration files are:

- !TMC5092.CFG (for the 3C579–TP adapter)
- !TMC5093.CFG (for the 3C579 adapter)

There is a configuration setting for maximum modem speed. If you plan to run a modem at speeds above 9600 baud, you should set the maximum modem speed accordingly.

Test utility

Additional configuration and testing of the 3C579 are done with a DOS utility program supplied by 3COM. The utility program provides an easy-to-use menu interface for both diagnostic and configuration functions.

This adapter is tested using a program called `menu.exe`. The menu program is provided on a diskette.

Use the xcopy command to copy the utility diskette and its subdirectories to a directory on your hard disk.

Example:

```
c:\>mkdir c:\3com
c:\>xcopy a:\ c:\3com /s
c:\>cd \3com
c:\3com>menu
```

3COM ETHERLINK 16 (3C507/3C507TP)

Configuration

The manual for the 3Com EtherLink 16 and 16TP card specifies that the base address of the card's shared RAM can be configured to several different addresses. Solaris does not support the configuration of the card at the following addresses listed in the EtherLink 16 manual:

- F0000
- F4000
- F8000
- FC000

The 3Com EtherLink 16 Ethernet adapter has an on-board buffer of 64K. Using the configuration utility supplied by 3Com, you can configure it to use the full 64K or a smaller amount.

The adapter itself may fail if it is configured for less than 64K of memory. This failure will be noticed as soon as Solaris attempts to access the network. When this happens, use the configuration utility to configure the adapter to use the full 64K of memory (even though your system may not have a valid 64K memory range available), then configure it back to the desired memory size. This workaround usually solves the problem.

INTEL ETHEREXPRESS 16

This adapter uses the Solaris `iee` driver.

Configuration

When using any version of the EtherExpress 16 adapter, you must use the SOFTSET configuration utility to manually configure which connector to use. This DOS program is supplied by the network card manufacturer and is contained on a diskette that comes with the board.

Known Problems

Auto-detect is currently not supported.

When you use the boot floppy to select booting from the Intel EtherExpress 16 Ethernet Adapter, on rare occasions you may see the error message:

```
AdapterISR(): wait scb failed
```

The next reboot usually recovers from this problem.

INTEL ETHEREXPRESS FLASH 32

This adapter uses the Solaris `ieef` driver.

Configuration

Be sure to disable Flash Memory using the EISA configuration utility that comes with your Intel EtherExpress Flash32 adapter. All other parameters should be left to their defaults.

Known Problems

The Solaris `ieef` driver does not support using either IRQ 3 or 5 on the Intel EtherExpress Flash32 Ethernet cards. Do not configure the card using IRQ 3 or 5.

If a system with an Intel EtherExpress Flash32 network card is booted without the network cable plugged in, the network will not come up, even if the cable is plugged in later. Make sure the cable connecting the Intel EtherExpress Flash32 to the system is connected before booting the system.

A system with two Intel EtherExpress Flash32 cards will not operate reliably as a gateway. The primary network interface will fail after some period of activity.

MADGE TOKEN RING ADAPTER

This adapter uses the Solaris `mtok` driver.

Configuration

The Madge SMART 16/4 AT Ringnode token ring adapter (ISA) has an onboard jumper for enabling or disabling the use of DMA and selecting DMA channels. DMA must be ENABLED under Solaris for proper operation.

The driver may produce error messages during booting and configuration. In those cases where error messages are expected, they will be preceded by the following message (the I/O location in the message will vary):

```
You may see some WARNING messages from the system.
Please ignore these as the driver is trying to find the
interrupt number of the Madge ISA card at I/O location
Oxa20.
```

Known Problems

Solaris supports the use of the Madge token ring for normal network operations. However, it may not be used by a client's machine to install Solaris from a network boot/install server. Once Solaris has been installed from another network adapter or from a CD–ROM, the Madge token ring network adapter can be used.

If a system with two Madge token ring cards is installed with the Driver Update, it fails to create /dev/mtok. If this occurs, you can create the link manually using the commands:

```
# cd /dev
```

```
# ln -s ../devices/pseudo/clone:mtok mtok
```

After rebooting the system, the network should then be available.

The Madge token ring card and driver (`mtok`) cannot be used on systems with an IBM–compatible Token Ring card installed.

When you boot a machine with a token ring card in it, you get the following message:

```
ip_rput: DL_ERROR_ACK for 29, errno 1, unix 0
ip: joining multicasts failed on mtok1 - will use link
layer broadcasts for multicast
```

This message can be ignored.

You cannot run snoop using a token ring device. When you try to run snoop on a token ring, you get the message:

```
snoop: Mac type = 2 is not supported
```

SMC ELITE AND ELITE ULTRA ADAPTERS (8216)

This adapter uses the Solaris `smc` driver.

Configuration

An updated driver is available to support the SMC Elite Ultra family of Ethernet adapters. See Appendix A for more information about the Solaris *driver update diskettes*.

This update driver specifically supports the SMC 8216 family of ISA bus Ethernet adapters. The updated Solaris `smc` driver supersedes the existing `smc` driver and continues to support all the previous SMC/WD 80x3 Elite family of ISA and MCA Ethernet adapters.

Newer SMC network adapters have a jumper labeled "SOFT" and should be configured using the software setup program provided by SMC. The shared memory address must be between C0000 and DE000.

SMC ELITE32 NETWORK ADAPTERS (8216)

This adapter uses the Solaris `smce` driver.

Configuration

The SMC Elite32 is a dual channel Ethernet adapter so you get two network interfaces for each board that you install in the system. Thus both `smce0` and `smce1` are available for the first board installed; `smce2` and `smce3` are available for the second board installed and so forth.

SMC Elite32 Ethernet adapters come in two possible network connector configurations. One configuration has both the AUI-type and the BNC-type connectors, while the other has both the

AUI-type and 10BaseT-type connectors. Both configurations allow channel 0 to have a choice of connectors, but channel 1 is limited to the use of the BNC-type or 10BaseT-type connector, not the AUI connector.

EISA Configuration

1. Specify the network connector for channel 0. You can use the EISA configuration utility to select which type of connector you've chosen for channel 0. If you have connected a transceiver to the AUI connector, the board will use the AUI connection regardless of what connector has been selected in the EISA configuration.
2. Set the IRQ level if needed. In the EISA configuration of the SMC Elite32 Ethernet board, the IRQ value is usually automatically determined by the system. It does this by finding the first available IRQ level that is known to the EISA configuration program. If the system contains ISA adapters whose IRQ settings have not been entered into the EISA configuration utility, however, the chosen IRQ level may conflict with that of an ISA adapter. This will impact system performance or render the network adapter unable to communicate on the network. You can override the automatic assignment of the IRQ level by manually editing the details and selecting an appropriate IRQ level for the Elite32 adapter.

Network Installation

Network installation must be performed through channel 0 of the first adapter. All installation questions regarding network configuration should be answered with respect to the channel 0 connection.

Known Problems

The `smce` driver hangs the system when snoop is run. Don't run snoop using the `smce` driver.

SMC ETHERCARD PLUS™ (8003)

The SMC EtherCard Plus network adapter is not a good choice unless you already have one and want to use it. It is difficult to configure and does not have a wide range of IRQ choices. This adapter is also very slow by current standards.

This card cannot be used to boot from the network.

Features

- Thick and thin Ethernet
- Manual setup using jumpers

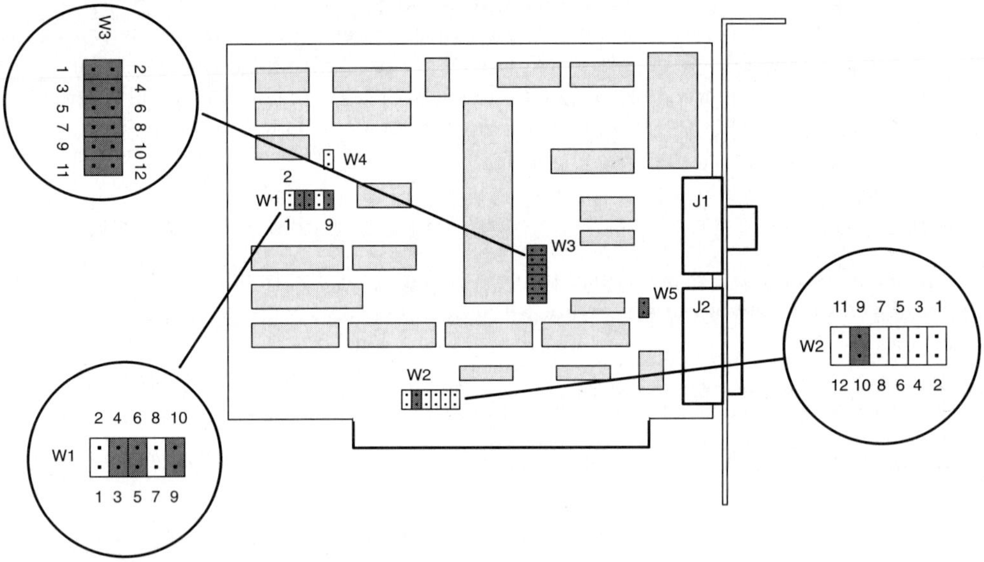

Configuration

Network Adapter Settings

	IRQ Level	DMA Channel	I/O Port Address	BIOS Address	RAM Address
Factory Defaults	3	N/A	280	N/A	C4000
Recommended	5	N/A	300	N/A	D4000

Configuration Notes

You will almost certainly have to change your configuration from the default.

The 8K RAM buffer area defaults to C4000 unless you use the SMC utility program to set it to a different value.

IRQ #	Jumper W2					
	1–2	3–4	5–6	7–8	9–10	11–12
IRQ 2	0	0	0	0	0	1
*IRQ3	0	0	0	0	1	0
IRQ4	0	0	0	1	0	0
IRQ5	0	0	1	0	0	0
IRQ6	0	1	0	0	0	0
IRQ7	1	0	0	0	0	0

I/O Port Address	Jumper W1			
	3–4	5–6	7–8	9–10
200	1	1	1	1
220	0	1	1	1
240	1	0	1	1
260	0	0	1	1
*280	1	1	0	1
2A0	0	1	0	1
2C0	1	0	0	1
2E0	0	0	0	1
300	1	1	1	0
320	0	1	1	0
340	1	0	1	0
360	0	0	1	0
380	1	1	0	0
3A0	0	1	0	0
3C0	1	0	0	0
3E0	0	0	0	0

Ethernet Media Type	Jumper W3					
	1–2	3–4	5–6	7–8	9–10	11–12
*Thin Ethernet	1	1	1	1	1	1
Thick Ethernet	0	0	0	0	0	0

Ethernet Version	Jumper W4
*Version 2	0
Version 1	1

AT CPU Clock	Jumper W1
	1–2
*8–16MHz	0
6MHz	1

Segment Length	Jumper W4
*Standard length	1
300 meters	0

Switches: 0=off
1=on
Jumpers: 0=not installed
1=installed

*=Default Settings

Known Problems

The 8003 board has a limited amount of on-board memory which causes very poor Solaris NFS performance. To avoid this problem, it is recommended that NFS mounts over the 8003 interface use a 4K read/write buffer size. This problem can also impact installation of Solaris over the network, causing occasional NFS warnings (which can be ignored).

SMC ELITE 16 (8013)

The SMC Elite 16 network adapters are good performers at a reasonable cost. They are readily available at most retail computer stores that sell network components. I used the SMC 8013 cards on many of my test systems.

Features

- Thick, thin, and UTP Ethernet
- Single jumper for quick configuration
- Software setup program
- Optional boot ROM
- Transmit and receive LEDs

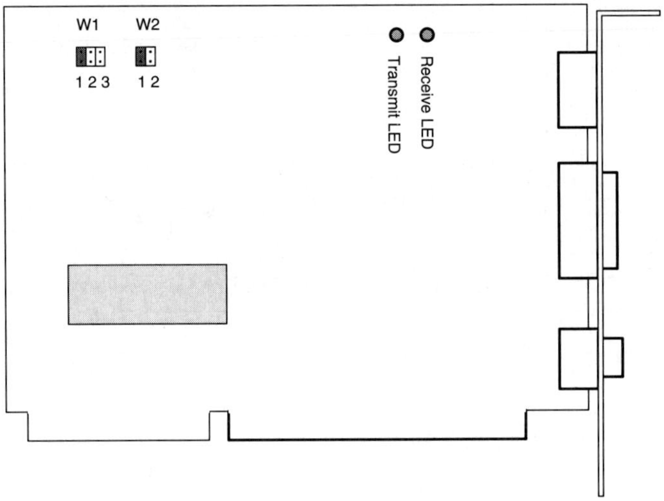

Configuration

Network Adapter Settings

	IRQ Level	DMA Channel	I/O Port Address	BIOS Address	RAM Address
Factory Defaults	3	N/A	280–29F	N/A	D0000
Recommended	10	N/A	300–31F	N/A	CC000

Configuration Notes

If you are willing to accept the preselected jumper defaults, you can easily configure this board by moving jumper W1 to the "300,10,CC000" setting. I do not recommend using the default jumper setting unless you plan to use the software configuration program to set your IRQ, RAM address, and I/O ports. The default IRQ 3 setting on this board will almost always cause a conflict with your serial port assignments.

Configuration Utility

Use the DOS utility program (called `ezsetup.exe`) provided by SMC to test and configure your board. If you use the software to configure your board, you will not have to move any jumpers from their default positions on the board.

Use the xcopy command to copy the utility diskette and its subdirectories to a directory on your hard disk.

Example:

```
c:\>mkdir c:\smc
c:\>xcopy a:\ c:\smc /s
c:\>cd \smc
c:\smc>ezsetup
```

Setup Configuration	Jumper W1			Optional ROM Address	Jumper W2	
	1	2	3		1	2
*Software Controlled	1	0	0	*Software Controlled	1	0
280, 3, D0000	0	1	0	D8000	0	1
300, 10, CC000	0	0	1			

Switches: 0=off
1=on
Jumpers: 0=not installed
1=installed

*=Default Settings

XIRCOM POCKET ETHERNET ADAPTER

This parallel port Ethernet adapter uses the Solaris `pe` driver.

Configuration

The Solaris `pe` driver is available as a driver update. See Appendix A for more information on the Solaris *driver update diskettes*.

The Xircom Ethernet adapters (models PE3 and PE2) are very easy to install: they have no switches or software-setable options and do not require any manual configuration. Make sure that the Ethernet adapter is powered up before Solaris tries to bring up its networking services.

Network booting is supported only for model PE3, not PE2. The Xircom driver automatically senses whether the parallel port is unidirectional or bidirectional, and takes advantage of the faster operation that is possible with a bidirectional parallel port.

For combo (BNC and 10Base-T) adapters, the adapter will automatically sense which connector has a cable connected, and the driver will automatically be configured for that type of connection.

Caution: *The system should be powered down to attach the adapter, following manufacturer's instructions.*

Appendix G

CD–ROM CONFIGURATION

Only SCSI CD–ROM drives that are connected to a supported SCSI controller are supported by Solaris x86. Do not connect your SCSI CD–ROM drive to a SCSI connector on a sound board.

CD–ROM Drives

The following SCSI CD–ROM drives are compatible with Solaris x86. If you are shopping for a CD–ROM drive, you should get the most recent hardware compatibility list and find a compatible drive that is double or triple speed. You should get a drive with a throughput rate of at least 300 KB/sec.

Manufacturer	Model	Description
Hitachi	CDR–1900S	
LMS	CM214	
NEC	Intersect CDR–74	
NEC	Intersect CDR–84	
NEC	Multispin 3X	
Phillips	CM425A	
Sony	CDU–7211	
Sony	CDU–6211	
Sun Microsystems Inc.	SunCD	
Texel	DM–5021	
Texel	DM–5024	
Texel	DM–5028	
Toshiba	TXM–3201	
Toshiba	TXM–3301	
Toshiba	TXM–3401	

Appendix H

I/O BOARD CONFIGURATION

I/O boards are inexpensive and easy to configure. They usually feature the same set of options and settings. For the most part you will use jumpers to set the names of the ports, the port addresses, and the IRQ numbers.

Proprietary motherboards usually come with embedded serial and parallel ports. The embedded ports are the same as those provided on optional adapter boards and must also be configured or disabled to avoid conflicts with other devices.

I/O Port Standard Configuration

The following table is an example of standard hardware port assignment. Most PC software applications will assume these standard default values.

Name	I/O Port Address	IRQ #
COM1 (Solaris x86 tty00)	3F8–3FF	IRQ 4
COM2 (Solaris x86 tty01)	2F8–2FF	IRQ 3
COM3 (Solaris x86 tty02)	3E8–3EF	IRQ 4
COM4 (Solaris x86 tty03)	2E8–2EF	IRQ 3
LPT1 (Solaris x86 lp1)	378–37F	IRQ 7
LPT2 (Solaris x86 lp2)	278–27F	IRQ 5

Note: *A parallel port using I/O port address 3BC will be designated Solaris x86 lp0. The use of I/O port address 3BC is rare. Port 3BC was the port assignment that was hard wired on early vintage monochrome adapter boards equipped with a parallel port.*

I/O Port Connections

I/O ports are connected to I/O devices via external cables, which come in a variety of lengths and styles and are readily available at computer retail outlets. There was a time when it was common to make your own cables, but those days are pretty much gone. You can, of course, still make your own cables, but there is no real need to do it.

Cables

For the benefit of the few out there who still want to work on their cables, here is some basic pinout information on serial and parallel ports.

Serial 25 Pin DB Cables

DB25 Pin #	Signal Name
1	Chassis Ground
2	Transmit
3	Receive
4	Request To Send
5	Clear To Send
6	Data Set Ready
7	Signal Ground
8	Carrier Detect
9	+DC Test Voltage
10	–DC Test Voltage
11	Equalizer Mode
12	Carrier Detect 2
13	Clear To Send 2
14	Transmit Data 2
15	Transmit Clock
16	Receive Data 2
17	Receive Clock
18	N/A
19	Request To Send 2
20	Data Terminal Ready
21	Signal Quality Detect
22	Ring Indicator
23	Data Rate Select
24	Transmit Clock (external)
25	N/A

Serial 9 Pin DB Cables

DB9 Pin #	Signal Name
1	Carrier Detect
2	Receive Data
3	Transmit Data
4	Data Terminal Ready

DB9 Pin #	Signal Name
5	Signal Ground
6	Data Set Ready
7	Request To Send
8	Clear To Send
9	Ring Indicate

Parallel Printer Cable connection

Please refer to Appendix N for details on the DB25 to Centronics cable.

Optional Features

Many I/O adapters come with optional features such as clocks, game ports, or IDE drive controllers. Disable the features you do not use. If you cannot disable a feature, make sure you check for conflicts before installing the I/O adapters.

Solaris 2.1

The following information is from a SunSoft technical note.

Sharable interrupts for COM1–COM4

Solaris x86 2.1 can support 4 COM with shared interrupts. COM1 is enabled by default. If you want to use other COM ports, you need to edit `/kernel/drv/asy.conf` file and uncomment (remove the # character from the begining of the line) 2 lines starting with "name=" for each COM port you wish to enable.

On most of the standard serial I/O cards, the IRQs are fixed for each port, and you cannot change them. The standard IRQs are 4 and 3. Some serial cards with more than 2 COM ports can share an IRQ. The standard IRQs are:

COM1	IRQ4
COM2	IRQ3
COM3	IRQ4
COM4	IRQ3

The Solaris x86 asy driver is configured by default to use sharable interrupts: interrupt 4 for COM1 and COM3, and interrupt 3 for COM2 and COM4. You can use these sharable interrupts if you have an I/O adapter that supports sharable interrupts.

Appendix I

MODEM AND FAX CONFIGURATION

I am amazed at how quickly performance has improved on FAX modems as their price continues to drop. If you have a slot available on your system, go out and get a FAX modem today! I recommend the internal type because it comes with equipped with a serial port. This is the lowest cost solution.

External FAX Modem

If you decide on an external FAX modem, be sure you have a high-speed serial port to handle the high transmission rates.

DB 25 Modem Cable

External FAX modems require a serial port and a cable to make the connection complete.

Computer DB25 Pin #	Signal Name	Modem DB25 Pin #
1	Ground	1
2	Transmit	2
3	Receive	3
4	Request To Send	4
5	Clear To Send	5
6	Data Set Ready	6
7	Signal Ground	7
8	Carrier Detect	8
20	Data Terminal Ready	20
22	Ring Detect	22

Configuration

The FAX modem is configured the same way you would configure a serial port. If you have several FAX modems on one machine you may have to use alternate IRQ numbers to avoid conflicts with other adapters.

I/O Port Standard Configuration

Name	I/O Port Address	IRQ #
COM1 (Solaris x86 tty00)	3F8–3FF	IRQ 4
COM2 (Solaris x86 tty01)	2F8–2FF	IRQ 3
COM3 (Solaris x86 tty02)	3E8–3EF	IRQ 4
COM4 (Solaris x86 tty03)	2E8–2EF	IRQ 3

Appendix J

TAPE DRIVES

Solaris x86 supports SCSI .25" (QIC 24/120/150/320/525), 4mm, and 8mm (DAT) tape devices.

The following SCSI tape drives have been tested by SunSoft:

Manufacturer	Model	Description
Archive	Viper 2525S	525 MB QIC
Archive	Viper 2150S/ES	150 MB QIC
Sun Microsystems	x660A	150MB QIC
Sun Microsystems	x814a	1.3GB 8mm
Tandberg	Panther 525S	525 MB QUI
Tandberg	TDC 3820	
Tandberg	TDC 4120	
Tandberg	TDC 4220	
Wangtek	5525ES	525 MB QUI

Configuration

SCSI tape drives are much the same as most SCSI devices. You must set:

- SCSI target address
- Termination (if connected to end of SCSI bus)
- Enable disconnect

The SCSI target ID is usually set to 4 or 5. Pick an address that does not conflict with your hard disk drives and CD–ROM.

You do not need to terminate your tape drive unless it is at the end of the SCSI bus cable.

The disconnect/reconnect feature should not be disabled on the tape drive or on the SCSI controller. If the SCSI controller cannot disconnect from the tape unit, you will experience long delays while the controller waits for the tape to complete each command.

Appendix K

INPUT DEVICES

The following mice are supported.

Manufacturer	Model	Description
Appoint	Thumbelina	Same as Microsoft 2 button mouse
Appoint	MousePen Pro	Same as Microsoft 2 button mouse
Dyna Point	DynaTrak	Same as Microsoft 2 button mouse
Interlink	PortaPoint	Same as Microsoft 2 button mouse
Kraft Systems	MicroTrack	Same as Microsoft 2 button mouse
Logitech	MouseMan	Serial/Bus 3 Button
Logitech	C7	Serial/Bus 3 Button
Logitech	C9	Same as Microsoft 2 button mouse
Logitech	Trackman	Serial/Bus Mice
Logitech	MouseMan	Cordless
Microsoft	Serial Mouse	Two Button
Microsoft	Bus Mouse	Two Button
Microsoft	PS/2 Mouse	Two Button
MicroSpeed	Microtrac	Trackball
Mouse Systems	New Point	

The mouse can be a problem to configure if you have a brand that is not listed above. When you choose a mouse, make sure to get one that is Microsoft serial or bus mouse compatible. Most clone mice are compatible with the Microsoft format.

KEYBOARDS

There is little to say about keyboards. I have not run into any compatibility problems with keyboards. It is relatively safe to use the keyboard of your choice.

Appendix L

MONITOR CONFIGURATION

Each monitor has unique operating characteristics. Most quality monitors are capable of adapting to a variety of resolutions and scan rates. This adaptability enables a monitor to be used with many different video adapter cards. This is good news for the consumer, but it is not always easy to understand.

When you match a monitor to your video adapter, you need to know a few key monitor specifications:

- Resolution in pixels (horizontal x vertical)
- Interlaced or noninterlaced (scans twice or once to complete a display)
- Vertical refresh rate (how many times per second the screen is scanned)

You must know the three characteristics listed above to match your monitor to your video adapter card. Although each monitor manufacturer provides this information in one format or another, it is not always easy to find. Some manufacturers seem to take great pride in disguising this information by finding unique ways to present it in their documentation. I have included a few examples of monitor specifications to give you an idea how to make a simple chart for your monitor. You will need such a chart when you are trying to find the best video adapter mode for your monitor.

Resolution

Resolution is measured in pixels. Each pixel is a dot on the screen that can be individually controlled by the video adapter. Each pixel can be displayed in a monochrome or in one of 256 colors. The number of colors can vary (into the millions), but for the sake of simplicity we can deal with a 256-color model. The more colors you have, the more video memory you need to display them. Systems that display more than 256 colors per pixel usually are specialized for applications such as medical imaging.

The most common pixel resolution for 17-inch color monitors is 1024x768. Pixel resolution is stated in horizontal by vertical format. 1024x768 would be 1024 pixels of horizontal resolution and 768 pixels of vertical resolution. In common terms, your screen is wider than it is tall.

Interlaced

If a monitor cannot scan fast enough to display each pixel in one continuous scan across its display surface, it can instead use interlacing to divide the pixels into odd and even scan lines.

The interlaced display can scan the odd half of the lines in one pass and then interlace the even lines in a second scan.

Noninterlaced

The best monitors are capable of operating in a noninterlaced mode for each resolution. All of the pixels are displayed in one scan across the display surface.

Vertical Refresh Rate

The vertical refresh rate is the number of surface scans per second. This is extremely important because scan rates slower than 70Hz can induce eye fatigue. Make sure you have a monitor and video adapter that display the selected resolution at 70Hz or better.

Some manufacturers have different ways of stating their vertical refresh rates for interlaced modes. It takes twice the number of vertical scans to display a picture when using interlaced mode. Look at the two examples below; they are the same and yet they are different:

- 1024x768 87Hz (interlaced)
- 1024x768 43Hz (interlaced)

In the first case the manufacturer is stating that the monitor is scanning half a picture at a rate of 87 times each second; in the second case the manufacturer is stating that the monitor is scanning a complete picture 43 times each second. This is just one more reason why you almost need a consultant to understand PC hardware specifications.

Monitor Specification Examples

CPD–1604 17-inch Monitor	**Resolution**	**I**	**NI**	**VF (Hz)**
	VGA		x	59.9
	VGA		x	70.1
	800x600		x	56
	1024x768		x	60
	1024x768		x	70
	1024x768	x		87

CPD–1791 17-inch Monitor	**Resolution**	**I**	**NI**	**VF (Hz)**
	VGA		x	59.9
	VGA		x	70.1
	800x600		x	56
	1024x768		x	60
	1024x768		x	70
	1024x768	x		87

ViewSonic 17-inch and 20-inch	Resolution	I	NI	VF (Hz)
	VGA 640x350		x	70
	VGA 640x400		x	70
	VGA 640x480		x	60
	VESA 640x400		x	84.1
	VESA 640x480		x	72.8
	800x600		x	60.3
	800x600		x	72
	8514/A 1024x768	x		87
	1024x768		x	60
	1024x768		x	70.1
	1280x1024		x	72

Your Monitor

You can use the template below to record your monitor specifications.

	Resolution	I	NI	VF (Hz)

Appendix M

DISK-DRIVE CONFIGURATION

Floppy-Disk Controller

Only one floppy-disk controller is allowed on a system. Most IDE controllers include a floppy-disk controller that uses IRQ 6. The floppy-disk controller can usually be disabled in the event that there is another floppy controller present, but it is recommended that you use the floppy-disk controller on the IDE controller and disable any other floppy controllers on your system.

This is usually not an issue unless you have a motherboard with a built-in floppy controller, or you have a secondary disk controller (such as a SCSI controller) with a built-in floppy disk controller.

Floppy-Disk Cable

The floppy disk cable is usually made with three connectors. There is a characteristic twist in the cable between two of the connectors and a stripe that runs along the length of one edge.

The colored stripe along the cable indicates the location of pin 1. It is important to match the pin 1 side of the cable with the corresponding pin 1 side of the connectors on the floppy drives and the floppy-drive controller.

Note: *Pin 1 is usually designated on cable connectors, devices, and adapters by a triangle, arrow, dot, square, numeral 1, or other such mark. Look closely at your cables, devices, and adapters to locate pin 1.*

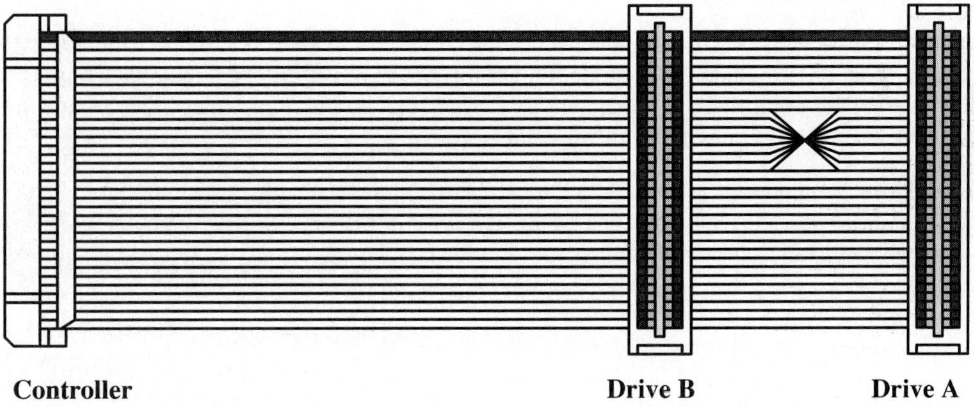

Floppy drive A is connected to the end of the cable after the twist. Some cables may have more than two floppy-drive connectors. This is to accommodate both the different style of connectors required to support some 1.44/2.88 MB floppy drives.

The floppy cable is designed to support only two drives — one on each side of the twist in the cable. If you are installing more than two drives, you will have to check your hardware documentation for details on how to customize your cable and floppy device addresses to accommodate three or four devices on the floppy controller.

Floppy Disk

Floppy-disk drives usually come from the factory preconfigured to the IBM PC standard floppy device address B. This is why the floppy drive cable has a twist in it. The drive connected before the twist is Drive B and the drive connected after the twist is Drive A. Now you know 99% of what you need to properly configure the floppy drive.

The most important aspect of floppy-drive configuration is to get the cables connected correctly. The cable is the first thing to check when the floppy drive does not work. Most often the cable is upside down or offset to the side. It is an unfortunate fact that all manufacturers do not key their cables and connectors to prevent improper installation.

Both 5.25-inch and 3.5-inch floppy drives are supported by Solaris x86. Floppy drives of 3.5-inches with capacities of 720K, 1.44MB, and 2.88MB are supported.

I recommend including both 5.25-inch and 3.5-inch floppy drives on your system. As long as manufacturers ship both formats, you will need to have both drives. I personally like the dual format drive that includes both formats into a single half-height 5.25-inch slot in my computer case.

Hard Disks (>1024 cylinders)

When installing Solaris x86 2.1, you may get the error message:

```
requested cylinder is beyond range of BIOS geometry
```

This type of error occurs when the hard-drive controller BIOS does not support the reading of sectors beyond 1023 cylinders. If you do not get this error message, you do not have a problem. For example, DPT controllers remap geometry for hard drives with more than 1024 cylinders, but in Adaptec controllers you will see the error message.

IDE drives can be reconfigured with less than 1023 cylinders by changing the number of heads or tracks in the CMOS setup for drive type (if the CMOS setup allows the user to manually enter the drive type). Reinstall Solaris x86 after correcting the problem.

SCSI drives with more than 1023 cylinders can be fixed by deleting slice 9 (ALTSCTR) from the hard disk VTOC (volume table of contents).

1. Reboot using Solaris x86 CD–ROM and boot diskette.

2. Exit to the shell when prompted to remove diskette.

3. Edit VTOC to remove slice 9:

```
# fmthard -i -n "" /dev/rdsk/c0t0d0s2 >/tmp/out
# vi /tmp/out
```

4. Remove last line in the /tmp/out file. The last line looks like:

```
9  9  01  ...  ...  ...

#fmthard -s /tmp/out -n "newlabel" /dev/rdsk/c0t0d0s2
```

5. Reboot.

The procedure listed above is not for novices. Call SunSoft Technical Support if you are not completely confident about executing this procedure.

Appendix N

PRINTER CONFIGURATION

Printer hardware configuration is not very difficult. Check your printer documentation to make sure you have the correct cable. The cable configurations listed in the tables below are common to most printers.

DB25 Female Serial CPU to DB25 Male Serial Printer (null modem connection)

Serial Computer DB25 Pin #	CPU Serial Signal Names	Printer Serial Signal Names	Serial Printer DB25 Pin #
1	Ground	Ground	1
2	Transmit	Receive	3
3	Receive	Transmit	2
4	Request To Send	Clear To Send	5
5	Clear To Send	Request To Send	4
6	Data Set Ready	Data Terminal Ready	20
7	Signal Ground	Signal Ground	7
8	Carrier Detect	Data Terminal Ready	20
20	Data Terminal Ready	Data Set Ready	6
20	Data Terminal Ready	Carrier Detect	8

DB9 Serial CPU to DB25 Male Serial Printer

Serial Computer DB9 Pin #	CPU Serial Signal Names	Printer Serial Signal Names	Serial Printer DB25 Pin #
1	Carrier Detect	Request to Send	4
2	Receive	Transmit	2
3	Transmit	Receive	3
4	Data Terminal Ready	Clear to Send	5
4	Data Terminal Ready	Data Set Ready	6
5	Signal Ground	Signal Ground	7

Serial Computer DB9 Pin #	CPU Serial Signal Names	Printer Serial Signal Names	Serial Printer DB25 Pin #
6	Data Set Ready	Data Terminal Ready	20
7	Request To Send	Carrier Detect	8
8	Clear To Send	Data Terminal Ready	20

DB 25 to Centronics Parallel Cable

Computer DB25 Pin #	Parallel Printer Signal Names	Printer Centronics Pin #
1	Strobe –	1
2	Data Bit 0 +	2
3	Data Bit 1 +	3
4	Data Bit 2 +	4
5	Data Bit 3 +	5
6	Data Bit 4 +	6
7	Data Bit 5 +	7
8	Data Bit 6 +	8
9	Data Bit 7 +	9
10	Acknowledge –	10
11	Busy +	11
12	Paper Empty +	12
13	Select +	13
14	Auto Feed –	14
15	Error –	32
16	Initialize Printer –	31
17	Select Input –	36
18–25	Ground	16, 33, 19–30

Appendix O

RESOURCE LIST

The computer systems and peripheral devices used for writing this book were provided courtesy of NCA Computer Products of Sunnyvale, California.

Company Name and Address	Sales	Service	FAX
NCA Computer Products 1202 Kifer Road Sunnyvale, CA 9408632	(408) 739–9010	(408) 739–4110	(408) 739–2420

Company Name and Address	Sales	Service	FAX
Acer America 2641 Orchard Parkway San Jose, CA 95134	(408) 922–2517	(800) 637–7000	(408) 456–0471
Adaptec Inc. 691 South Milpitas Blvd. Milpitas, CA 95035	(408) 945–8600	(408) 945–8600	(408) 262–2533 BBS (408) 945–7727
Advanced Logic Research (ALR) 9401 Jeronimo Irvine, CA 92718	(714) 581–6770	(714) 581–6770	(714) 581–9240
American Megatrends Inc. (AMI) 1346 Oakbrook Drive Suite #120 Norcross, GA 30093	(800) 828–9264	(404) 263–8181	(404) 263–9381
Arnet	(800) 366–8844	(800) 366–8844	(800) 366–8844
AST Research Inc. 16215 Alton Parkway P.O. Box 19658 Irvine, CA 92713	(714) 727–4141	(800) 876–4278	(714) 727–9355
ATI Technologies Inc. 3761 Victoria Park Avenue Scarborough, Ontario, Canada	(416) 756–0718	(416) 756–0711	(416) 756–0720 BBS (416) 756–4591
Avnet Works	(813) 573–5967	(813) 573–5967	(813) 573–5967

Company Name and Address	**Sales**	**Service**	**FAX**
Buslogic Inc. (Formerly BusTek) 4151 Burton Drive Santa Clara, CA 95054	(408) 492–9090	(408) 492–9090	(408) 492–1542
Chantal	(619) 621–2810	(619) 621–2810	(619) 621–2810
Chinon America 615 Hawaii Avenue Torrance, CA 90503	(310) 533–0274	(800) 441–0222	(310) 533–1727
Compaq Computer Corp. 20555 State Highway 249 Houston, TX 77070	(800) 888–5816	(800) 345–1518	(713) 374–1740
CompuAdd 12301 Technology Blvd. Austin, TX 78727	(800) 925–8077	(800) 999–9901	(512) 219–2890
Connor 3081 Zanker Road San Jose, CA 95134	(800) 426–6637	(800) 426–6637	(408) 456–4903
Corollary Inc. 2802 Kelvin Irvine, CA 92714	(800) 338–4020	(800) 338–4020	(714) 250–4043
Creative Labs Inc. 1901 McCarthy Boulevard Milpitas, CA 95035		(408) 428–6622	(408) 428–6633 BBS (408) 428–6660
Dell Computer Corp. 9505 Arboretum Blvd. Austin, TX 78759	(800) 846–3749	(800) 624–9896	(512) 343–3653
Diamond Computer Systems 1130 East Arques Avenue Sunnyvale, CA 94086	(408) 736–2000	(408) 736–2000	(408) 773–8000
DigiBoard 6400 Flying Cloud Drive Eden Prairie, MN 55344	(612) 943–9020	(800) 344–4273	(612) 922–4287
Distributed Processing Technology (DPT) 140 Candace Drive Maitland, FL 32751	(407) 830–5522	(407) 830–5522	(407) 260–5366
DTK	(818) 810–8880	(818) 810–8880	(818) 810–8880

Company Name and Address	Sales	Service	FAX
Equinox	(305) 255–3500	(305) 255–3500	(305) 255–3500
Fujitsu	N/A	(800) 826–6112	(408) 428–0456
Gateway 2000 Inc. 610 Gateway Drive P.O. Box 2000 North Sioux City, SD 57049	(800) 846–2065	(800) 846–2000	(605) 232–2023
Grid Systems Corp. 7 Village Circle, Suite 100 Westlake, TX 76262	(800) 934–4743	(800) 654–4743	(817) 347–7679
IBM Old Orchard Road Armonk, NY 10504	(800) 426–2968	(800) 727–2227	N/A
ICL Inc. 9801 Muirlands Blvd. P.O. Box 19593 Irvine, CA 92713	(714) 458–7282	(714) 458–7282	(714) 458–6257
Intel	(408) 765–8080	(408) 765–8080	(408) 765–8080
Laser Magnetics	(714) 588–5730	(714) 588–5730	(714) 588–5730
Madge Networks	(408) 441–1300	(408) 441–1300	(408) 441–1300
Maxtor Corporation 211 River Oaks Parkway San Jose, CA 95134	N/A	(800) 262–9867	(303) 678–2618
Maynard Electronics Inc. 36 Skyline Drive Lake Mary, FL 32746	(800) 821–8782	(800) 227–6296	(407) 263–3536
Mobius	(510) 460–5252	(510) 460–5252	(510) 460–5252
Mountain Computer	(408) 379–4300	(408) 379–4300	(408) 379–4300

Company Name and Address	Sales	Service	FAX
Mylex	(510) 796–6100	(510) 796–6100	(510) 796–6100
NCA Computer Products 1202 Kifer Road Sunnyvale, CA 94086	(408) 739–9010	(408) 739–4110	(408) 739–2420
NEC Technologies Inc. 1414 Massachusets Ave Boxborough, MA 01719	(800) 374–8000	(800) 388–8888	(508) 264–8673
Olivetti USA 765 U.S. Highway 202 P.O. Box 6945 Bridgewater, NJ 08807	(800) 527–2960	(908) 704–6501	(908) 526–8405
Orchid Technology Inc. 45365 Northport Loop West Fremont, CA 94538	(800) 767–2443	(510) 683–0323	(510) 490–9312
Philips Information Systems Co. 1435 Bradley Lane Suite #100 Carrollton, TX 75007	(800) 527–0204	(800) 835–3506	(214) 991–6572
Procomp	(216) 234–2233	(216) 234–2233	(216) 234–2233
Quantum Corporation	N/A	N/A	N/A
Racore Computer Products Inc. 170 Knowles Drive Los Gatos, CA 95030	(800) 635–1274	(408) 374–8290	(408) 374–6653
Seagate Technology, Inc. 920 Disc Drive Scotts Valley, CA 95066	N/A	(408) 438–8222	(408) 438–2620
SMC	(800) 833–4762	(800) 833–4762	(800) 833–4762
Specialix	(408) 378–7919	(408) 378–7919	(408) 378–7919
Sun Microsystems Computer Corp 2550 Garcia Avenue Mountain View, CA 94047	(800) 873–7869	(800) 874–4786	(800) 873–7869
SysKonnect	(408) 725–4650	(408) 725–4650	(408) 725–4650
Tatung Co. 2850 El Presidio Street Long Beach, CA 90810	(800) 827–2850	(800) 827–2850	(310) 637–8484

Company Name and Address	Sales	Service	FAX
3COM	(408) 764–5673	(408) 764–5000	(408) 727–7021
Toshiba America 9740 Irvine Blvd. Irvine, CA 92713	(800) 334–3445	(714) 455–0407	(714) 587–6382
Trident	(415) 691–9211	(415) 691–9211	(415) 691–9211
U&X Technology	(714) 248–9597	(714) 248–9597	(714) 248–9597
UltraStor Corp. 47061 Warm Springs Blvd. Fremont, CA 94539	(510) 623–8955	(510) 623–8955	(510) 623–8953
Wangtek Inc. 41 Moreland Road Simi Valley, CA 93065	(800) 992–9916	(805) 583–5233	N/A
WYSE Technology Inc. 3471 North First Street San Jose, CA 95134	(800) 438–9973	(408) 922–5700	(408) 473–1212
Zenith Data Systems 2150 East Lake Cook Road Buffalo Grove, IL 60089	(800) 582–0524	(800) 553–0331	(708) 808–4434

Glossary

abort

To terminate in a controlled manner a processing activity in a computer system because it is impossible or undesirable for the activity to proceed.

agent

In the *client–server model*, the part of the system that performs information preparation and exchange on behalf of a client or server application.

allocate

To reserve memory for use by a program. Programs often need certain system resources such as memory or disk space, and they request them as needed from the operating system. The process of responding to a request for a resource is called *allocation*. The two basic types of allocation are *static allocation*, in which memory is set aside when the program starts and remains allocated while the program is running, and *dynamic allocation*, in which memory is allocated and deallocated while the program is running.

American National Standards Institute (ANSI)

An organization that reviews and approves product standards in the United States. In the electronics industry , its work enables designers and manufacturers to create and support products that are compatible with other hardware *platforms* in the industry.

American Standard Code for Information Interchange (ASCII)

The standard binary encoding of alphabetical characters, numbers, and other keyboard characters.

ANSI

See *American National Standards Institute (ANSI).*

AnswerBook on-line documentation

Sun's on-line documentation for use with OpenWindows.

application

A software program specially designed for a particular task or the specific use of a software program.

architecture

The specific components of a computer system and the way they interact with one another.

ASCII

See *American Standard Code for Information Interchange (ASCII).*

ASIC

(Pronounced *ā–sic.*) An application–specific integrated circuit. A *gate array* or other nonstandard chip design for proprietary use.

asynchronous

(1) Without regular time relationship; unexpected and unpredictable with respect to the execution of a program's instructions. Contrast with synchronous. (2) A form of data transmission in which information is sent one character at a time, with variable time intervals between characters; generally used in communication via modem. Asynchronous transmission does not use a separate clock signal to enable the sending and receiving units to separate characters by specific time periods. Instead, each transmitted character consists of a number of data bits (the character itself) preceded by a "begin character" signal, called a start bit, and ending with an optional parity bit followed by one or more "end character" signals, called stop bits.

backbone

The primary connectivity mechanism of a hierarchical distributed system. All systems that have connectivity to an intermediate system on the backbone are assured of connectivity to each other. This does not prevent systems from setting up private arrangements with each other to bypass the backbone for reasons of cost, performance, or security.

backup

A copy on a diskette, tape, or disk of some or all of the files from a hard disk. There are two types of backup: a full backup and an incremental backup. Synonymous with "dump."

baud rate

The rate at which information is transmitted between devices; for example, between a terminal and the computer.

Berkeley software distribution (BSD)

UNIX version developed at the University of California, Berkeley. They bear names such as BSD 2.7 and BSD 4.2.

bit

Short for "binary digit." Indicates the smallest unit of information stored in a digital memory. Binary digits indicate two possible values: on and off. A single bit is represented in memory as 0 (off) and 1 (on).

block

A unit of data that can be transferred by a device, usually 512 bytes long.

boot

To load the system software into memory and start it running.

boot server

A server system that provides client systems on the network with the programs and information that they need to start up.

bps

Bits per second.

bridge

A device that joins two or more physical networks and forwards packets between them.

BSD

See *Berkeley software distribution (BSD)*.

bug

An error in the hardware or software of a computer system.

bus

A circuit over which data or power is transmitted, one that often acts as a common connection among a number of locations.

byte

A group of eight adjacent binary digits (bits) operated on by the computer as a unit.

cache

A buffer of high-speed memory filled at medium speed from main memory, often with instructions and programs. A cache increases the effective memory transfer rates and processor speed.

cathode-ray tube (CRT)

A video monitor based on cathode-ray tube technology.

CD–ROM

An optical disc.

central processing unit (CPU)

The central processing unit of a computer.

checksum

The sum of a group of data items associated with the group for checking purposes. The data items are either numerals or other character strings regarded as numerals during the process of calculating the checksum.

chip

(1) A small chunk of silicon bearing the equivalent of a large number of electrical components. (2) An integrated circuit (IC).

client

In the client–server model for file systems, the client is a machine that remotely accesses resources of a computer server, such as compute power and large memory capacity.

closed architecture

Any computer design with specifications not freely available. Such proprietary specifications make it difficult or impossible for third-party vendors to create ancillary devices that work correctly with the closed-architecture machine; usually, only its original master can build peripherals for such a machine. Contrast with *open architecture*.

command

An instruction to the computer. A command is typically a character string typed at a keyboard and interpreted by the computer as a demand for a particular action.

console

A terminal, or dedicated window on the screen, where system messages are displayed.

controller

An adapter board, chip, or electronic circuit that controls the operation of a peripheral device. The controller receives and responds to requests (commands) from the computer system, and in turn translates the requests into control and data signals that are sent to the peripheral device. The controller also responds to requests from the peripheral device, and in turn translates the requests into control and data signals to the computer system. The term controller is commonly used in reference to an adapter board such as a SCSI controller, a floppy disk controller, or a hard disk controller.

CPU

See *central processing unit (CPU)*.

CRT

See *cathode–ray tube (CRT)*.

CSMA/CD

Abbreviation for "carrier sense multiple access with collision detection." The access method used by local area networking technologies such as Ethernet.

daisy chain

A specific method of propagating signals along a bus. This method is often used in applications in which devices not requesting a daisy-chained signal respond to a signal by passing it on.

dataless client

A client system that relies on a server system for its home directory, and on a local disk for its root directory and swap space. See also *diskless client* and *diskfull client*.

default

An alternative value, attribute, or option assumed when none has been specified.

degauss

The process of removing magnetization from objects such as magnetic tape drives and monitors.

devconfig

A Solaris x86 utility program used to identify keyboard, mouse, video display, and SCSI controller configuration.

device

A hardware component, such as a printer or disk drive, acting as a unit to perform a specific function.

direct memory access (DMA)

The transfer of data directly into memory without the supervision of the processor. The data is passed on the bus directly between the memory and another device.

directory

A type of file that can contain other files and directories.

disc

Note the spelling (as opposed to "disk"). This particular spelling is reserved for optical discs, as opposed to magnetic disks, in keeping with the common spelling used in the CD (compact disc) market. A CD–ROM is an optical disc.

disk

A round platter, or set of platters, of a magnetized medium organized into concentric tracks and sectors for storing data such as files.

diskette

A 3.5-inch or 5.25-inch removeable storage medium.

diskfull client

A client on the network that relies on a server for resources, such as files, but has its own local disk storage. Some of its files are local and others are remote. The remote files can be obtained from any machine running as a file network file server. Contrast with *diskless client* and *standalone*.

diskless client

A client on the network that relies on a server for all of its disk storage. Contrast with *diskfull client* and *standalone*.

disk partition

A portion of the *disk* reserved for a specific file system and function.

display

(1) A visual presentation of data. (2) To present a display image on a display surface. (3) Abbreviated term for *display device*.

display device

The hardware device that displays windows, text, icons, and graphical pictures.

distributed file system

A file system that exists on more than one machine, enabling each user to access files on other machines.

DMA

See *direct memory access (DMA)*.

domain

In the Internet, a part of a naming hierarchy. Syntactically, an Internet domain name consists of a sequence of names (labels) separated by periods (dots). For example, "eng.sun.com."

dpi

Abbreviation for dots per inch.

DRAM

Acronym for "dynamic random-access memory."

driver

A software subsystem that controls either a hardware device (device driver) or another software system.

dump

See *backup*.

EISA

See *Extended Industry Standard Architecture (EISA)*.

e-mail

Abbreviation for electronic mail.

environment

The conditions under which a user works while using the DOS or UNIX system.

Ethernet

A type of local area network that enables real–time communication between machines connected directly together through cables. Ethernet was developed by Xerox in 1976, originally for linking minicomputers at the Palo Alto Research Center. A widely implemented network from which the IEEE 802.3 standard for contention networks was developed, Ethernet uses a bus topology (configuration) and relies on the form of access known as CSMA/CD to regulate traffic on the main communication line.

execute

(1) To run a file as a program. (2) To perform one or more instructions. In programming, execution implies loading the machine language code of the program into memory and then performing the instructions.

export

The process by which a server advertises the file systems that it allows hosts on the network to access.

Extended Industry Standard Architecture (EISA)

An industry standard bus architecture used to connect I/O adapter cards to a computer. The EISA architecture extends the capability of the ISA bus while at the same time maintaining compatibility with ISA bus adapters.

file

A sequence of bytes constituting a unit of text, data, or program. A file can be stored in system memory or on an external medium such as tape or disk.

file transfer protocol (FTP)

The Internet protocol (and program) used to transfer files between hosts.

flag

An argument to a command indicating a particular option or modification. UNIX flags usually are indicated by a leading hyphen (-). DOS flags usually are indicated by a leading forward slash (/).

floppy disk

See *diskette*.

formatting

Preparing a disk for use.

frame

In video, the time interval of a video signal that contains exactly one complete picture, with all of its associated sync elements.

frame buffer

Display memory that temporarily stores (buffers) a full frame of picture data at one time. Frame buffers are composed of arrays of *bit* values that correspond to the display's *pixels*. The number of bits per pixel in the frame buffer determines the complexity of images that can be displayed.

FTP

See *file transfer protocol (FTP)*.

gate array

See *ASIC*.

gateway

The original Internet term for what is now called a router or more precisely, IP router. In modern usage, the terms "gateway" and "application gateway" refer to the systems that do translations from some native format to another.

Gbyte

Abbreviation for gigabyte; 1,073,741,824 bytes.

gigabyte (Gbyte)

One billion bytes.

global

Having extended or general scope. For example, a global substitution of one word for another in a file affects all occurrences of the word.

graphical user interface (GUI)

The graphical user interface, or GUI, provides the user with a method of interacting with the computer and its special applications, usually via a mouse or other selection device.

GUI

See *graphical user interface (GUI)*.

guru

Anyone who knows more about something than you do!

hard disk

See *disk*.

hardware

The mechanical and electrical components of a computer.

HBA

Abbreviation for host bus adapter. A host bus adapter is one that connects a particular type of computer bus to another general type of controller. This term is commonly used in reference to a SCSI host bus adapter. See *controller*.

heterogeneous network

A network composed of systems of more than one architecture. Contrast with *homogeneous network.*

hexadecimal

Pertaining to a fixed-radix numeration system having a radix of sixteen (a base sixteen number).

High Sierra file specification (HSFS)

An industry-wide format specification for CD–ROM data. The High Sierra file specification defines the logical structure, file structure, and record structures of a CD–ROM disc; it served as the basis for the ISO 9660, an international format standard for CD–ROM.

homogeneous network

A network composed of systems of only one architecture. Contrast with *heterogeneous network.*

HSFS

See *High Sierra file specification (HSFS).*

IDE

See *intelligent drive electronics (IDE).*

incremental backup

A duplicate copy of the files that have changed since a certain date. An incremental backup is used for archival purposes.

incremental dump

See *incremental backup.*

industry standard

Elements of a computer system hardware or software subsystem that have been standardized and adopted by the industry at large.

Industry Standard Architecture (ISA)

An industry standard bus architecture used to connect I/O adapter cards to a computer.

input device

A hardware device that enables a user to communicate with the computer system. Examples of input devices are keyboard, mouse, track ball, light pen, and joystick.

intelligent drive electronics (IDE)

Intelligent drive electronics controllers and disk drives are lower performance alternatives to the more expensive, high-performance SCSI disk drives and controllers.

IDE drives are easy to configure and install, but only one IDE controller and two IDE disk drives are allowed on a system.

interactive

(1) Allowing the computer and user to carry on a dialog. (2) Describes an operating system, such as UNIX, that can handle immediate-response communication between the user and the computer.

interlace

A scanning standard in which alternate raster lines of a frame are displaced vertically by half the scan line pitch and displaced temporally by half the frame time, to form an odd field and an even field.

internet

A collection of networks interconnected by a set of routers that enables them to function as a single, large virtual network.

Internet

(Note the capital "I.") The largest internet in the world consisting of large national backbone nets (such as MILNET, NFSNET, and CREN) and a myriad of regional and local campus networks all over the world. The Internet uses the internet protocol suite.

interrupt

(1) To break off a command or other process, thus terminating it. (2) A signal that accomplishes this.

interrupt request (IRQ)

A signal used by a device requesting service from the cpu. Interrupt requests are assigned priorities and are serviced by the cpu in order of highest priority.

I/O

Input/output. Refers to equipment used to communicate with a computer, the data involved in that communication, the media carrying the data, and the process of communicating that information.

IP

Internet protocol. The network layer protocol for the Internet protocol suite.

IP address

A unique number that identifies each host on a network.

IRQ

See *interrupt request (IRQ).*

ISA

See *Industry Standard Architecture (ISA).*

ISV

Abbreviation for independent software vendor.

Kbyte

Abbreviation for *kilobyte (Kbyte)* (1024 bytes).

kernel

The core of the operating system software. The kernel manages the hardware (for example, processor cycles and memory) and supplies fundamental services such as filing that the hardware does not provide.

KHz

Abbreviation for kilohertz (1000 hertz).

kill

To terminate a process before it reaches its natural conclusion.

kilobyte (Kbyte)

A unit of measure equal to 1024 bytes.

LAN

See *local area network (LAN).*

loading

Putting the machine-language instructions of a program into memory.

local area network (LAN)

A group of computer systems in close proximity that can communicate with one another via some connecting hardware or software.

local bus

A high-speed 32-bit CPU bus that provides direct CPU memory access for local bus adapters such as video display adapters and SCSI (Small Computer System Interface) bus adapters. Direct data transfer between the CPU and adapter boards on the CPU bus bypasses the slower ISA I/O bus. See *VESA*.

login name

The name by which a computer knows a user.

login prompt

The string of characters that a system displays to let the user know that it is ready to accept the user name.

MB/s

Abbreviation for megabytes per second.

Mbyte

Abbreviation for megabyte; one million bytes.

MCA

See *Micro Channel Architecture (MCA).*

megabyte (Mbyte)

A megabyte is 1,048,576 bytes or 1024 kilobytes; or roughly 1 million bytes or 1000 kilobytes.

menu

A list of options from which a program user can select to perform a desired action.

MHz

Megahertz. One million cycles per second.

Micro Channel Architecture (MCA)

An industry standard bus architecture used to connect I/O adapter cards to a computer. The MCA bus is not compatible with either ISA or EISA architectures.

MIPS

An acronym for millions of instructions per second.

modem

Short for modulator/demodulator. A device that enables a machine or terminal to establish a connection and transfer data through telephone lines.

monitor

The video display that is part of a workstation. The term monitor usually refers to the video display and its housing. The monitor is attached to the workstation by a cable.

mounting

The process of making a file system accessible over the network by executing a `mount` command.

mouse

An input device connected to the computer that determines the position of the pointer. The basic features of the mouse are a casing with a flat bottom, designed to be gripped by one hand; one or more buttons on the top; a directional detection device on the bottom, such as a ball or optical sensor; and a cable that attaches the mouse to the computer.

multiprocessor

A computer employing two or more processors under integrated control. The processing units are roughly equal, and each carries out one or more processes in tandem.

multitasking

(1) Enabling more than one user to access the program at the same time. (2) Pertaining to the concurrent execution of two or more tasks by a computer. (3) A mode of operation offered by an operating system in which the computer works on more than one task at a time.

multithreading

A technique that enables multiprocessing applications to run more efficiently by breaking sequences of instructions (threads) into multiple sequences that can be executed from the kernel simultaneously.

multiuser system

Any computer system that can be used concurrently by more than one person. Although a computer shared by several people can be considered a multiuser system, the term is generally reserved for machines that are accessed by several or many people through communications facilities or via network terminals.

network

Technically, the hardware connecting various systems enabling them to communicate. Informally, the systems so connected.

network information service (NIS)

A distributed network database containing key information about the systems and the users on the network. The NIS database is stored on the master NIS server and all the slave NIS servers.

NIS

See *network information service (NIS)*.

NIS+

See *network information service (NIS)*.

NeWS

Network extensible window system. A window system based on PostScript that Sun Microsystems developed and licenses.

NFS

A distributed file system developed by Sun Microsystems that enables a set of computers to cooperatively access each other's files in a transparent manner.

node

An addressable point on a network. Each node in a Sun Microsystems network has a different name. A node can connect a computing system, terminal, or various other peripheral devices to the network.

noise

Irrelevant data that hamper the recognition and interpretation of the data of interest.

noninterlace

Display refresh of all raster lines on the CRT during each scan. Contrast with *interlace*.

null modem

A cable that connects two computers so they can communicate without the use of modems. A null modem cable accomplishes this by crossing the sending and receiving wires so that the wire used for transmitting by one device is used for receiving by the other and vice versa.

on-line

Connected to the system and operational.

on-line documentation

A disk-based form of documentation provided by many application programs, consisting of advice or instructions on using program features. On-line documentation can be accessed directly without the need to interrupt work in progress or leaf through a manual.

open architecture

A term used to describe any computer or peripheral design that has published specifications. A published specification enables third parties to develop add-on hardware for an open-architecture computer or device. Contrast with *proprietary* or *closed architecture*.

open systems interconnection (OSI)

An international standardization program to facilitate communications among computers from different manufacturers.

operating system (OS)

A collection of programs that monitosr the use of the system and supervises the other programs executed by it.

option

A variation on or modification to a command, usually requested by the use of a *flag*.

OS

See *operating system (OS)*.

OSI

See *open systems interconnection (OSI)*.

output

Information produced by a command, program, or such, and sent elsewhere; for example, to the terminal, a file, or a line printer.

package

(1) A collection of software grouped for modular installation. (2) A computer application consisting of one or more programs created to perform a particular type of work; for example, an accounting package or a spreadsheet package.

packet

Data in a fixed-disk format that is transmitted as a unit over communication lines.

page

(1) A block of 8192 contiguous byte locations used for memory mapping and protection. (2) The data between the beginning of a file and a page marker, or between two markers, or between a marker and the end of a file. (3) To advance text on the screen by one screenful (or page) at a time.

page frame

A physical address to which a page of virtual memory may be mapped. In a system with 4096-byte pages, page frame 0 corresponds to physical address 0 through 4095.

paging

The process of replacing the contents of a page frame with different pages.

parameter

A special type of variable used within shell programs to access values related to the arguments on the command line.

parity

A method used by a computer for checking that the data received matches the data sent. In typical modem-to-modem communications, parity is one of the parameters that must be agreed upon by sending and receiving parties before the transmission can take place.

partition

The unit into which the disk space is divided by the software.

path name

The location of a file or directory in the UNIX and DOS file systems.

peer

In networking, any functional unit in the same layer as another entity.

permissions

The attribute of a file or directory that specifies who has read, write, or execution access.

physical layer

The first, or lowest level of the seven layers in the International Organization for Standardization's open systems interconnection model for standardizing computer-to-computer communications. The physical layer is totally hardware oriented and deals with all aspects of establishing and maintaining a physical link between communicating computers. Among specifications covered in the physical layer are cabling, electrical signals, and mechanical connections.

physical media

Any means in the physical world for transferring signals between OSI systems. Considered to be outside the International Organization for Standardization's open systems interconnection (OSI) model, and therefore sometimes referred to as "Layer 0." The physical connector to the media can be considered as defining the bottom interface of the physical layer, i.e., the bottom of the OSI reference model.

physical memory

Main memory. The memory connected to the processor that stores instructions, which the processor directly fetches and executes, and any other data the processor must manipulate.

pixel

Short for picture element. In a raster grid, the pixel is the smallest unit that can be addressed and given a color or intensity. The pixel is represented by some number of bits in the frame buffer, and is illuminated by a collection of phosphor dots on the CRT that are struck by the beam(s) of the electron gun.

platform

The foundation technology of a computer system. Because computers are layered devices composed of a chip-level hardware layer, and an applications program layer, the bottom layer of a machine is often called a platform, as in "an x86 platform." However, designers of application software view both the hardware and systems software as the platform because both provide support for an application.

pointing device

A mechanical or electronic device, such as a *mouse*, used to manipulate the screen pointer.

port

In computer hardware, a location for passing data in and out of a computing device. Microprocessors have ports for sending and receiving data bits; these ports are usually dedicated locations in the memory. Full computer systems have ports for connecting peripheral devices such as printers and modems.

POSIX

An acronym created from the phrase "portable operating system interface," an IEEE standard that defines a set of operating-system services.

POST

See *power-on self test (POST).*

PostScript

A page description language published by Adobe Systems Incorporated. PostScript describes the appearance of text and graphics on printed pages. The best-known page-description language, PostScript uses English-like commands to control page layout and to load and scale outline fonts. Because PostScript uses scalable outline fonts, it can create a font of any size, giving the user flexibility in creating documents. PostScript is used in many printers, either as the only print mode or as one alternative among several.

power-on self test (POST)

A set of routines stored in a computer's read-only memory (ROM) that tests various system components such as RAM, the disk drives, and the keyboard to see if they are properly connected and operating. If problems are found, the POST routines alert the user by displaying a message, often accompanied by a diagnostic numeric value, to the standard output device. If the POST is successful, it passes control to the system's bootstrap loader.

power user

A computer user that pushes the limits of the computer and application programs. High-end system performance is critical to a power user.

print queue

A temporary lineup of print jobs waiting to be printed on a printer.

print spooler

Computer software that intercepts a print job on its way to the printer and and sends it to the disk or memory instead, where the print job is held until the printer is ready for it. The term "spool" is an acronym for "simultaneous peripheral operations on-line."

program

A sequence of instructions telling a computer how to perform a task. A program can be machine language or can be in a higher-level language that is translated into machine language.

prompt

The string of characters a system displays to tell the user it is ready to accept and interpret the next command line.

proprietary architecture

See *closed architecture*.

protocol

A formal description of messages to be exchanged and rules to be followed for two or more systems to exchange information.

QIC

Working group for quarter–Inch cartridge drive compatibility. A number of standard interfaces to 1/4-inch tape drives.

quit

To stop in an orderly manner; to execute the normal shutdown of a program, or return control to the operating system.

RAM

Semiconductor-based memory that can be read or written by the CPU or other hardware devices. The storage locations can be accessed in any order. Note that the various types of ROM memory are capable of random access. The term RAM, however, is generally understood to refer to volatile memory, which can be written as well as read. Compare with ROM.

raster

A rectangular grid of picture elements, or pixels. The graphical data to be displayed on the raster is stored by the *frame buffer*.

raster display

A video monitor (generally a CRT) that displays an image on the screen from top to bottom as a series of horizontal scan lines.

readme file

A file containing information that a user either needs or will find informative and that might not have been included in the documentation. Readme files are placed on disk in plain-text form (such as ASCII) so that they can be read easily by word-processing programs.

refresh rate

The rate at which successive frames of a raster display are swept by the scanning beam.

release

As a noun, a particular version of a piece of software, most commonly associated with the most recent version (as in the "latest release"). Some companies use the term *release* as an integral part of the product name.

remote file system (RFS)

A distributed file system, similar to NFS, developed by AT&T and distributed with their UNIX System V operating system.

remote system

A system other than the one on which the user is working.

repeater

A device that propagates electrical signals from one cable to another without making routine decisions or providing packet filtering.

resolution

(1) The number of pixels in the horizontal and vertical dimensions of a display, taking into account the size of the display, and thus the size of the pixels. (2) The number of

elements per unit length available for display or printing by a particular device. For example, 1200 dots per inch is considered to be excellent print resolution.

RFS

See *remote file system (RFS).*

robust

Reliable and dependable. Not prone to error. Usually used in reference to an application program.

ROM

Read-only memory.

root directory

One file system residing on the root device (a device predefined by the system at initialization) designated to anchor the overall file system.

root file system

The base directory from which all other directories stem, directly or indirectly.

root user name

SunOS user name that grants special privileges to the person that logs in with that ID. The user who can supply the correct password for the root user name is given *superuser* privileges for the particular machine.

router

A system responsible for making decisions about which of several paths network (or internet) traffic will follow. To do this it uses a routing protocol to gain information about the network, and the algorithms to choose the best route based on several criteria known as "routing metrics."

routing

The process of determining a pathway for data to get from one machine in a network to another machine through a gateway.

RS-232-C standard

An accepted industry standard for serial communications connections. Adopted by the Electronic Industry Association (EIA), this recommendation standard (RS) defines specific lines and signal characteristics used by serial communications controllers to standardize the transmission of serial data between devices. The letter C denotes that the current version of the standard is the third in a series. See also *RS-422/423/449 standard.*

RS-422/423/449 standard

Standards for serial communications with transmission distances over 50 feet. RS-449 incorporates RS-422 and RS-423. See also *RS-232-C standard.*

scan line

The parallel lines that are defined by the scan of the electron beam inside the *CRT*. Also, one line of *pixels* in the *frame buffer* corresponding to the above.

scanner

A hardware device that converts a hard copy image, such as a photograph, into digital data for display on the graphics system.

script

A type of program that consists of a set of instructions to an application or utility program. A script usually consists of instructions expressed using the application's or utility's syntax, combined with simple control structures such as loops and if/then expressions.

SCSI

(Pronounced "scuzzy.") See *small computer systems interface (SCSI)*.

seek

Usually refers to a disk seek, that is, positioning the read/write head of the disk so that data can be read or written.

serial port

A port for *serial transmission*.

serial transmission

A method in which bits that compose a character are transmitted sequentially as contrasted with parallel or simultaneous transfer.

server

In the client–server model for file systems, the server is a machine with compute resources (and is sometimes called the compute server) and large memory capacity. Client machines can remotely access and make use of these resources.

shadow mask

A metal plate with tiny holes carefully positioned inside the CRT hardware. The electron beam passes from the *electron gun*, through a hole in the shadow mask, which guides the beam and insures its precise placement on the inside of the display surface. The mask insures that electrons from the red gun hit the red *phosphor*, that electrons from the green gun hit the green phosphor, and that electrons from the blue gun hit the blue phosphor.

shell

A programmable command interpreter. The shell provides direct communication between the user and the operating system.

SIMM

See *single in-line memory module (SIMM)*.

single in-line memory module (SIMM)

A small circuit designed to accommodate surface–mount memory chips. SIMM components use less board space and are more compact than more conventional memory-mounting hardware.

small computer systems interface (SCSI)

An industry standard bus used to connect disk and tape devices to a workstation.

source code

The uncompiled version of a program written in a language such as C or Pascal. The source code must be translated to machine language by a program known as the *compiler* before the computer can execute the program.

SPARC

The 32-bit Scalable Processor ARChitecture from Sun Microsystems. SPARC is based on a reduced instruction set computer (RISC) concept. The architecture was designed by Sun Microsystems and its suppliers in an effort to significantly improve price and performance.

spooler

See *print spooler.*

standalone

A computer that does not require support from any other machine. It must have its own disk; it may or may not be attached to an Ethernet network. It must have some type of medium, such as CD–ROM or tape drive, for software installation.

standard input

Short for "standard output device." The device from which a program or system normally takes input. Usually a terminal or keyboard.

standard output

Short for "standard input device." The device from which a program or system normally sends its output. Usually a terminal or the display.

subdirectory

A directory that resides within another directory.

subnet

A working scheme that divides a single logical network into smaller physical networks to simplify routing.

SunOS

The best operating system in the world!

superuser

A special user who has privileges to perform all administrative tasks on the system. Also known as *root*.

swap space

The memory used for the transfer of a currently operating program from system memory to an external storage device. Also known as swapping area.

syntax

The order in which you type the parts of an operating system command.

system

A computer that enables a user to run computer programs.

target address

On a SCSI bus, the unique number (ID) that identifies a device from others on the same bus. Each device on the bus must have a unique target address between 0 and 6.

task

A standalone application or a subprogram that is run as an independent entity.

TCP

See *transport control protocol (TCP).*

TCP/IP

Acronym for transport control protocol/interface program (the protocol suite originally developed for the Internet). It is also called the Internet protocol suite. SunOS networks run on TCP/IP by default.

terminator

A device that is connected to the end of an electrical cable, thereby providing a resistance (load) that reduces noise.

thick Ethernet cabling

Thick Ethernet coaxial cabling is 1 centimeter (about 0.4 inch) in diameter that can be used to connect network stations over a distance of 1000 meters.

thin Ethernet cabling

Thin Ethernet coaxial cabling is 5 millimeters (about 0.2 inch) in diameter that can be used to connect network stations over a distance of 300 meters.

thread

In programming, a process that is part of a larger process or program.

token ring network

A local area network formed in a ring (closed loop) topology that uses token passing as a means of regulating traffic on the line.

toolkit

A set of programs and predefined routines that a programmer can use in writing a program for a particular machine, environment, or application.

transceiver

Transmitter–receiver. The physical device that connects a host interface to a local area network, such as Ethernet. Ethernet transceivers contain electronics that apply signals to the cable and sense collisions.

transport control protocol (TCP)

The major transport protocol in the Internet suite of protocols providing reliable, connection-oriented, full-duplex streams. Uses IP for delivery. See *TCP/IP.*

trap

A software mechanism that causes control of the machine to be instantly transferred to the kernel, even if a user process is currently running.

twisted-pair wiring (UTP)

Wiring that uses two separately insulated strands twisted together. Twisted–pair wiring is used to reduce signal interference introduced by a strong radio source such as a nearby cable.

UART

Universal asynchronous receiver–transmitter. A module, usually composed of a single integrated circuit, that contains both the receiving and transmitting circuits required for asynchronous serial communications.

user name

A combination of letters and possibly numbers that identifies a user to the system.

utility

A standard program, usually furnished at no charge with the purchase of a computer or computer product, that does housekeeping functions.

UTP

See *twisted–pair wiring (UTP).*

VESA

See *Video Electronic Standards Association (VESA).*

Video Electronic Standards Association (VESA)

Association of manufacturers responsible for the development of local bus standards to extend the useful life of the ISA bus by providing high-speed 32-bit CPU bus access for local bus adapters such as video display adapters and SCSI (Small Computer System Interface) bus adapters. By allowing data transfer between the CPU and adapter boards on the CPU bus, the older and slower ISA I/O bus can be completely bypassed.

video RAM (VRAM)

A special type of dynamic RAM (DRAM) used in high-speed video applications. With conventional DRAM, both the processor and the video circuitry must access

RAM by sharing the same control pins on the RAM chips. VRAM provides separate pins for the processor and the video circuitry.

VL

Abbreviation for *VESA* local bus.

wait state

A pause of one or more clock cycles during which a microprocessor waits for data from an input/output device or from memory. Wait states are most often used to control the speed at which the microprocessor receives data from random-access memory (RAM).

window

In applications and graphical interfaces, a portion of the screen that can contain its own document or message. In window-based programs, the screen can be divided into several windows, each of which has its own boundaries, and can contain a different document (or another view of the same document). Each window might also contain its own menu or other controls, and the user might be able to enlarge and shrink individual windows at will.

Index

A

B

C

D

E

F

G

H

K

L

M

N

Q

R

S

U

V

W

X